About This Book

Why is this topic important?

Communication is the very life's blood of an organization, vital at every level. Leaders must clearly articulate the organization's mission and its values. Managers must set clear expectations and give coherent and consistent directions. Workers must understand one another and pull together toward the same ends. Without this clarity, the organization becomes dysfunctional and begins to thrash blindly, like a creature with many arms and no brain. An enterprise full of people who cannot communicate effectively with one another cannot communicate well with its customers. That scenario is a recipe for disaster.

What can you achieve with this book?

This "book" is actually a working resource. It is a ready-made tool kit for trainers and consultants charged with improving communication in organizations. It contains articles, experiential learning activities, and survey instruments specially selected as the best and most useful in the thirty-year history of the *Pfeiffer Annuals*. You are free to reproduce and use all of the material for legitimate training purposes. The experiential learning activities are complete, time-tested training packages designed to let learners explore and practice a wide variety of communication skills. The questionnaires and survey instruments, also complete and ready to use, measure skills and attitudes with regard to communication. The articles can be used for self-education or as informative handouts in training sessions.

How is this book organized?

The opening section, Presentations and Discussion Resources, offers articles that establish a context for the improvement of interpersonal communication and explain how to go about improving it. The middle section, comprising the heart of the book, contains experiential learning activities to use in training sessions. The activities come complete with instructions for the facilitator and the learners, all necessary handouts are included, and the exercises' creators suggest variations to serve particular training situations. The final section contains self-scoring instruments and questionnaires to provide measurements and insights into the beliefs, attitudes, and practices that influence communication at both individual and organizational levels.

About Pfeiffer

Pfeiffer serves the professional development and hands-on resource needs of training and human resource practitioners and gives them products to do their jobs better. We deliver proven ideas and solutions from experts in HR development and HR management, and we offer effective and customizable tools to improve workplace performance. From novice to seasoned professional, Pfeiffer is the source you can trust to make yourself and your organization more successful.

Essential Knowledge Pfeiffer produces insightful, practical, and comprehensive materials on topics that matter the most to training and HR professionals. Our Essential Knowledge resources translate the expertise of seasoned professionals into practical, how-to guidance on critical workplace issues and problems. These resources are supported by case studies, worksheets, and job aids and are frequently supplemented with CD-ROMs, websites, and other means of making the content easier to read, understand, and use.

Essential Tools Pfeiffer's Essential Tools resources save time and expense by offering proven, ready-to-use materials—including exercises, activities, games, instruments, and assessments—for use during a training or team-learning event. These resources are frequently offered in looseleaf or CD-ROM format to facilitate copying and customization of the material.

Pfeiffer also recognizes the remarkable power of new technologies in expanding the reach and effectiveness of training. While e-hype has often created whizbang solutions in search of a problem, we are dedicated to bringing convenience and enhancements to proven training solutions. All our e-tools comply with rigorous functionality standards. The most appropriate technology wrapped around essential content yields the perfect solution for today's on-the-go trainers and human resource professionals..

Pfeiffer
www.pfeiffer.com

Essential resources for training and HR professionals

The Pfeiffer Book of Successful Communication Skill-Building Tools

The most enduring, effective, and valuable training activities for improving interpersonal communication

The Pfeiffer Book of Successful Communication Skill-Building Tools

The most enduring, effective, and valuable training activities for improving interpersonal communication

Edited by Jack Gordon

Pfeiffer
A Wiley Imprint
www.pfeiffer.com

ISBN-13: 0-978-0-4701-8180-5 (paperback)
ISBN-10: 0-4701-8180-X (paperback)
ISBN-13: 0-978-0-7879-6926-4 (alk. paper)
ISBN-10: 0-7879-6926-5 (alk. paper)

Acquiring Editor: Martin Delahoussaye
Director of Development: Kathleen Dolan Davies
Production Editor: Nina Kreiden
Manufacturing Supervisor: Bill Matherly
Composition: Leigh McLellan Design

Originally published as *Pfeiffer's Classic Activities for Interpersonal Communication.*

Printed in the United States of America

HB Printing 10 9 8 7 6 5 4 3 2

PB Printing 10 9 8 7 6 5 4 3 2 1

Contents

Introduction

Getting the Most from This Resource

The recipe for effective interpersonal communication, in the workplace or elsewhere, is really quite simple: two or more people who trust each other's motives speak honestly and listen attentively as they discuss the subject in question.

Given those three elements—trust, plain speaking, and a sincere attempt to hear and understand the other's point of view—it makes no difference what the subject of the conversation is or whether the two people agree or disagree about it. Even if they're arguing, both parties will emerge from the conversation understanding clearly what the argument is about and why they're on opposite sides of it. That puts them way ahead of most arguers.

In other words, while the goal of most attempts at workplace communication may be to achieve agreement, effective communication isn't necessarily about agreement. It's about accuracy. It requires a symbiotic relationship between the sender and the receiver of a message. The goal of the relationship is that the receiver should accurately perceive the honest message that the sender intends to transmit. (If the message is dishonest, the sender may be a skillful liar, but he or she will not long be an effective communicator.)

If the recipe is simple, why is communication a sorry mess in so many organizations? Because one or more of the three main ingredients are often missing. Justifiably or not, we don't trust the motives of our managers, our subordinates, our co-workers, or our customers. Even if trust is present, we find it difficult to express ourselves clearly and openly. And as for our ability or willingness to listen attentively for thirty seconds to what someone else is saying—well, the less said about that the better.

In most organizations, there are so many needs and opportunities for improved communication skills at all levels that trainers hardly know where to start.

That's where this resource comes in.

THIRTY YEARS OF EXPERTISE

This handbook is a compilation of material chosen from three decades of the Pfeiffer *Annuals* and *Handbooks*. Since 1972, trainers and consultants have found in these volumes a treasure chest of resources for a wide range of training and organization-development needs. The books offer not just ideas or educational reading but tools meant to be put to work for training and development purposes.

Like the books that provided its content, this one is organized into three sections: Presentation and Discussion Resources (articles); Experiential Learning Activities; and Inventories, Questionnaires, and Surveys. The selections presented here were picked as the all-time best the *Annuals* and *Handbooks* have to offer on matters pertaining to a particular topic: interpersonal communication.

A WIDE NET

We chose the material not only for quality but with an eye toward serving a broad range of objectives falling under the umbrella of communication skills. We looked for presentations, experiential activities, and instruments designed for groups at all levels of the organization—managers and nonmanagers, intact work teams and front-line customer-service reps.

We also cast a wide net for the types of communication skills these tools address. You will find help in teaching the skills of both speaking and listening that apply in a number of situations. You'll find some experiential activities that build awareness of nonverbal communication habits and others designed to encourage trust and openness in work groups. You'll find information and tools that offer insight into how personality types, as well as cultural and gender differences, affect communication attempts.

While the best techniques for achieving effective face-to-face communication are timeless, computer technology has added a new wrinkle to the picture. Not only does a lot of workplace communication now take place via e-mail, but a lot of workers now must communicate routinely with remote "teammates" they rarely or never meet in person. We've included information and tools to help address the new challenges of high-tech communication as well as the old challenges that arise when people meet in the flesh.

The Sections

The articles in the *Presentations* section can be used for self-education, as workshop handouts, or both. Most of them were selected because they provide a quick, solid, and insightful grounding in a classic theme of communication-skills training.

Here you'll find some excellent background reading to expand or refresh your understanding of several core issues. These issues include emotional factors that interfere with clear speaking and effective listening, how to give performance feedback to subordinates, why trust and openness are preconditions for effective communication, and why and how personality typologies are often used in communication-skills training.

Two of the presentations address different aspects of high-tech communication: the uses and abuses of e-mail, and the limitations of computer-based channels for communicating with employees about sensitive issues.

The *Experiential Learning Activities* in the second section form the heart of the book. These are complete, ready-made training exercises designed to meet a variety of needs for different audiences.

We have grouped the experiential activities into two categories: those intended to build skills strictly in individuals and those that have implications touching on the organization's management practices, structure, or policies. See the introduction to the experiential-activities section for a more thorough description.

The final *Inventories* section contains questionnaires and instruments designed to do three things: to provide insight into trainees' own communication habits and how they are perceived by others, to measure the health of actual relationships within work groups or between managers and subordinates, or to shed light on communication practices within the broader organization.

How to Use This Resource

Following are a few examples of the book's intended uses.

Situation 1

Suppose you're teaching managers or supervisors how to communicate more effectively with subordinates about job-performance issues. From the handbook's Inventories section you might choose the "Organization Behavior

Describer Survey" as a self-scoring instrument to give trainees some insight into the way they currently communicate. Or, before the workshop, you might ask these managers' subordinates to provide feedback by completing an instrument such as the "Communication Climate Inventory."

After discussing the results, you might lead the group through an experiential learning activity such as "Resistance: A Role Play" or "Defensive and Supportive Communication."

To prepare your own remarks for this workshop beforehand, you might turn to the Presentations section and read the chapter titled "The Lost Art of Feedback." You also may decide to run off some copies of the chapter and use them as handouts.

Situation 2

Suppose you're facilitating a meeting of a group charged with developing policies, procedures, or a list of best practices for communicating with co-workers via e-mail. The Presentations section offers a chapter called "E-Mail Basics: Practical Tips to Improve Communication," which includes guidelines designed to help a group decide for itself what kinds of norms will work best.

To demonstrate in a concrete way some of the challenges and pitfalls this group's recommendations must address, you might select the experiential learning activity called "Mediated Message Exchange: Exploring the Implications of Distance Communication in the Workplace."

CHOOSE WISELY

These are just two of many possible training situations. Only you can select the best tools for a given job. Surveys can be grouped with different exercises and presentations to address any particular circumstance. And we don't mean to suggest that you will want to use items from all three sections of the book for every training challenge that arises. Sometimes you'll want only a survey or an experiential exercise—or maybe just some first-rate background reading.

It is of course up to you, the facilitator, to learn as much as possible about the situation you're trying to address and the people involved in it before you devise a strategy for setting things right.

A TOOLBOX

This is not a book meant to be read from cover to cover. It is a resource—a collection of working tools. The experiential learning activities and surveys are complete packages: duplicate the materials, use them, and adapt them as you see fit for training purposes (the experiential activities all suggest variations, and you can invent your own). You also may duplicate the articles in the Presentations section for use as handouts or background reading.

There are just two exceptions to the liberal copyright policy. If noted, reprint permission must be obtained from the primary sources. And if the materials are to be reproduced in publications for sale or are intended for large-scale distribution (more than one hundred copies in twelve months), prior written permission is required. Please contact Jossey-Bass/Pfeiffer if you have questions.

This volume is a distillation of thirty years of expertise in the teaching of communication skills. We offer it in the hope that the contents will help build healthier organizations for working people everywhere.

Jack Gordon
Editor

Part 1
Presentation and Discussion Resources

The ten articles in this opening section are offered as recommended reading for trainers and consultants intending to teach communication skills. Look here for a good crash course in the subject of a workshop you're about to facilitate; nothing creates credibility faster than knowing what you're talking about.

Much of what we know about effective communication comes not just from experience but from research. The authors of these articles have the experience, and they cite the research.

Most of the presentations lay out fundamental, time-proven concepts and principles of effective communication and the factors that inhibit it. The articles deal with such topics as speaking and listening, giving performance feedback, influencing others, attending to the emotional undercurrents of conversations, and coping with angry people.

Two selections provide background information and insight into the uses of training tools commonly employed in communication workshops: personality typologies and the Johari Window. (The latter is a model used to illustrate the foundations of open communication in working groups and, usually, to encourage more of it.)

Finally, two presentations have valuable things to say about communication in the computer age. "Communicating Organizational Change: Information Technology Meets the Carbon-Based Employee Unit" is not only our favorite title, it's also a penetrating analysis of when *not* to rely solely on electronic means to communicate volatile information to employees. "E-Mail Basics" is a practical guide that can help a team or an organization work though its own problems with e-mail communication and decide how to address them.

Following are short descriptions of the individual presentations.

1. **Conditions That Hinder Effective Communication.** How preoccupation, emotional blocks, hostility, and other factors can prevent us from hearing what another person is really trying to say.

2. **The Lost Art of Feedback.** Clear, classic advice for managers about how to give both supportive and corrective feedback to subordinates.

3. **The Influence Continuum.** Describes a five-step process for "selling" your proposals to others in the organization, from the birth of your idea to completion of the project.

4. **Communicating Communication.** Tips for speakers and listeners about how to communicate effectively, with an emphasis on awareness of one's own and the other's emotions.

5. **The Johari Window: A Model for Eliciting and Giving Feedback.** Solid explanation of the classic Johari model for illustrating the degree of openness in a group's communication patterns.

6. **Using Personality Typology to Build Understanding.** An analysis of the Myers-Briggs inventory and other typologies often used in communication-skills training.

7. **Communicating Organizational Change: Information Technology Meets the Carbon-Based Employee Unit.** An analysis of how and why corporate communication must take particular forms when employees perceive threats in changing conditions.

8. **Confrontational Communication.** Presents a step-by-step process for dealing effectively with angry customers or co-workers.

The Pfeiffer Book of Successful Communication Skill-Building Tools © 2004 John Wiley & Sons, Inc.

9. **Assertion Theory.** Assertiveness training developed a bad reputation, but the original idea remains valid today: You can stand up for yourself without trampling the other person.

10. **E-Mail Basics: Practical Tips to Improve Communication.** Solid background information and suggested guidelines to help a work group decide how to communicate via e-mail.

1

Conditions That Hinder Effective Communication

J. William Pfeiffer

A person's interpersonal life is dependent on that person's facility for making his or her thoughts, feelings, and needs known to others and on that person's receptiveness to the attempts of others to share similar data with him or her. Communication, a multifaceted phenomenon, is the result of efforts by individuals toward this end. Communication can be considered in simplistic terms as the sending and receiving of messages, as both elements must be present for communication to take place. However, the fundamental transaction of message sent and received does not presuppose that communication has occurred. Often, it has only partially occurred or has been aborted entirely as a result of the circumstances surrounding the occasion when the communication attempt was made. These circumstances may be environmental, emotional, verbal-skill oriented, phenomenological, or resulting from a host of conditions present within the individuals who are attempting to relate.

An analogy may help to clarify the concept of the effect of circumstances on the effectiveness of sending and receiving messages. In the late afternoon when you observe a sunset, the sun often appears to be a deep red, larger and less intense than it seems at midday. This is due to the phenomenon of *refraction,* the bending of the light rays as they pass through the earth's atmosphere, and the higher density of dust in the air through which the light passes as the sun goes down. The sun has already moved below the horizon, but it is still in sight because its emissions are distorted by the conditions of the medium through which they must travel. In a similar way the messages that we send to one another are often refracted by intrapersonal, interpersonal, and environmental conditions that contribute to the atmosphere in which we are relating. I may distort my message to you by giving out mixed messages verbally and symbolically, and you may distort what you hear because of your own needs and experiences. The two of us may be located in an environment, physical and psychological, that contributes to the difficulty in clearly sharing what we intend. In an atmosphere of suspicion, for example, we may both become unduly cautious in our communication.

Although it is unlikely that totally nonrefracted communication is a possibility over time between any two people or with significant others with whom we must deal interpersonally, an awareness of conditions that block and alter the intention of sent and received messages may produce less refraction and better communication in the long run.

Some of the conditions that cause refraction can be labeled and examined in light of their impact on effective communications:

- preoccupation
- emotional blocks
- hostility
- charisma
- past experiences
- hidden agendas
- inarticulateness
- stereotyping
- physical environment
- mind wandering
- defensiveness
- relationships
- status

1. *Preoccupation.* A person who is focusing on internal stimuli may listen in such a way that none of the message comes through or so little of it that he or she cannot grasp the message appropriately and may respond in such a way that the blocking of the message is apparent. A story is told of a columnist in New York who attended numerous cocktail parties and had come to believe that a certain socialite was so preoccupied with making an outstanding impression on her guests that she was unable to hear anything they were saying. To test his theory he came late to her next party; when he was greeted effusively at the door by the hostess, he said, "I'm sorry to be late, but I murdered my wife this evening and had a terrible time stuffing her body into the trunk of my car." The super-charming hostess beamed and replied, "Well, darling, the important thing is that you *have* arrived, and now the party can really begin!"

2. *Emotional blocks.* A second condition may be an emotional block to the direction that the message is taking. Words may have become charged with emotion for a person, possibly due to that person's conditioning in childhood or to current circumstances in his or her life at the time the communication attempt is made. An example might be of the well-intentioned but unaware adult white male, who, in speaking to an adult black male, makes reference to "you colored boys." Similarly, a woman who is having difficulty in conceiving a child may not be able to discuss Aunt Mary's comment, "Now that you and Bob have been settled for a few years, it would be nice to start a family"; or she may find herself responding irrationally to a lecture on population control.

3. *Hostility.* Hostility may create refraction of messages. This can occur when communicating with a person with whom you are angry, or it may be a carryover from a recent experience. It may also be the subject matter that arouses hostility. When two people are engaged in a hostile confrontation, each often distorts messages from the other in such a way that provides fuel for further venting of hostility. A husband and a wife may have the following type of exchange of messages: *He:* "I really thought I was helping you when I . . ." *She:* "Are you trying to tell me that I was incapable of . . ." *He:* "You aren't capable of much of anything! Just look at the state of our finances." The husband's intended message was "I know I've made you angry by my action. Where did I go wrong?" The angry wife chose to interpret the word "help" as an accusation that she lacked the resources to handle the situation. Her message elicits further distortion and hostility from the husband. In another example, a woman may come home from

just having had a confrontation with her boss and may carry over her hostility to her family by overreacting to her husband's messages concerning the day's irritations, or she may simply filter out all messages and respond in monosyllables to any attempts at communication. The subject matter being dealt with may engender hostility and thereby distort the message. A father may comment that his son should plan to have his hair trimmed for his sister's wedding and find that his message has been refracted as an all-encompassing criticism of his son's life style.

4. *Charisma.* The charisma of the sender of a message may affect how the message is received. Political candidates are often chosen more for their possession of this quality than for their other attributes. A charismatic person can often make tired, trivial messages seem new and important to the recipient; however, this too can become detrimental to communication, as the receiver of the message is less likely to question or ask for clarification of the message. How often have we come away enthusiastically from having heard a dynamic speaker, only to discover that we cannot actually remember the content of the speech? Conversely, a person who has something important and unique to say to us may not be able to hold our attention in such a fashion that we hear the message he or she is sending.

5. *Past experience.* Our experience can predispose us to refraction. If our weekly staff meetings have always been a waste of time, we may come into each succeeding meeting expecting not to give the messages that are sent much consideration or to hear them as having no relevant implications. Staff meetings may also nurture another kind of condition that may create message refraction.

6. *Hidden agendas.* A person with a special interest, that is, a hidden agenda, may hear all messages only in reference to his or her own needs or may not be able to hear messages that do not relate to his or her own interest. If the hidden agenda is in competition with the message of another employee, he or she may reject all suggestions made by that other employee or may attempt to manipulate others into distorting the other employee's messages. The person with the hidden agenda might make such comments as "Of course, Chris has no real expertise in this area" or "We all know that the administration will never buy that, Chris." He or she may dismiss an excellent idea from someone with a fresh perspective.

7. *Inarticulateness.* Simple inarticulateness, or lack of verbal skill, may distort the intention of the sender. As clarity is essential for the true message to be received, a person may never be able to communicate effectively if he

The Pfeiffer Book of Successful Communication Skill-Building Tools © 2004 John Wiley & Sons, Inc.

or she has never developed verbal skills. If the receiver of the message is unaware of the sender's difficulty, he or she may dismiss the messages or distort them. Verbal patterns that are culturally determined may also hinder communication, as they could function as lack of skill when the message is received. A person from a minority culture may be quite articulate within his or her peer group but may fail to get messages through when speaking to a person from another culture. It is at this point that verbally administered standardized intelligence tests become invalid. An Appalachian child was once being tested by a psychometrist, who asked that the child name the seasons of the year. The child replied, "Deer season, possum season, fishing season . . ." The child showed an excellent grasp of seasonal variation throughout the year; but because his response was not the standard one, his score on the test was reduced.

8. *Stereotyping.* Culturally determined verbal patterns may lead to another type of communication distortion—stereotyping. Eliza Doolittle in the musical *My Fair Lady* was "heard" and understood as a charming, if unconventional, lady once her speech patterns had been altered from their original cockney flavor. However, Eliza had not changed her values or increased her worth as a person in changing her speech patterns; the only change was in her ability to send messages as a refined lady rather than as the stereotype of a thoroughly dismissable guttersnipe. Another type of stereotyping that causes adjustments in a person's perceptual prism is that of the visual impact of the speaker. A very conventional person may "hear" all attempts at communication as radical if the speaker has an unconventional physical appearance. A conservative member of the faculty at an urban university in the United States may hear a bearded colleague say "Perhaps some of the experimental programs, such as the bachelor's degree in general studies, would serve the needs of our particular group of students better than the traditional degree programs seem to do," and may angrily dismiss the idea as an attempt to downgrade the "standards" of the university. Yet a colleague with a conservative appearance might make the identical proposal, and the faculty member might respond with "Yes, we need to have more flexibility for our particular student population."

9. *Physical environment.* The environment alone may create conditions under which communication cannot take place effectively. A stuffy, warm room may make it impossible to send and receive messages accurately. A person's physical state may also be detrimental to communication. Any teacher will expound at length on the decline in understanding on the part of students as summer approaches in a classroom that is not air conditioned. Physical

environment may contribute to another condition that may get in the way of communications.

10. *Mind wandering.* This is a state to which all are susceptible. It distracts from the message sent in much the same way that preoccupation distracts, but the internal stimulus may never focus on any topic for more than a few seconds. This inability to focus for long on internal stimuli will generalize to the external stimulus of a sender's message.

11. *Defensiveness.* This leads to continual refraction of messages received. The insecurity of the person tends to distort questions into accusations and replies into justifications. A wife may ask her husband if he happened to pick up a loaf of bread on his way home from work. Her intention is informational, that is, she is planning to go out anyway and will pick up some bread at the same time, if he has not already bought some. The issue is duplication of effort. The insecure husband, however, may respond as if the issue were his ability to meet her needs. "No, I didn't. I can't think of everything, you know, when I'm busy with a huge project at work. I suppose you think my buying a loaf of bread is more important than concentrating on my job!"

12. *Relationships.* When we are attempting to communicate with another person, we are giving out two sets of messages simultaneously, content and relationship. The other person may be so preoccupied with hearing any cues about the latter that the content is lost or seriously refracted. For example, a boss tells her secretary that she has a set of instructions for her and that she wants her to be sure that she gets them right. If the secretary is insecure in her relationship with the boss, she may hear an implication that she is being evaluated negatively. Consequently, the secretary may distort her hearing of the boss's instructions.

13. *Status.* Perhaps the most difficult condition to overcome in communications is that of status, as it encompasses most of the elements that have already been discussed. A person in a position of high status may find communication difficult with most of the people with whom he or she must interact, as his or her perceived power differentially affects various people. One person may be preoccupied with impressing the source of power, while another may be defensive, feeling that his or her job or status is threatened by the powerful person. In addition, any high-status person must deal with the hostility of the envious, the stereotyping of the power worshiper, the past experiences with other high-status individuals that people may be generalizing from, and the emotional elements generated by all of these conditions.

The means of alleviating these conditions that interfere with the communication process are as varied as the people who must deal with them. The key, however, is in becoming aware of the conditions that are interfering with the process and attempting to modify behavior in such a way that messages are less often and less severely refracted.

Originally published in The 1973 Annual.

2

The Lost Art of Feedback

Hank Karp

The ability and the willingness to communicate effectively are the keys to supervisory success. Although communication effectiveness is based on the ability to make and maintain effective contact, regardless of the situation, specific areas of communication require some additional thought and planning.

One of the most important tools for maintaining control and developing people is the proper use of feedback. Although feedback has been categorized as positive and negative, another way of viewing it is to classify it into *supportive* feedback (which reinforces an ongoing behavior) and *corrective* feedback (which indicates that a change in behavior is appropriate). In this sense, all feedback is positive. The purpose of all feedback should be to assist a person in maintaining or enhancing his or her present level of effectiveness.

Some feedback, by definition, is better than no feedback. There are, however, ways to give feedback well and ways to give it superbly; there are also ways to receive it effectively. This article presents some guidelines that can help to sharpen the processes of giving and receiving feedback. The most important function of feedback is to help the person who is receiving that feedback to keep in touch with what is going on in the environment.

Supportive Feedback

Supportive feedback is used to reinforce behavior that is effective and desirable. An axiom of effective supervision is "Catch them doing something right and let them know it" (Blanchard & Johnson, 1982). One of the most damaging and erroneous assumptions that many supervisors make is that good performance and appropriate behavior are to be expected from the employee and that the only time feedback is needed is when the employee does something wrong. Therefore, these supervisors never give supportive feedback. If a supervisor, however, were determined to give only one kind of feedback, he or she would do well to choose supportive feedback and let corrective feedback go. In other words, if a supervisor stressed errors only, the end result would be—at most—an attempt by employees to do standard, error-free work. This accomplishment would not be *bad,* but there is a better way.

If a supervisor concentrated on what employees were doing well, then superior work is what those employees would become aware of. They would begin to view their work in terms of performing as well and as creatively as possible. What is reinforced has a tendency to become stronger; what is not reinforced has a tendency to fade away. If excellence is actively reinforced and errors are simply mentioned, employees will focus on excellence and tend to diminish errors. The following example of the two types of feedback illustrates the difference.

> *Focus on errors:* "The last three pieces in that batch contained wrong figures. We cannot have that kind of sloppy work in this department."
>
> *Focus on good work:* "This batch looks good, except for the last three pieces, which contain wrong figures. You probably used the wrong formula. Take them back and check them out, just the way you did the first group."

Fortunately, however, no one has to make a choice between using only supportive or only corrective feedback. Both are essential and valuable, and it is important to understand how each works so that the maximum gain can be received from the process.

Corrective Feedback

Corrective feedback is used to alter a behavior that is ineffective or inappropriate. It is as essential to the growth process as supportive feedback. A corrective feedback session, although never hurtful if done properly, is not a particularly pleasant experience. Under the best of circumstances, the subordinate will probably feel a little defensive or embarrassed.

In giving corrective feedback, the manager should have an option ready to present. When the employee is made aware of the inappropriate behavior, having an immediate alternative can be effective and powerful in shaping behavior. By presenting the alternative immediately after the corrective feedback, the manager is helping the subordinate to come out of a personally uncomfortable situation in the shortest possible time. This protects the dignity of the subordinate. The manager also is establishing himself or herself as a supporter of good work and good workers, which goes a long way in developing strong, productive, and supportive working relationships. Also very important, the manager is presenting an alternative that the employee might never have considered—or that was considered and rejected. This provides for immediate learning. Most important, however, is the fact that the manager is making the employee aware that an alternative was available at the time the employee chose to act otherwise. This awareness can help the employee to take responsibility for his or her own choices. In other words, the employee would realize, "That's right; I could have done it that way." The following example shows how an alternative can be effectively added to the feedback: "When you snapped at Ann in front of the group, she appeared to be very embarrassed and angry. *When you must remind an employee to be on time, it's less embarrassing for everyone to discuss it with the employee privately after the meeting.*"

Guidelines for Effective Feedback

The following guidelines are helpful for managers who are trying to improve their feedback skills, and they may also be used as a review prior to giving feedback.

1. Deal in Specifics

Being specific is the most important rule in giving feedback, whether it is supportive or corrective. Unless the feedback is specific, very little learning or reinforcement is possible. The following examples illustrate the difference in general and specific statements.

> *General:* "I'm glad to see that your work is improving."
> *Specific:* "I'm pleased that you met every deadline in the last three weeks."
>
> *General:* "You're a very supportive person."
> *Specific:* "I appreciate your taking time to explain the contract to our new employee."
>
> *General:* "You're falling down on the job again."
> *Specific:* "Last month most of your cost reports were completely accurate, but last week four of your profit/loss figures were wrong."

The last set is, of course, an example of corrective feedback. General statements in corrective feedback frequently result in hostile or defensive confrontations, whereas specific statements set the stage for problem-solving interaction. Carrying the last illustration one step further, the manager could add an alternative: "Start checking the typed report against the computer printouts. Some of the errors may be typos, not miscalculations."

If the employee is to learn from feedback and respond to it, then he or she must see it in terms of *observable* effects. In other words, the employee must be able to see clearly how his or her behavior had a direct impact on the group's performance, morale, and so on. When the employee sees the point of the feedback objectively, the issue will be depersonalized, and the employee will be more willing to continue with appropriate behaviors or to modify inappropriate behaviors. Although the manager's personal approval ("I'm glad to see . . .") or disapproval ("I'm disappointed that . . .") can give emphasis to feedback, it must be supported by specific data in order to effect a change in behavior.

2. Focus on Actions, Not Attitudes

Just as feedback must be specific and observable in order to be effective, it must be nonthreatening in order to be acceptable. Although subordinates—like their supervisors—are always accountable for their *behavior,* they are never accountable for their attitudes or feelings. Attitudes and feelings cannot be measured, nor can a manager determine if or when an employee's feelings have changed. For feedback to be acceptable, it must respect the dignity of the person receiving the feedback.

No one can attack attitudes without dealing in generalities, and frequently attacks on attitudes result in defensive reactions. The following example illustrates the difference between giving feedback on behavior and giving feedback on attitudes.

Feedback on attitude: "You have been acting hostile toward Jim."

Feedback on behavior: "You threw the papers down on Jim's desk and used profanity."

An attitude that managers often try to measure is loyalty. Certain actions that *seem* to indicate loyalty or disloyalty can be observed; but loyalty is a *result,* not an action. It cannot be demanded; it must be earned. Whereas people have total control over their own behavior, they often exercise little control over their feelings and attitudes. They feel what they feel. If a manager keeps this in mind and focuses more energy on things that can be influenced (that is, employee behavior), changes are more likely to occur.

The more that corrective feedback is cast in specific behavioral terms, the more it supports problem solving and the easier it is to control. The more that corrective feedback is cast in attitudinal terms, the more it will be perceived as a personal attack and the more difficult it will be to deal with. The more that supportive feedback is cast in terms of specific behaviors, the higher the probability that those behaviors will be repeated and eventually become part of the person's natural way of doing things.

3. Determine the Appropriate Time and Place

Feedback of either type works best if it is given as soon as feasible after the behavior occurs. Waiting decreases the impact that the feedback will have on the behavior. The passage of time may make the behavior seem less important to the manager; other important events begin to drain the energy of the manager, and some of the details of the behavior might be forgotten. On the other hand, dwelling on it for a long period could blow it out of proportion. From the subordinate's viewpoint, the longer the wait for the feedback, the less important it must be. The following example illustrates this point.

Tardy feedback: "Several times last month you fell below your quota."

Immediate feedback: "There are only ten products here; your quota for today was fourteen."

Enough time should be allotted to deal with the issues in their entirety. A manager can undercut the effectiveness by looking at the clock and speeding up the input so that an appointment can be met. Answering the telephone or allowing visitors to interrupt the conversation can have the same effect. The manager can also cause unnecessary stress by telling an employee at ten o'clock in the morning, "I want to see you at three this afternoon." A more appropriate procedure would be to say, "Would you please come to my office now" or "When you reach a stopping point, drop by my office. I have something good to tell you."

In addition to an appropriate time, the setting for the feedback is important. The old proverb "Praise in public, censure in private" is partially correct. Almost without exception, corrective feedback is more appropriately given in private. In the case of supportive feedback, however, discretion is needed. In many instances, praise in public is appropriate and will be appreciated by the subordinate. In other instances, privacy is needed to keep the positive effect from being short-circuited. For example, some people make a virtue out of humility; any feedback that reinforces their sense of worth is embarrassing. Rather than appreciating an audience, this type of employee would find it painful and perhaps resent it.

Sometimes a norm arises in a work group that prevents anyone from making a big deal out of good work. This does not mean that the group does not value good work, but supportive feedback in private might prevent the employee from feeling he or she was responsible for breaking the norm. In other instances, public praise can cause jealousy, hostility, or tense working relationships. Therefore, a conscious decision should be made about whether or not to give the supportive feedback publicly.

Another important consideration is the actual location selected for giving the feedback. The delivery of the feedback should match its importance. If the feedback concerns an important action, the manager's office would be better than an accidental encounter in the hall. On the other hand, the manager might convey a quick observation by telling someone at the water fountain, "Say, that was beautiful art work on the Madison report." Choosing the time and place is a matter of mixing a little common sense with an awareness of what is going on.

4. Refrain from Inappropriately Including Other Issues

Frequently when feedback is given, other issues are salient. When supportive feedback is given, any topic that does not relate to the specific feedback point should not be discussed if it would undercut the supportive feedback. For example, the manager could destroy the good just accomplished by adding, "And by the way, as long as you are here, I want to ask you to try to keep your files a little neater. While you were away, I couldn't find a thing."

When corrective feedback is given, however, the situation is different. The manager will want the feedback to be absorbed as quickly and as easily as possible, with the employee's negative feelings lasting no longer than necessary. Therefore, as soon as the feedback has been understood and acknowledged, the manager is free to change the subject. The manager may want to add, "I'm glad that you see where the error occurred. Now, as long as you are here, I'd like to ask your opinion about . . ." This type of statement, when used appropriately, lets the subordinate know that he or she is still valued. Obviously, the manager should not contrive a situation just to add this type of statement; but when the situation is naturally there, the manager is free to take advantage of it.

In certain situations, it is appropriate to give supportive and corrective feedback simultaneously. Training periods of new employees, performance-appraisal sessions, and times when experienced employees are tackling new and challenging tasks are all good examples of times when both types of feedback are appropriate. Nevertheless, some cautions are necessary:

Never follow the feedback with the word "but." This word will negate everything that was said before it. If it is appropriate to give supportive and corrective feedback within the same sentence, the clauses should be connected with "and." This method allows both parts of the sentence to be heard clearly and sets the stage for a positive suggestion. The following examples illustrate the difference:

> *Connected with "but":* "Your first report was accurate, but your others should have measured up to it."
>
> *Connected with "and":* "Your first report was accurate, and your others should have measured up to it."
>
> *Connected with "but":* "You were late this morning, but Anderson called to tell you what a great job you did on the Miller account."
>
> *Connected with "and":* "You were late this morning, and Anderson called to tell you what a great job you did on the Miller account."

Alternate the supportive and corrective feedback. When a great deal of feedback must be given, it is frequently better to mix the supportive feedback with the corrective feedback than to give all of one type and then all of the other. If all of one type is given first, regardless of which type comes first, the latter will be remembered more clearly. If a chronic self-doubter is first given supportive feedback and then only corrective feedback, he or she is likely to believe the supportive feedback was given just to soften the blow of the other type. Alternating between the two types will make all of the feedback seem more genuine.

When feasible, use the supportive feedback to cushion the corrective feedback. When both types of feedback are appropriate, there is usually no reason to start with corrective feedback. However, this does not mean that corrective feedback should be quickly sandwiched between supportive feedback statements. Each type is important, but frequently supportive feedback can be used as an excellent teaching device for areas that need correcting. This is especially true if the employee has done a good job previously and then failed later under similar circumstances. For example, the manager might say, "The way you helped Fred to learn the codes when he was transferred to this department would be appropriate in training the new employees."

PRINCIPLES OF FEEDBACK

Two major principles govern the use of feedback. The first principle, which relates to how feedback is conducted, can be paraphrased as "I can't tell you how you are, and you can't tell me what I see." In other words, the person giving the feedback is responsible to relate the situation as he or she observes it; and the person receiving the feedback is responsible for relating what he or she meant, felt, or thought. The second principle is that feedback supports growth.

Giving Feedback: "You Can't Tell Me What I See"

The object of giving feedback is not to judge the other person, but to report what was seen and heard and what the effects of the behavior were. Personal approval or disapproval, even if important, is secondary.

Feedback should be given directly to the person for whom it is intended. When others are present, the manager sometimes addresses them almost to the exclusion of the intended recipient, who sits quietly and gathers information by eavesdropping. Good contact with the recipient is an essential element in giving feedback.

It is never necessary to apologize for giving corrective feedback. Corrective or otherwise, feedback is a gift; apologies will discount its importance and lessen its impact. Nevertheless, corrective feedback must be given in a way that does not jeopardize the recipient's dignity and sense of self-worth.

It is sometimes helpful to offer an interpretation of the behavior or a hunch about what the behavior might indicate. What is of paramount importance is that the interpretation be offered as a suggestion and *never* as a judgment or clinical evaluation of the person. Only the recipient is capable of putting it into a meaningful context. For example, the manager might say, "When Pete showed you the error you made, you told him it was none of his concern. I wonder if you were mad at Pete for some other reason." This statement shows the recipient the behavior and allows him or her to consider a possible cause for that behavior.

Receiving Feedback: "You Can't Tell Me How I Am"

From the recipient's viewpoint, the first principle is "You can't tell me how I am, and I can't tell you what you see." Although most people realize that giving feedback correctly requires skill and awareness, they are less aware of the importance of knowing how to receive feedback. When receiving feedback, many people tend to argue about, disown, or justify the information. Statements like "I didn't say that," "That's not what I meant," and "You don't understand what I was trying to do" are attempts to convince the person giving the feedback that he or she did not see or observe what he or she claims. However, the recipient needs to understand that the observer—whether manager, peer, or subordinate—is relating what he or she experienced as a result of the recipient's behavior. The giver and the recipient may well have different viewpoints, and there is nothing wrong with that. The purpose of feedback is to give a new view or to increase awareness. If an argument ensues and the observer backs down, the recipient is the loser.

The appropriate response, as a rule of thumb, is to say "thank you" when either type of feedback is received. It is also appropriate, of course, to ask for clarity or more detail on any issue.

The purpose of feedback is to help the recipient. Feedback can be thought of as food. It is very nourishing. When people are hungry, food is what they need; but when they are full, food is the last thing they want or need. The same applies to ingesting feedback. When people have had enough, they should call a halt. Attempting to absorb all of the feedback that might be available, or that various people would like to give, is like forcing food into a full stomach just because someone says, "Please have some more."

The recipient is responsible for demanding specificity in feedback. No feedback should be accepted as legitimate if it cannot be clearly demonstrated by an observable behavior. For example, if someone says, "You're very arrogant," an appropriate response would be "What specifically have I said or done to cause you to think that?" If that response is countered with "I don't know; I just experience you that way," then the accusation should be immediately forgotten. People cannot afford to change just to meet everyone's personal likes or expectations.

In fact, it is impossible to change to meet *everyone's* expectations, and the situation becomes compounded as more and more people give the feedback. A single act can generate disparate feedback from different people who observe the behavior. For example, a loud exclamation could be viewed as appropriately angry by one person, overly harsh by another, and merely uncouth by a third. Each person will see it from his or her unique perspective. Therefore, feedback requires action from both the giver and the recipient. Only the giver can tell what he or she observed or experienced, and only the recipient can use the information in deciding whether or not to change the behavior.

For feedback to be effective, the recipient must hear what the giver is saying, weigh it, and then determine whether or not the information is relevant. The following example illustrates how this can be done:

> *Department manager:* "Waste in your unit is up by 4 percent. Are you having any problems with your employees?"
>
> *Supervisor:* "I was not aware of the waste increase. No, I am not having trouble with my employees. I suppose I have been focusing on the quality so much that I lost sight of the waste figures. Thanks for bringing this to my attention."

Feedback Supports Growth

The second major principle, "feedback supports growth," is important, because we cannot always see ourselves as others see us. Although a person may be the world's foremost authority on himself or herself, there are still parts of that person that are more obvious to other people. Although people may be more aware of their own needs and capabilities and more concerned about their own welfare than other people are, they are able to stretch themselves and grow if they pay attention to feedback from others. Although feedback may be extremely uncomfortable at the time, a person can look back later and recognize such feedback as the spark that inspired a directional change in his or her career or personal life. If the feedback is not rejected or avoided, recipients can discover and develop ways to behave that they did not think were available.

Feedback Strategies

The strategies suggested here are not step-by-step procedures to be blindly followed. Their purpose is to help in planning and organizing an approach to dealing with an issue. They offer a logical and effective sequence of events for the feedback session. The person planning the session must decide on the desired future objective. (The "future," however, could be five minutes after the session or two years later.) During the feedback session, attention must be focused on what is happening in terms of the outcome. In other words, the focus must be on obtaining the goal, not on sticking to the strategy. This focus allows the giver to change tactics or even modify the original strategy if conditions change or unforeseen events occur. After the strategy has been selected, the following three rules should be kept in mind:

1. Be clear about what you want in terms of specific, identifiable outcomes for yourself, your subordinate, and the organization.

2. Plan what you intend to say and how you intend to conduct the meeting, according to the particular strategy you will use.

3. Have the strategy in mind as you engage the person, but keep it in the background.

Supportive Feedback Strategy

The following steps are suggested as a strategy for supportive feedback:

1. *Acknowledge the specific action and result to be reinforced.* Immediately let the subordinate know that you are pleased about something he or she did. Be specific and describe the event in behavioral terms. "You finished the project (*action*) on time (*result*)."

2. *Explain the effects of the accomplishment and state your appreciation.* For the behavior to be reinforced, the person must be able to see the effects of that behavior in specific, observable ways. Your appreciation is important but as an additional reinforcing element. The main reinforcement is the effect. "What you did on the project was a major factor in getting the contract (*effect*), and I am pleased with your outstanding work (*appreciation*)."

3. *Help the subordinate to take full responsibility for the success.* If the employee acknowledges the feedback, this step is accomplished. If the employee seems overly modest, more work is needed. Unless he or she can, to some degree,

internalize the success and receive satisfaction from it, very little growth will occur. One approach would be to ask how the success was accomplished or if any problems were encountered and how they were overcome. In talking about what happened, the employee is likely to realize how much he or she was really responsible for. It is important for both you and the employee to hear how the success was accomplished.

4. *Ask if the subordinate wants to talk about anything else.* While the employee is feeling positive and knows that you are appreciative and receptive, he or she may be willing to open up and talk about other issues. The positive energy created by this meeting can be directed toward other work-related issues, so take advantage of the opportunity.

5. *Thank the subordinate for the good performance.* The final step, again thanking the subordinate for the accomplishment, ensures that your appreciation will be uppermost in his or her mind as he or she leaves and returns to the work setting.

Corrective Feedback Strategy

The following steps are suggested as a strategy for corrective feedback:

1. *Immediately describe the event in behavioral terms and explain the effect.* Relate clearly in specific, observable, and behavioral terms the nature of the failure or behavior and the effect of the failure or behavior on the work group or organization. If you can appropriately say something to reduce the employee's embarrassment, the employee is more likely to accept the feedback nondefensively.

2. *Ask what happened.* Before assuming that the subordinate is at fault, ask what happened. In many instances, the subordinate is not at fault or is only partially responsible. At the worst, the employee is given an opportunity to explain before you proceed; at the best, you may receive information that would prevent you from censuring the employee.

3. *Help the subordinate to take full responsibility for the actions.* The more time spent in step 2 (finding out what happened), the easier step 3 will be. The subordinate needs to learn from the experience in order to reduce the probability of a recurrence. Unless this step is handled effectively, the subordinate will see himself or herself as a victim rather than as someone who made a mistake and is willing to correct it.

4. *Develop a plan to deal with the issues.* Once the subordinate has accepted responsibility, the next step is to help rectify the situation. Now that the employee is willing to be accountable for errors, you can jointly devise a plan that will help eliminate them. In other words, both of you must agree to take action. If you both want the same thing (that is, better performance from the subordinate), then both of you are obligated to do something about it. This is also an excellent opportunity to build on the subordinate's strengths (for example, "I'd like for you to show the same fine attention to safety regulations that you show to job specifications").

5. *State your confidence in the subordinate's ability.* Once the issue is resolved, end the session by stating your confidence in the ability of the employee to handle the situation. The object is to allow the subordinate to reenter the work setting feeling as optimistic about himself or herself as the situation permits. The subordinate must also understand that you will follow up and give additional feedback when the situation warrants it.

Reference

Blanchard, K., & Johnson, S. (1982). *One minute manager.* New York: Morrow.

Originally published in The 1987 Annual.

3

The Influence Continuum

Marlene Caroselli

Abstract: To work is to sell, regardless of whether you are "in sales" and whether you hold a position of authority over others. When you interact with people, generally you are either presenting an idea or listening to the ideas of others—either selling or being sold on something. To sell successfully, you must convince others that it is worth their time to listen to a proposal and to take action in accordance with it. This article offers a process for influencing others, consisting of five stages: balk, talk, caulk, walk, and stalk. Recommendations are given for each stage: for influencing others, for overcoming negative reactions and obstacles that may be encountered, and for fostering successful implementation of the idea being sold.

THE INFLUENCE CONTINUUM

Often when you want people to comply with your wishes, you will either not have or not want to use position power to accomplish your goal; instead, you will want to influence them. This article offers an approach to influencing that can be used by anyone in an organizational or team setting. With some adaptation, the approach can also be used in one-on-one situations. The process of influencing is separated into five stages, each named for the characteristic action of that stage (on the part of the audience, the influencer, or both): Balk, Talk, Caulk, Walk, and Stalk. Figures 1 and 2 illustrate the five stages. Figure 1 presents them as a continuum. Figure 2 shows that, during the process of influencing, investment in terms of time and effort is greatest at the beginning and gradually decreases, as those influenced become increasingly committed.

STAGE 1: BALK

When you want to influence others to listen to an idea and to take action that is different from their accustomed behavior, you must anticipate resistance. During the first stage, called "balk" because of this characteristic audience reaction, prepare to present your idea in ways that lower resistance.

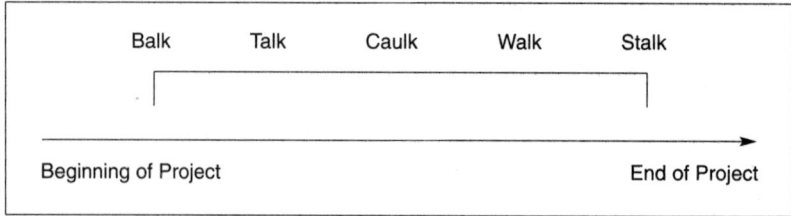

Figure 1.   The Five-Stage Influence Continuum

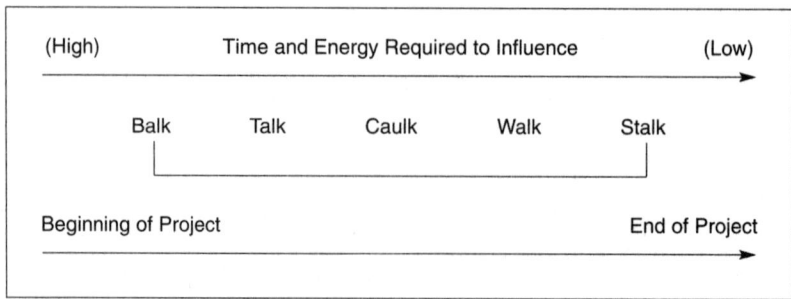

Figure 2.   Time and Energy Required to Influence During the Five Stages

Most people do not feel a need to give up a current practice and adopt another unless they believe that the new practice will be significantly better in some way. Reactions may range from hesitation or agreement on a surface level only ("It sounds okay, but let me think it over") to questions about potential benefits ("What's in it for me?") or direct challenges ("The way I'm doing things now works just fine; I don't need to change"). Influencing others successfully during the "balk" stage, when people know little or nothing about your proposal and probably do not care to know more, calls for preparing an introduction to your idea that will create interest.

Lay the Groundwork.   Before you unveil your proposal, set a tone of anticipation. Let people know that they can look forward to the change as a positive experience.

Prepare for Resistance.   Develop strategies for handling resistance to the change. Anticipate people's questions and qualms; devise appropriate responses and rehearse them before you meet with people to present the change.

Gather Precedents to Cite.   Collect facts, figures, and benchmarking data from comparable situations to include in your initial presentation of the idea. These precedents will go a long way toward persuading others of the validity of your idea.

Plan a Powerful Presentation.   Work on making your presentation powerful or dramatic. You might try an experiential approach. Let's say you previously trained three colleagues from another department in a new problem-solving technique that you now want your team to adopt. You could invite these colleagues to a team meeting, explaining to them in advance that you want them to use the technique for solving a particular problem. At the meeting you would ask the team members to suggest a real workplace problem that needs to be solved. You would form three subgroups, each to be led by one of the colleagues. Then you would give each colleague a specific amount of time to come up with a solution and walk through it with the subgroup members. After the subgroups finished the task, you would reassemble the entire group to review the new technique, discuss ways in which it may be superior to techniques currently being used, and answer any questions. Also, you would encourage your three colleagues to share their experiences with the technique, its benefits, any difficulties they encountered, how they overcame those difficulties, and their personal reactions to the technique.

Stage 2: Talk

The "talk" stage refers to the actual presentation of your idea, during which you not only explain it but also engage your audience in a discussion of it. To make your presentation as effective as possible, consider the following questions and incorporate resulting insights:

- What draws my attention?
- What factors are compelling enough for me to try something despite my belief that I don't need it?
- What persuades me? How am I persuaded?

Seasoned influencers often begin their presentations by acknowledging the negative emotions that people experience when confronted with change. One approach to exploring these emotions involves offering some simple snacks that most people in your audience are not likely to have tried. Examples of foods that are largely unfamiliar to an American audience, for example, are plantain chips and sesame tahini spread. Minutes before you start your presentation, place the food items along with any necessary serving utensils, napkins, and so forth on a table. Tell people to help themselves; then deliberately occupy yourself with paperwork or some other unrelated activity. Meanwhile, have an observer make notes about who tries the food, who avoids it, and what comments people make. After everyone has had a chance to sample or refuse the food, ask the observer to share his or her notes. Then start a discussion by stating that you fully understand people's preference for what is familiar over what is unfamiliar, in eating as well as other activities. Lead people to the realization that trying something new can yield gains, regardless of whether those gains are apparent at the outset. Following are recommendations of ways to influence successfully during the "talk" stage, when you are ready to present your idea to people who are willing to listen to it and discuss it.

Use Visual Aids. Use visual aids to supplement your message, but make sure that they do not constitute more than half of your presentation. Visual aids can be highly effective, but they cannot replace a passionate proposal and an effective rationale for implementing that proposal. Remember that visual aids are only one of the three essential "V's" of an influential presentation: voice, verbiage, and visuals.

Paint a Vivid Picture.   Use metaphors and vivid verbal pictures to engage the members of your audience and to help them envision your idea. When your purpose is to inspire and motivate rather than simply to edify, you need to appeal not only to people's minds but also to their emotions and imaginations.

Acknowledge Disadvantages and Risks.   Present and explain any potential disadvantages and risks associated with your idea. People know that every new venture has a "downside." By readily acknowledging the particulars of that downside, you will be seen as honest, and you will probably preclude some audience attacks on your idea. Discussing disadvantages and risks also allows you to appeal to the courage and adventurous spirit of others in trying your idea.

Encourage Discussion.   Make sure that you establish a dialogue with your audience. By inviting and welcoming feedback, you will arouse people's interest and enhance the likelihood of buy-in.

Ensure Viability and Value.   First ensure that the idea you are proposing is both doable and worth doing. Then assure your audience that it is viable and beneficial. Don't worry about aiming slightly higher than existing comfort levels; that is the basis of continual improvement.

STAGE 3: CAULK

The third stage, "caulk," extends throughout the process of implementing your idea. At the beginning of implementation you scrutinize your idea, looking for and "caulking" or repairing cracks or weak spots that might jeopardize the outcome. For example, if you find that you lack essential organizational support, you can cultivate a relationship with a top manager who is willing and able to champion your idea. Then, once implementation has begun, you and others involved in the process continue to assess progress. The "caulking" responsibilities that must be fulfilled consist of solving any problems that arise, obtaining any additional resources that are needed, and strengthening commitment when it begins to wane. Recommendations for successfully influencing others during the "caulk" stage, when you and they are working to reinforce implementation, are as follows:

Agree on Measurements of Success.   Because we human beings have such a capacity for misunderstanding one another, it's important that you establish clear and measurable gauges of success. Quantitative measures, although they need not be used exclusively, will tell you when and where caulking is needed.

Focus on Accomplishments.   When setbacks occur, remind people of their accomplishments to date. Sometimes during implementation the future seems too far away, the goal less distinct than it once was, the need for your idea less pressing. If you are to be effective as an influencer, expect such developments and be prepared to caulk any fissures by restoring people's flagging spirits. For example, Jack Kahn, CEO of Manco Inc., a manufacturer of duct tape, spurs his sales staff to ever-greater achievement by making "fun" promises (*Incentive,* 1997). In one case he promised that if sales quotas were met, he would let his staff shave his head. Altered pictures of the executive, with hair deleted, were posted throughout the workplace. A new record was set in sales and, as promised, the staff shaved the head of their chief executive.

Avoid Defensiveness.   Don't let defensiveness impair your ability to identify and solve problems. You won't be able to caulk if you don't know where the leaks are, and you won't know where the leaks are if you refuse to listen to feedback. If you doubt the importance of paying attention to feedback, consider the following news story: As reported in *USA Today,* "If repairs had been made when leaks in the city's infrastructure were first noted, the cost would have been about $10,000. However, the problems were not addressed; caulking was not done. Consequently, 250 million gallons of water from the Chicago River spilled into faulty underground pipes and then into the city, causing a loss of $1.5 billion attributable to repairs, lost revenue, and property damage."

Identify the Real Causes of Problems.   Use what is called the "five-why technique" to determine causes. This method consists of asking why a problem exists and continuing to ask why as each answer is received until you are certain that you have uncovered the real causes, rather than superficial reasons. You scrape through the various layers on the surface until you can clearly identify the cracks; then you can caulk appropriately.

STAGE 4: WALK

Eventually you will cease to be the impetus behind your idea; after implementation the idea continues on the strength of its own momentum. By the time you reach this fourth stage, known as "walk," you have conceived the idea, nurtured it through a period of gestation, helped to give it birth, facilitated its continued growth, and seen it reach maturity. Your idea has become standard operating procedure; now you can walk away and turn your attention to another project. Recommendations for influencing others during the "walk" stage, the process of releasing yourself from the day-to-day execution of your idea, are as follows:

Recognize People's Efforts. Think of appropriate ways to recognize those who helped you to implement your idea. For example, you might write a formal letter of commendation to everyone who participated in the process and then send a copy to each person's supervisor.

Celebrate Successful Implementation. It is important to hold some kind of celebration or ceremony to signify the end of the project. Not only does the hard work of those involved deserve public and lavish praise, but such a ritual also helps the participants to achieve closure and move on. People often remember the closing celebrations or ceremonies with as much intensity as they remember the many months preceding the project's conclusion.

Encourage Networking. Encourage networking among those who have been part of the project. Frequently, all people need is a nudge in the right direction. Keep in touch with them, and ensure that they keep in touch with one another. Some teams find the initial success so heady an experience that they decide to undertake a second project. Other teams disband after the initial success, but their members network to keep alive their memories of the past, to learn about opportunities for other projects, and to encourage their hopes for the future.

Connect Implementers with Influencers. Make plans to inform your implementers when new opportunities arise, in connection with either your own new projects or the developing projects of others. Such referrals are appreciated by those being referred, as well as by those who need implementers.

STAGE 5: STALK

Despite the usual negative connotation of the word "stalk," it is used here in a positive sense to designate the fifth and final stage of influencing. It consists of dropping in on those who have implemented your idea and who continue to support it and maintain the implementation.

Recommendations for influencing others during the "stalk" stage, during which you strive to catch others in the act of doing the right things in the right way, are as follows:

Seek Periodic Progress Reports.　Even though you are no longer associated with the day-to-day operation of your project, you will want to keep apprised of progress. Periodically seeking progress reports will assure you that the plan is being executed as you envisioned and that those responsible are able to function without your intervention. Your "stalking" efforts need not consume much of anyone's time or effort. You may make phone calls, visit people's offices, or hold "reunion" social gatherings; or you may choose to receive occasional memos. Keeping yourself updated in this way allows you to monitor progress and to continue to show your interest in the project.

Publish What Has Been Learned.　After you have witnessed that the right things are being done in the right way, spread the word about what has been learned. For example, you might oversee the publishing and disseminating of special reports or articles in the organization's newsletter. Another idea is to set up a system whereby other employees who are interested in influencing can meet with and receive advice from those who served on the implementation team. In this way you can help to spread the knowledge gained from implementation.

Encourage Continual Improvement.　Meet with your implementers to discuss ways of continually improving on the progress that's been made. You might create and maintain a record of the team members' suggestions during implementation or a log of lessons learned and insights gained; then make that record or log available to all of your implementers as well as others in the organization who are interested in similar pursuits.

CONCLUSION

It's long been observed that if you fail to plan, you can plan to fail. This adage serves as the philosophy behind the five-stage model presented in this article. Whether you use this model in influencing others or in teaching others to influence, your emphasis at each stage needs to be on careful planning to accomplish a goal.

References

A hairy challenge. (1997, December). *Incentive,* p. 12.

The Chicago flood. (1992, April 21). *USA Today,* p. 10A.

Lewin, K. (1982). Group decision and social change. In G.E. Swanson, T.M. Newcomb, & E.L. Hartley (Eds.), *Readings in social psychology.* New York: John Wiley.

Originally published in The 2000 Annual, Volume 1, Training.

4

Communicating Communication

J. Ryck Luthi

Effectiveness of management personnel of all grades is very dependent upon the ability to communicate orally not only the policy of the company but suggestions as to how work should be done, criticism of poor work, and the application of discipline, and of course the general field of human relationships (Lull, Funk, & Piersol, 1955, p. 17).

It seems safe to conclude from research studies that, by and large, the better supervisors (better in terms of getting the work done) are those who are more sensitive to their communication responsibilities. They tend to be those, for example, who give clear instructions, who listen empathically, who are accessible for questions or suggestions, and who keep their subordinates properly informed (Redding & Sanborn, 1964, p. 60).

Research leads to the conclusion that there is a positive correlation between effective communication and each of the following factors: employee productivity, personal satisfaction, rewarding relationships, and effective problem solving. Two major components of effective communication are sending messages and receiving messages. Techniques of listening and verbalizing help in both of these dimensions.

FACTORS AFFECTING THE SENDER

Self-Feelings

In the context of each communicating situation, the sender's feelings about self will affect how the message is encoded. The following questions are conscious and subconscious tradewinds that affect the effectiveness of the message: "Do I feel worthwhile in this situation? Am I safe in offering suggestions? Is this the right time (place)? Am I the subordinate or the boss in this situation?" In everyday jargon, such questions might be phrased in these ways: "Am I O.K.? Do I count?" Usually, the more comfortable or positive the self-concept, the more effective the sender is in communicating.

Belief in Assertive Rights

Linked to self-concept is the belief that one has some rights, such as the right to change one's mind; the right to say "I don't understand" or "I don't know"; the right to follow a "gut" or intuitive feeling without justifying reasons for it; the right to make mistakes and to be responsible for them; and the right to say "I'm not sure now, but let me work on it." Believing in such rights can help strengthen the sender's self-concept and avoid the defensive maneuvering that hinders communication in exchanging information. It would be wise to remember that assertive rights are not complete without responsibility. For example, one has the right to say "I don't know"; but one probably also has the responsibility to find out.

The Sender's Perception of the Message

The sender's perception of the message is encompassed in the following questions: "Do I feel the information I have is valuable? Is it something I want to say or do not want to say? How do I feel it will be received? Is the topic interesting or not interesting to me? Do I understand the information correctly, at least well enough to describe it to others, and do I know the best way to say it?"

The Sender's Feelings About the Receiver

The probability of effective communication is increased if the sender feels positive or respectful toward the receiver. Positive or respectful feelings usually carry a built-in commitment and/or desire to share communication. Negative or non-respectful feelings require conscious effort to communicate effectively. For the sender it is important to know it is all right not to like everyone, or, for the optimist, to like some people less than others. It is also important to know that we live in a world in which not everyone is going to like or respect us and that is all right, too.

Suggestions for Effective Expression

In order to send messages effectively, you should consider the following points:

1. *Become aware of your thoughts and feelings.* Do not be quick to brand them "good," "bad," "wrong," or "right." Accept them as a reflection of the present "you," and let them become best friends by giving support and feedback to your effectiveness and to your needs; consider what they are whispering or shouting to you. By increasing your awareness of your feelings, you can better decide what to do with them.

2. *Feel comfortable in expressing your feelings.* Such expression, when congruent with the situation and appropriate, can enhance communication.

3. *Be aware of the listener.* Try to verbalize your message in terms of the listener's understanding and indicate why you feel the message is important to him or her. Does it have a specific significance for the listener, or is it just "general information"?

4. *Focus on the importance of the message* and repeat key concepts and essential aspects of the information.

5. Use as few words as possible to state the message.

POINTS FOR THE LISTENER

Effective listening is as important to communication as effective sending. Effective listening is an active process in which the listener interacts with the speaker. It requires mental and verbal paraphrasing and attention to non-verbal cues like tones, gestures, and facial expressions. It is a process of listening not to every word but to main thoughts and references.

Nichols (1952) listed the following as deterrents to effective listening:

1. Assuming in advance that the subject is uninteresting and unimportant;

2. Mentally criticizing the speaker's delivery;

3. Getting overstimulated when questioning or opposing an idea;

4. Listening only for facts, wanting to skip the details;

5. Outlining everything;

6. Pretending to be attentive;

7. Permitting the speaker to be inaudible or incomplete;

8. Avoiding technical messages;

9. Overreacting to certain words and phrases; and

10. Withdrawing attention, daydreaming.

The feelings and attitudes of the listener can affect what he or she perceives. How the listener feels about herself or himself, how the message is perceived, and how the listener feels about the speaker all affect how well the recipient listens to the message. As a listener, you should keep the following suggestions in mind:

1. *Be fully accessible to the speaker.* Being preoccupied, letting your mind wander, and trying to do more than one thing at a time lessen your chances of hearing and understanding efficiently. In the words of Woody Allen, "It is hard to hum a tune and contemplate one's own death at the same time." Interrupting a conversation to answer the phone may enhance your perceived ego, but the interrupted speaker feels of secondary importance.

2. *Be aware of your feelings as a listener.* Emotions such as anger, dislike, defensiveness, and prejudice are natural; but they cause us not to hear what is being said and sometimes to hear things that are not being said.

According to Reik (1972), listening with the "third ear" requires the listener to do the following things:

1. Suspend judgment for a while;

2. Develop purpose and commitment to listening;

3. Avoid distraction;

4. Wait before responding;

5. Develop paraphrasing in his or her own words and context, particularly to review the central themes of the messages;

6. Continually reflect mentally on what the speaker is trying to say; and

7. Be ready to respond when the speaker is ready for comments.

Responses That Block Communication

The following kinds of responses can block effective communication:

Evaluation response. The phrases "You should . . . ," "Your duty . . . ," "You are wrong," "You should know better," "You are bad," and "You are such a good person" create blocks to communication. There is a time for evaluation; but if it is given too soon, the speaker usually becomes defensive.

Advice-giving response. "Why don't you try . . . ," "You'll feel better when . . . ," "It would be best for you to . . . ," and "My advice is . . ." are phrases that give advice. Advice is best given at the conclusion of conversations and generally only when one is asked.

Topping response, or "my sore thumb." "That's nothing, you should have seen . . . ," "When that happened to me, I . . . ," "When I was a child . . . ," and "You think you have it bad" are phrases of "one-upmanship" or assuming superiority. This approach shifts attention from the person who wants to be listened to and leaves him or her feeling unimportant.

Diagnosing, psychoanalytic response. "What you need is . . . ," "The reason you feel the way you do is . . . ," "You don't really mean that," and "Your problem is . . ." are phrases that tell others what they feel. Telling people how they feel or why they feel the way they do can be a double-edged sword. If the diagnoser is wrong, the speaker feels pressed; if the diagnoser is right, the speaker may feel exposed or captured. Most people do not want to be told how to feel and would rather volunteer their feelings than to have them exposed.

Prying-questioning response. Why, who, where, when, how, and what are responses common to us all. But these responses tend to make the speaker feel "on the spot" and therefore resistant to interrogation. At times, however, a questioning response is helpful for clarification; and in emergencies it is needed.

Warning, admonishing, commanding response. "You had better . . . ," "If you don't . . . ," "You have to . . . ," "You will . . . ," and "You must . . ." are used constantly in the everyday work environment. Usually such responses produce resentment, resistance, and rebellion. There are times, of course, when this response is necessary, such as in an emergency situation when the information being given is critical to human welfare.

Logical, lecturing response. "Don't you realize . . . ," "Here is where you are wrong," "The facts are . . . ," and "Yes, but . . ." can be heard in any discussion with two people of differing opinions. Such responses tend to make the other person feel inferior or defensive. Of course, persuasion is part of the world we live in. In general, however, we need to trust that when people are given correct and full data they will make logical decisions for themselves.

Devaluation response. "It's not so bad," "Don't worry," "You'll get over it," and "Oh, you don't feel that way" are familiar phrases used in responding to others' emotions. A listener should recognize the sender's feelings and should not try to deny them to the owner. In our desire to alleviate emotional pain, we apply bandages too soon and possibly in the wrong places.

Whenever a listener's responses convey nonacceptance of the speaker's feelings, the desire to change the speaker, a lack of trust, or the sense that the speaker is inferior or at fault or being "bad," communication blocks will occur.

AWARENESS OF ONE'S OWN FEELINGS

For both senders and listeners, awareness of feelings requires the ability to stop and check what feelings one is presently experiencing and to make a conscious decision about how to respond to the feelings. At first this technique may be uncomfortable and easy to forget, but only by using it will it become second nature. The individual should picture three lists:

Behaviors	$\longrightarrow$	Feelings	$\longrightarrow$	Responses
_____		_____		_____
_____		_____		_____
_____		_____		_____

At a given time, the person stops and mentally asks, "What am I feeling?" A person usually experiences a kaleidoscope of emotions simultaneously but can work on focusing on one present, dominant feeling. After the feeling has been identified, the person asks himself or herself, "What perceived behaviors are causing this feeling? Do I feel this way because of what the other person is saying or how he or she is saying it, or do I feel this way because I do not want to be bothered?"

The next step is for the person to choose how he or she wants to react to the feeling. There is much written about letting others know one's feelings in order to bring congruence to actions and words. One can choose, however, not to express a feeling because of inappropriate time, place, or circumstances. For example, I may identify a feeling of annoyance at being interrupted. To share that feeling may not be worthwhile in the situation. The main thing is that *I am aware of my annoyance* and what caused the feeling and can now *choose whether or not to let it be a block to my listening.* I may tell myself that I am annoyed but that my feeling is not going to get in the way of my listening. I can decide if my feeling is to be a listening block; and I can keep it from becoming one, if I so choose.

Another way of becoming aware of feelings is "hindsight analysis." After any given situation, the person can recheck his or her responses and/or feelings: "What happened to cause those feelings? What was I feeling during my responses? Why do I tend to avoid certain people and why do I enjoy being around others?" "Why?" is very helpful in finding feelings and behaviors that cue those feelings. As a person works with this technique, identification and decision making will become better, resulting in more effective communication.

CONCLUSION

The communication process is complex but vital to effective problem solving and meaningful personal relationships. It is a process that is never really mastered; one can continually improve on it. It requires certain attitudes, knowledge, techniques, common sense, and a willingness to try. Effective communication happens when we have achieved sufficient clarity or accuracy to handle each situation adequately.

References

Lull, P.E., Funk, F.E., & Piersol, D T. (1955). What communications means to the corporation president. *Advanced Management, 20,* 17–20.

Nichols, R.G. (1952). *Listening is a ten part skill.* Chicago: Enterprise Publications.

Redding, W.C., & Sanborn, G.A. (Eds.) (1964). *Business and industrial communication: A sourcebook.* New York: Harper & Row.

Reik, T. (1972). *Listening with the third ear.* New York: Pyramid.

Originally published in The 1978 Annual.

5

The Johari Window: A Model for Eliciting and Giving Feedback

Philip G. Hanson

The process of giving and receiving feedback is one of the most important concepts in laboratory training. It is through feedback that we implement the poet's words, "to see ourselves as others see us." It is also through feedback that other people know how we see them. Feedback is a verbal or nonverbal communication to a person (or a group) that provides that person with information as to how his or her behavior is affecting you or the state of your here-and-now feelings and perceptions (giving feedback). Feedback is also a reaction on the part of others, usually in terms of their feelings and perceptions, as to how your behavior is affecting them (receiving feedback). The term was originally borrowed from electrical engineering by Kurt Lewin, one of the founders of laboratory training. In the field of rocketry, for example, each rocket has a built-in apparatus that sends messages to a steering mechanism on the ground. When the rocket is off target, these messages come back to the steering mechanism, which makes adjustments and puts the rocket back on target again. In laboratory training, the group acts as a steering or corrective mechanism for individual members who, through the process of feedback, can be kept on target in terms of their own learning goals.

The process of giving and receiving feedback can be illustrated through a model called the Johari Window (see Figure 1). The window was originally developed by two psychologists, Joseph Luft and Harry Ingham, for their program in group process. The model can be looked on as a communication window through which you give information about yourself to others and receive information about yourself from them.

Looking at the four panes in terms of vertical columns and horizontal rows, the two columns represent the self and the two rows represent the *group*. Column one contains "things that I know about myself"; column two contains "things that I do not know about myself." Row one contains "things that the group knows about me"; row two contains "things that the group does not know about me." The information contained in these rows and columns is not static but moves from one pane to another as the level of mutual trust and the exchange of feedback vary in the group. As a consequence of this movement, the size and shape of the panes within the window will vary.

The first pane, called the "arena," contains things that I know about myself and about which the group knows. It is an area characterized by free and open exchange of information between me and others. The behavior

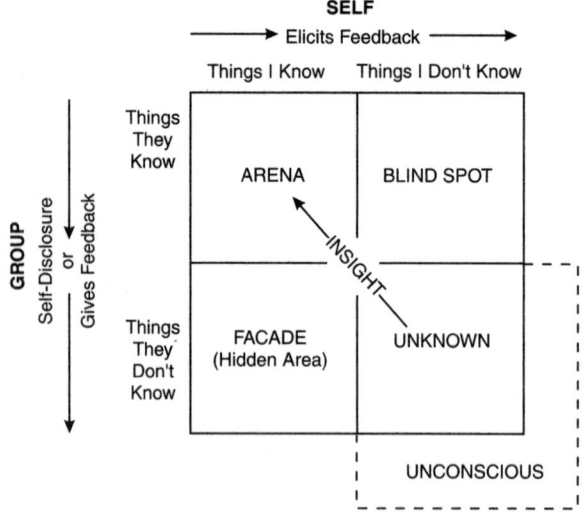

Figure 1. The Johari Window

The Pfeiffer Book of Successful Communication Skill-Building Tools © 2004 John Wiley & Sons, Inc.

here is public and available to everyone. The arena increases in size as the level of trust increases between people or between a person and his or her group and, therefore, as more information—particularly personally relevant information—is shared.

The second pane, the "blind spot," contains information that I do not know about myself but about which the group may know. As I begin to participate in the group, I communicate all kinds of information of which I am not aware, but that is being picked up by other people. This information may be in the form of verbal cues, mannerisms, the way I say things, or the style in which I relate to others. The extent to which we are insensitive to much of our own behavior and what it may communicate to others can be quite surprising and disconcerting. For example, a group member once told me that every time I was asked to comment on some personal or group issue, I coughed before I answered.

In pane three are things that I know about myself but of which the group is unaware. For one reason or another I keep this information hidden from them. My fear may be that if the group knew of my feelings, perceptions, and opinions about the group or individual members of the group, they might reject, attack, or hurt me in some way. As a consequence, I withhold this information. This pane is called the "facade" or "hidden area." One of the reasons I may keep this information to myself is that I do not see the supportive elements in the group. My assumption is that if I start revealing my feelings, thoughts, and reactions, group members might judge me negatively. I cannot find out, however, how members will really react unless I test these assumptions and reveal something of myself. In other words, if I do not take some risks, I will never learn the reality or unreality of my assumptions. On the other hand, I may keep certain kinds of information to myself when my motives for doing so are to control or manipulate others.

The last pane contains things that neither I nor the group knows about me. Some of this material may be so far below the surface that I may never become aware of it. Other material, however, may be below the surface of awareness to both me and the group but can be made public through an exchange of feedback. This area is called the "unknown" and may represent such things as intrapersonal dynamics, early childhood memories, latent potentialities, and unrecognized resources. As the internal boundaries can move backward and forward or up and down as a consequence of eliciting or giving feedback, it would be possible to have a window in which there would be no unknown. As knowing *all* about oneself is extremely unlikely, the unknown in the model illustrated is extended so that part of it will always remain unknown. If you are inclined to think in Freudian terms, you can call this extension the "unconscious."

One goal we may set is to decrease our blind spots, that is, move the vertical line to the right. How can I reduce my blind spot? As this area contains information that the group members know about me but of which I am unaware, the only way I can increase my awareness of this material is to get feedback from the group. As a consequence, I need to develop a receptive attitude to encourage group members to give me feedback. I need to actively elicit feedback from group members in such a way that they will feel comfortable in giving it to me. The more I do this, the more the vertical line will move to the right. See Figure 2.

Another goal we may set for ourselves, in terms of our model, is to reduce our facade, that is, move the horizontal line down. How can I reduce my facade? As this area contains information that I have been keeping from the group, I can reduce my facade by giving feedback to the group or group members concerning my reactions to what is going on in the group and inside me. In this instance, I am giving feedback or disclosing myself in terms of my perceptions, feelings, and opinions about things in myself and in others. Through this process the group knows where I stand and does not need to guess about or interpret what my behavior means. The more self-disclosure and feedback I give, the farther down I push the horizontal line. See Figure 3.

You will notice that while we are reducing our blind spots and facades through the process of giving and eliciting feedback, we are, at the same time, increasing the size of our arena or public area.

In the process of giving and asking for feedback, some people tend to do much more of one than the other, thereby creating an imbalance of these two behaviors. This imbalance may have consequences in terms of the person's effectiveness in the group and group members' reactions to him or her.

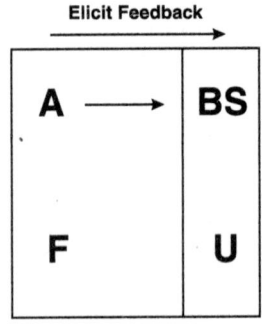

Figure 2. Reducing Blind Spots

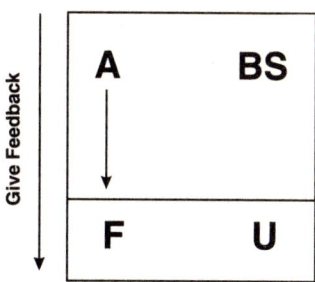

Figure 3. Reducing the Façade

The *size* and *shape* of the *arena,* therefore, is a function of both the amount of feedback shared and the ratio of giving versus eliciting feedback. In order to give you some idea of how to interpret windows, I would like to describe four different shapes that characterize an ideal window and three extreme ratios in terms of eliciting and giving feedback. These descriptions will give you some idea of how people, characterized by these windows, might appear to others in a group setting. See Figure 4.

Window number 1 is an "ideal window" in a group situation or in any other relationship that is significant to the person. The size of the arena increases as the level of trust in the group increases, and the norms that have been developed for giving and receiving feedback facilitate this kind of exchange. The large arena suggests that much of the person's behavior is aboveboard and open to other group members. As a consequence, there is less

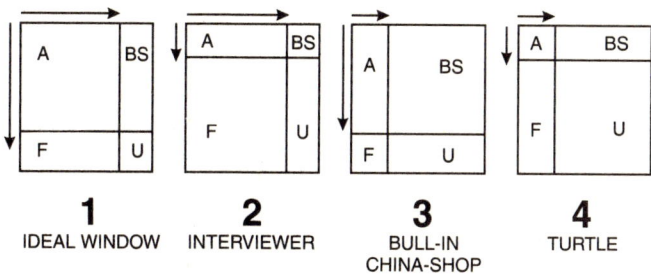

Figure 4. Ideal Window and Extreme Ratios

tendency for other members to interpret (or misinterpret) or project more personal meanings into the person's behavior. Very little guesswork is needed to understand what the person is trying to do or communicate when his or her interactions are open both in terms of eliciting and giving feedback. It is not necessary, however, to have a large arena with everyone. The people with whom you have casual acquaintances may see this kind of openness as threatening or inappropriate. It is important to note, however, in your group or with some of your more significant relationships, that when most of your feelings, perceptions, and opinions are public, neither person has to engage in game behavior.

The large facade in window 2 suggests a person whose characteristic participation style is to ask questions of the group but not to give information or feedback. Thus, the size of the facade is inversely related to the amount of information or feedback flowing from the individual. He or she responds to the group norm to maintain a reasonable level of participation, however, by eliciting information. Many of his or her interventions are in the form of questions such as these: "What do you think about this?" "How would you have acted if you were in my shoes?" "How do you feel about what I just said?" "What is your opinion about the group?" The person wants to know where other people stand before committing himself or herself. You will notice that his or her "eliciting feedback" arrow is long, whereas the "giving feedback" arrow is short. As this person does not commit himself or herself in the group, it is hard to know where the person stands on issues. At some point in the group's history, other members may confront him or her with a statement similar to "Hey, you are always asking me how I feel about what's going on, but you never tell me how you feel." This style, characterized as the "Interviewer," may eventually evoke reactions of irritation, distrust, and withholding.

Window number 3 has a large blind spot. This person maintains his or her level of interaction primarily by giving feedback but eliciting very little. The person's participation style is to tell the group what he or she thinks of them, how he or she feels about what is going on in the group, and where he or she stands on group issues. Sometimes the person may lash out at group members or criticize the group as a whole, believing that he or she is being open and aboveboard. For one reason or other, however, the person either does not hear or appears to be insensitive to the feedback given to him or her. The person either may be a poor listener or may respond to feedback in such a way that group members are reluctant to continue to give him or her feedback; for example, he or she may become angry, cry, threaten to leave. As a consequence, the person does not know how he or she is coming across to other people or what his or her impact is on them. Because the person does not appear to utilize the corrective function (reality) of group feedback, many of his or her reactions or self-

The Pfeiffer Book of Successful Communication Skill-Building Tools © 2004 John Wiley & Sons, Inc.

disclosures appear out of touch, evasive, or distorted. The result of this one-way communication (from him or her to others) is that the person persists in behaving ineffectively. As the person is insensitive to the steering function of the group, he or she does not know what behaviors to change. The person's "eliciting feedback" arrow is very short, while his or her "giving feedback" arrow is long. This style of interaction comes across as a "bull-in-a-china-shop."

Window number 4, having the large unknown, represents the person who does not know much about himself or herself, nor does the group know much about him or her. This person may be the silent member or the "observer" in the group, who neither gives nor asks for feedback. As you can see in window number 4, the "eliciting" and "giving feedback" arrows are very short. He or she is the mystery person in the group because it is difficult for group members to know where this person stands in the group or where they stand with him or her. The person appears to be surrounded by a shell that insulates him or her from other group members. When confronted about the lack of participation, he or she may respond with a comment such as "I learn more by listening." Group members who are not actively involved in the group or who do not participate receive very little feedback because they do not provide the group with any data to which they can react. The person who is very active in the group exposes more facets of himself or herself and provides the group members with more information about which they can give feedback. While this kind of exchange may cause the active participant some discomfort, he or she learns considerably more than the inactive participant who does not give or elicit feedback. The person characterizing this window is called the "turtle" because a shell keeps other people from getting in and him or her from getting out. It takes a considerable amount of energy to maintain an arena this small in a group situation because of the pressure that group norms exert against this kind of behavior. Energy channeled in maintaining a closed system is not available for self-exploration and personal growth.

The goal of eliciting feedback and self-disclosure or giving feedback is to move information from the blind spot and the facade into the arena, where it is available to everyone. In addition, through the process of giving and receiving feedback, new information can move from the unknown into the arena. A person may have an "aha" experience when he or she suddenly perceives a relationship between a here-and-now transaction in the group and some previous event. Movement of information from the unknown into the arena can be called "insight" or "inspiration."

It is not an easy task to give feedback in such a way that it can be received without threat to the other person. This technique requires practice in developing sensitivity to other people's needs and being able to put oneself in other people's shoes. Some people feel that giving and receiving feedback cannot be learned solely by practice; instead, giving and receiving feedback require a basic philosophy or set of values that must first be learned. This basic philosophy is that the person be accepting of himself or herself and others. As this acceptance of self and others increases, the need to give feedback that can be construed as evaluative or judgmental decreases.

Originally published in The 1973 Annual.

6

Using Personality Typology to Build Understanding

Toni La Motta

Understanding how others function is a first step in working with them. Organizations consist of people who differ from one another on almost every dimension possible. Diversity certainly is a challenge that is here to stay.

However, diversity also offers an opportunity to appreciate differences. In the face of constant change, organizations need the differing strengths of different types of people. Increasingly organizations are turning to human resource development (HRD) professionals to guide them in managing change and managing diversity. The HRD professional then acts as a bridge between past and future technologies and as a facilitator between employees and managers and among various teams within an organization. As such, an HRD professional plays roles ranging from teacher to technician to prophet to psychologist.

In a dynamic environment, the most important and least understood HRD role may be that of psychologist. People react in many ways to changes around them; some adjust well, but others see change as threatening and react defensively. An effective way to diminish the defensiveness that occurs with change is to define roles clearly and to make personnel feel acknowledged and appreciated. Understanding theories of personality type can help an HRD professional in these endeavors.

This article begins with brief reviews of three related theories of personality typology: Jung, Myers and Briggs, and Keirsey and Bates. Jung's work formed the basis of the later work of Myers and Briggs; the work of Myers and Briggs, in turn, formed the basis of Keirsey and Bates' work. Next the article describes the four dimensions of personality that provide the structure for these three theories. These dimensions are extraverts/introverts, sensors/intuitors, thinkers/feelers, and judgers/perceivers. The article subsequently outlines Jung's functional types and then provides detailed explanations of the more widely recognized Myers-Briggs types and Keirsey and Bates temperaments.

The explanatory material is important to an understanding of the next section, the role of temperament and management style. Following that, four case studies of how personality typology can be used in an organizational setting are presented. Finally, the article describes action steps that can be taken by managers and HRD practitioners who want to use personality typology to enhance understanding in the workplace.

HISTORICAL PERSPECTIVE ON PERSONALITY TYPOLOGIES

Jung's Theory of Type

Carl Gustav Jung was a Swiss psychiatrist whose theory of psychological types (Pfeiffer, 1991) helps people to recognize and to understand basic personality differences. In essence, this theory describes people's ranges of orientations to *perceiving* (sensing versus intuitive), *interpreting* (thinking versus feeling), and *responding* (extraversion versus introversion). By becoming aware of these basic differences, people can better understand others' motivations and behaviors and can expand tolerance and respect for those whose styles are different.

Jung recognized that people make clear choices from infancy on as to how they use their minds. Although each person has some of each kind of orientation, he or she generally favors one type over the other. Furthermore, types seem to be distributed randomly with regard to sex, class, level of education, and so on.

The Myers-Briggs Type Indicator

In the early 1940s, Isabel Briggs Myers and her mother, Katherine Briggs, began to explore ways to use Jung's theories to explain personality differences. With World War II as a backdrop for their work, the women saw peace in the world as the ultimate goal of understanding personality types. Their paper-and-pencil instrument for determining personality type became known as the *Myers-Briggs Type Indicator* (MBTI). The MBTI is based on a psychometric questionnaire whose results seem to determine accurately a person's viewpoint and style of behavior in all aspects of work and personal interaction. Use of the MBTI is extremely widespread; to date, several million Americans have taken it. The instrument also has been translated into Japanese, Spanish, and French, helping many people around the world to understand and accept themselves and others.

Using Jung's theories as a starting point, Myers and Briggs designated three sets of letter pairs: E/I (extraversion/introversion), S/N (sensing/intuitive), and T/F (thinking/feeling). To these they added a fourth letter-pair set, J/P (judging/perceiving). The MBTI classifies each person in one of sixteen personality types, based on that person's preferences for one aspect from each of the four sets of letter pairs.

The Keirsey and Bates Sorter

David Keirsey and Marilyn Bates (1984), in their book *Please Understand Me,* use the same four dimensions that are found in the MBTI to outline four "temperaments." They define temperament to be "that which places a signature or thumb print on each of one's actions, making it recognizably one's own" (Keirsey & Bates, 1984, p. 27). Temperament is based first on the S/N dimension; differences on this dimension are "the source of the most miscommunication, misunderstanding, vilification, defamation, and denigration" (Keirsey & Bates, 1984, p. 17). People with an S (sensing) preference gather information in concrete ways, based on facts in the here-and-now; temperament theory then subdivides them based on how they act on this information (judging or perceiving). People with an N (intuitive) preference gather information in abstract ways, based on intuition and possibilities; the temperament sorter then subdivides them based on how they make decisions about this information (thinking or feeling). Thus, according to the Keirsey and Bates Sorter, a person is characterized as SJ, SP, NT, or NF.

THE LETTER PAIRS

The dimensions used by Jung, by Myers and Briggs, and by Keirsey and Bates represent tendencies rather than absolute choices. In most situations, a person prefers one approach over another. A person who understands his or her own approach then can use this information to improve communication with others.

Extraverts and Introverts (E and I)

Jung identified two basic "attitude types," which describe the direction of a person's interest: extravert and introvert. In the context of personality typology, an extravert is a person whose energy source is the external world of people and things, whereas an introvert is a person whose energy source is the internal world of ideas.

An extravert generally appears friendly and easy to know; he or she tends to think aloud and to express emotions openly. An extravert often acts first and reflects later. In contrast, an introvert is most productive in private and tends to reflect first and act later. An introvert generally internalizes emotions and appears to be less self-revealing and to need a great deal of privacy. Contrary to popular notions, however, a healthy extravert may need time alone and a healthy introvert may have highly developed communication skills.

Sensors and Intuitors (S and N)

The S/N preference concerns the mental function of how a person takes in data from the outside world. The letter "S" is used for sensing, and the letter "N" is used to represent intuition.

A person is a sensor if he or she takes in information in parts, noticing fine details by means of the five senses. A sensor is a very practical individual who wants, trusts, and remembers facts. He or she is highly attuned to details and is usually very orderly and organized. For this person, learning is a linear process in which data are collected sequentially and facts are believed only when experience bears them out. A sensor values order and truth; often he or she is a hard worker who values perspiration more than inspiration. A sensor enjoys the present moment, takes directions easily, and may be most comfortable with tasks that are highly detailed and require repetition.

In contrast, a person is an intuitor if he or she perceives a situation in its entirety rather than piecemeal. An intuitor has a global perspective and is often described as living by a sixth sense. He or she is imaginative and is always anticipating future events. An intuitor looks primarily for relationships and patterns in the information taken in. He or she is an innovator who believes in and excels in hunches, visions, and dreams. An intuitor is adept at long-range planning and can recognize all of the complexities in a given situation.

 The Pfeiffer Book of Successful Communication Skill-Building Tools © 2004 John Wiley & Sons, Inc.

Taken to the extreme, the sensing function causes a person to miss the forest for the trees, and the intuitive function causes a person to miss the trees for the forest.

Thinkers and Feelers (T and F)

Once data have been collected, decisions often must be made, a process that is determined by one's T/F preference. The letter "T" represents thinking, and the letter "F" represents feeling. Although this preference is based on how logic is used, thinking should not be equated with intelligence or intellectualism, nor should feelings be equated with emotion.

A thinker processes data in a formalized, linear fashion and can be described as logical. He or she uses an impersonal basis to make decisions in an exacting, structured, analytical manner. The thinker's actions are apt to be deliberate and based on cause and effect. A thinker is ruled by the intellect and will fight for principles; such a person is drawn to jobs that do not depend heavily on interpersonal dynamics.

In contrast, a feeler makes decisions based on a process that more closely reflects personal values or concerns for others. He or she looks at extenuating circumstances rather than rigid laws. A feeler often is artistic and sensitive to the opinions and values of others; consequently, he or she is best suited to a job that requires strong communication and interpersonal skills.

Judgers and Perceivers (J and P)

Jung's discussion of temperament actually dealt only with the S/N, T/F, and E/I preferences, emphasizing that each person has preferred styles of perceiving and judging that are best done in either the outer or inner world. Myers and Briggs built from Jung's theory and created a fourth pair of opposites for the MBTI, concerning the style in which a person lives life (J/P). The J/P preference represents the weight that each of the mental functions (S/N and T/F) is given. In general terms, this preference refers to lifestyle.

A judger prefers situations that are orderly and well planned; and the judging function is dominant in the decision-making dimension, regardless of whether the person is a thinker or a feeler. Such a person prefers a decided, settled path and tends to be neat and orderly. A judger must know priorities and works best when his or her attention is dedicated to one assignment. He or she likes to be prepared for any situation, runs life by making and adhering to lists, thrives on deadlines, and always sees a task through to the end. However, because of a strong desire for stability, a judger may find change troubling.

A perceiver, on the other hand, lives life in an open, fluid, and spontaneous fashion. The perceiving function is dominant in his or her actions, regardless of whether the person is a sensor or an intuitor. A perceiver sees life's possibilities and is always ready for the unexpected. He or she remains open to sudden changes and is comfortable with letting things happen by chance; this person adapts well to changing environments and usually enjoys being given a variety of tasks.

COMBINING ATTITUDE AND FUNCTION

Jungian Functional Types

Jung categorized people according to the psychological functions of thinking, feeling, sensation, and intuition; each of these functions then could be found in either extraverted or introverted individuals. In this way, Jung recognized eight functional types: extraverted sensing, extraverted intuitive, extraverted thinking, extraverted feeling, introverted sensing, introverted intuitive, introverted thinking, and introverted feeling.

The Myers-Briggs Types

The sixteen four-letter type indicators that classify types in the Myers-Briggs Type Indicator (MBTI) consist of one letter representing a trait from each pair. Thus, the possible sixteen combinations are ISTJ, ESTJ, INTJ, ENTJ, ISTP, ESTP, INTP, ENTP, ISFJ, ESFJ, INFJ, ENFJ, ISFP, ESFP, INFP, and ENFP. Each of these types has certain characteristics and preferences that distinguish it from other types.

ISTJ *(Introverted-Sensing-Thinking-Judging)*. The ISTJ type is dependable and decisive. Attention to detail, combined with dependability, draws a person of this type to careers in which he or she can work alone and can focus on results, objective thinking, and procedures.

ESTJ *(Extraverted-Sensing-Thinking-Judging)*. People of this type perceive through their senses rather than through their intuition and can be described as practical and oriented toward facts. Because of their focus on visible, measurable results, this type is ideally suited to organizing and directing the production of products.

INTJ *(Introverted-Intuitive-Thinking-Judging)*. The INTJ type is naturally good at brainstorming and excels at turning theory into practice. People of this type often choose careers that allow them to create and apply technology, and they often rise rapidly in an organization because of their abilities to focus on both the overall picture and the details of a situation.

ENTJ *(Extraverted-Intuitive-Thinking-Judging)*. The ENTJ type uses intuition rather than sensing to explore possibilities and relationships between and among things. People of this type have a strong desire to lead and tend to rise quickly to upper-management levels.

ISTP *(Introverted-Sensing-Thinking-Perceiving)*. An ISTP type excels in technical and scientific fields because he or she uses sensing and thinking to analyze and organize data. Not wasting time is a key value for a person of this type, who tends to become bored by tasks that are too routine or too open ended.

ESTP *(Extraverted-Sensing-Thinking-Perceiving)*. The ESTP type makes decisions based on logic more than on feelings. Such a person prefers to learn as he or she goes along, as opposed to becoming familiar with an entire process in advance. An ESTP type has excellent entrepreneurial abilities but quickly tires of routine administrative details.

INTP *(Introverted-Intuitive-Thinking-Perceiving)*. The INTP person uses intuition to explore possibilities, preferring new ideas and theories to facts. This person's love of problem solving means that he or she is well suited to research and other scholarly endeavors.

ENTP *(Extraverted-Intuitive-Thinking-Perceiving)*. The ENTP type is attracted to work that allows the exercise of ingenuity. Such a person learns best by discussing and challenging and has little tolerance for tedious details.

ISFJ *(Introverted-Sensing-Feeling-Judging)*. An ISFJ type combines an ability to use facts and data with sensitivity to others. Although uncomfortable in ambiguous situations, a person of this type is a hard worker and prefers work in which he or she can be of service to others, both within the organization and outside it.

ESFJ *(Extraverted-Sensing-Feeling-Judging)*. The ESFJ type is probably the most sociable of all types and thus is highly effective in dealing with others. He or she often leans toward a career that serves others, such as teaching or the ministry.

INFJ *(Introverted-Intuitive-Feeling-Judging)*. The INFJ type has a natural gift for facilitating groups. Although interpersonal interactions are important to a person of this type, he or she can be comfortable with any work that allows opportunities to grow and to learn.

ENFJ *(Extraverted-Intuitive-Feeling-Judging)*. An ENFJ person is a born leader who places highest priority on people. This preference, combined with his or her strong verbal-communication skills, makes the ENFJ type ideally suited for motivating others.

ISFP *(Introverted-Sensing-Feeling-Perceiving)*. People whose type is ISFP excel at tasks that require long periods of concentration and have senses that are keenly tuned. They prefer to express themselves in concrete, nonverbal ways and are especially inclined toward the fine arts.

ESFP *(Extraverted-Sensing-Feeling-Perceiving)*. An ESFP type uses sensing and feeling to live in the here-and-now and is most challenged by activities that are new and require some special effort. He or she prefers work that provides instant gratification, an opportunity to work with others, and avenues for learning and growing.

INFP *(Introverted-Intuitive-Feeling-Perceiving)*. People of this type are best described as idealists; they value integrity, hard work, and concern for others. Although they are adaptable to most work situations, they are best suited for careers that involve service to others.

ENFP *(Extraverted-Intuitive-Feeling-Perceiving)*. The ENFP type is most interested in finding new solutions to problems and is attracted to work that involves people. Such a person tends to be impatient with rules and procedures and serves better as a mentor for employees than as a boss.

Keirsey and Bates Temperaments

The Keirsey and Bates Sorter classifies people by temperament rather than by type. Based on Jungian definitions, the sorter lists the four temperaments as sensing perceiver (SP), sensing judger (SJ), intuitive thinker (NT), or intuitive feeler (NF). Sensing perceivers and sensing judgers each make up between 35 and 40 percent of the population, while intuitive thinkers and intuitive feelers each constitute between 10 and 15 percent.

Sensing Perceiver (SP). An SP, or sensing perceiver, constantly seeks adventure and freedom and is open to whatever is new and changing. This person lives for the moment and makes an excellent negotiator. In a work setting, he or she may deal well with vendors and may be useful in keeping the staff abreast of new products and new releases. Such a person often is known as a troubleshooter who likes to resolve crises and to rally the support of others in solving a problem. Hot-line programs are often well served by people with SP temperaments.

Sensing Judger (SJ). A sensing judger (SJ) believes in rules, regulations, and rituals. He or she works best in a formalized, structured situation and often is well qualified to institute the structure that is needed in the workplace. A sensing judger would make a good librarian, inventory controller, scheduler, or administrator. He or she thrives on setting standards, whether in reference to resource selection or the day-to-day operating procedures of a department.

Intuitive Thinker (NT). A person who wants to understand, control, explain, and predict events is an intuitive thinker (NT). He or she is an intellectual purist and a self-motivated learner. An intuitive thinker can best serve an organization as a visionary and planner. He or she is a determined learner and will pursue something until it is mastered. An intuitive thinker makes an excellent system designer because of his or her conceptual ability and may be well suited to customer support because of a need to strive for resolution. Newsletter production may also be a good outlet for an intuitive thinker's skills.

Intuitive Feeler (NF). An intuitive feeler (NF) is enthusiastic and often has strong communication and interaction skills. Such a person often excels at public relations and can be effective as a liaison to other companies or departments. An intuitive feeler also often makes a good teacher, especially on the elementary level, because of his or her patience and understanding. Such a person is excellent at setting the atmosphere necessary for quality learning and training.

PERSONALITY TYPOLOGY AND MANAGEMENT STYLE

Because all temperament types bring their own strengths and weaknesses to the workplace, managers need to be aware of their own temperaments before they attempt to understand and lead the rest of the staff. Temperament, according to Keirsey and Bates (1984), is a prime determinant of management style. To use personality typing within a department, a manager must first look at the corporate culture in which the department exists, its particular mission, and the objectives of the available positions. He or she must consider whether the department is new, is seeking greater recognition, or is a mature group looking to improve or to maintain services.

Managers need to assess their own temperaments and personality styles and their inherent strengths and weaknesses before assessing the behavior exhibited by current or potential staff members. Most managers will need staff members with similar personalities to support them. However, opposite types are also needed to compensate for existing weaknesses. The best teams seem to be composed of people who have some personality differences but who are not total opposites. Differences can encourage group growth, while similarities can facilitate understanding and communication. When a team of complete opposites does exist, an understanding of type theory can go a long way toward alleviating disagreements and recognizing the need for team integration.

When looking for a clear vision of how to plan for the future, the manager should keep in mind that sensors are best at practical, detail tasks; that intuitors are best at creative, long-range tasks; that thinkers' skills are appropriate for analysis tasks; and that the skills of feelers are suited to interpersonal communications. A successful staff demands that all skills be used in the right place at the right time. A good manager will recognize the type of task that needs to be done and will assign the best and most appropriate talents to accomplish the job in harmony.

The Sensing-Judging (SJ) Manager

The SJ manager is a stabilizer or consolidator who excels at establishing policies, rules, schedules, and routines. Such a person is usually patient, thorough, and steady. An SJ manager will provide a sense of permanence that encourages industriousness and responsibility in a staff. A sensing-judging manager is a task master who feels that every person must earn his or her keep and therefore tends to be very reluctant to praise. Operational costs are carefully monitored, but true costs often are not. An SJ manager is impatient with delays, may decide issues too quickly, and often complicates matters by preserving rules that are unnecessary and by adapting slowly to change. On the other hand, this type of person has a strong understanding of policy and is a good decision maker. He or she runs meetings efficiently; is always punctual; and can absorb, remember, manipulate, and manage a great deal of detail—traits that certainly are useful to an organization.

The Sensing-Perceiving (SP) Manager

Unlike the SJ manager who sets up rules, regulations, and procedures, the SP manager excels at putting out fires. An SP manager has a good grasp of potential situations and is an excellent diplomat. The SP type is crisis oriented and makes decisions based on expediency; neither regulations nor interpersonal relations are so sacred that they cannot be negotiated by an SP manager. An SP manager is concerned with getting the job done and is very reluctant to pay attention to theory or abstractions. Such a person often makes commitments that he or she has difficulty carrying out when something comes up that is more current or more pressing. An SP manager can be unpredictable and, when not troubleshooting, can resist changes that are imposed by someone else. However, such a person adapts well when a situation changes, always seeming to be one step ahead. He or she is very practical and often sees break-

The Pfeiffer Book of Successful Communication Skill-Building Tools © 2004 *John Wiley & Sons, Inc.*

downs before they occur. Beginning or struggling organizations are ideally suited to the SP manager.

The Intuitive-Thinking (NT) Manager

An NT manager is the true architect of change, questioning everything and basing answers on proven laws and principles. Although he or she is not good at managing maintenance or consolidation projects, an intuitive-thinking manager excels at and takes pride in technical knowledge. An NT manager avoids crisis at all costs because everything must make sense to him or her. The NT manager may delegate the execution of organizational plans but afterward rarely feels that these plans were carried out satisfactorily. Such a person often has difficulty with interpersonal transactions because of his or her impatience and reluctance to show appreciation. A need to escalate standards continually results in the NT manager's feeling restless and unfulfilled. An NT manager sees the long- and short-term implications of a decision, can recognize the power base and the structure of an organization, and can make decisions based on impersonal choices. More than any other type, an intuitive thinker seems to have the vision to see all dimensions of a system, making him or her a very capable planner and constructor.

The Intuitive-Feeling (NF) Manager

A manager who is an intuitive feeler is probably inclined toward personnel management. He or she is committed to the personal progress of the staff, to seeing possibilities for others' growth, and to helping others to develop their potentials. An NF manager is democratic and encourages participation; in fact, he or she often is overly concerned with the staff's personal problems. Interpersonal relationships often drain the time and energy that an NF manager needs for his or her personal and professional life. However, an NF manager's ability to show appreciation can encourage staff; verbal fluency and enthusiasm make him or her an excellent spokesperson for an organization. An NF manager is often a good judge of the organizational climate; he or she shows great patience, despite a tendency to opt for stopgap solutions. Such a person can find himself or herself in conflict if the qualities of subordinates do not match the tasks required by the manager's superiors. In such situations, an NF manager can become frustrated at not being able to please all of the people all of the time; often, however, he or she learns to turn liabilities into assets.

PERSONALITY TYPOLOGY IN THE WORKPLACE

Personality typology can be used to classify a person's behavioral type in very general terms. Despite significant differences within each type, recognizable similarities are apparent. The purpose of studying types is not to judge others or to change their behavior, but rather to understand and to appreciate why people respond differently to the same stimuli. No preference is right or wrong; each has its own strengths and weaknesses. Effective decision making in the workplace can hinge on exploiting the strengths and minimizing the weaknesses of each type. For example, on a team project, an S (sensor) will note essential details and apply practicality. However, an N (intuitive) will exercise ingenuity, see the possibilities, and give a clear vision of the future. In addition, a T (thinker) will provide incisive analyses, and an F (feeler) will supply the necessary interpersonal skills. Together all four will be effective in bringing the project to fruition.

Being typed, therefore, should not limit people but rather uncover their possibilities. Living or working with a person of the opposite type can generate friction, but understanding may help opposites to accept and to take advantage of each other's differences.

Case Study 1: Extraverted Feeler and Introverted Thinker

The following example illustrates how a manager and an employee used personality typology to resolve a conflict. The manager, Helen, showed a strong preference for extraversion and feeling; in contrast, the employee, Marie, tended toward introversion and thinking. When Helen would ask Marie how she felt about issues they had been discussing, Marie never expressed an opinion. Later, however, Marie would complain or express disagreement about the same issues to Helen or to another staff member. Once she understood the concept of personality types, Helen learned that the best way to encourage Marie's feedback in a positive manner was to ask Marie to consider the situation and to express her opinions within a few hours or days. This approach gave Marie the time she needed to sort through her ideas and to substantiate her viewpoint. Meanwhile, through typing, Marie began to understand Helen's need to verbalize and to monitor the environment around her.

Case Study 2: Training Extraverts and Introverts

In creating a training environment, an HRD professional must be aware that extraverts and introverts learn differently. For an extravert, concepts must follow experience; in other words, extraverts learn by example or trial and error. In contrast, an introvert wants to learn the theory or the concepts behind a lesson before trying to put them into practice.

For example, a trainer who teaches conflict-management skills to introverts might first familiarize them with theories of conflict and encourage them to read on the subject; then the trainer could conduct activities that involve group processes. A trainer teaching conflict-management skills to extraverts might need the opposite approach: Group experience would precede any written text or theory because extraverts learn best by trial and error and tend to have shorter attention spans.

The same consideration of E/I preference holds true for the working environment. Extraverts may experience a distracting loneliness when not in contact with people. They usually do not mind noise around the workplace, and some may even need noise (such as music) in order to work. The introvert, however, is more territorial. He or she may desire a defined space and may show a true need for privacy in the physical environment. Understanding and accommodating these needs and differences will foster the highest-possible productivity.

Case Study 3: A Perceiver and a Judger

Veronica, a perceiver, and Wayne, a judger, worked together on a project. Each time they met for strategic planning sessions, Wayne felt that nothing of value had been accomplished. However, Veronica felt satisfied that the sessions had unveiled many possibilities—but she also sensed Wayne's discomfort. Because they were aware of their differences on the J/P scale, they resolved the conflict by establishing a clearly defined agenda and setting strict time limits for each meeting; this satisfied the judger's needs. To satisfy the perceiver's needs, they agreed to explore as many areas as possible on a given topic and to reopen the topic at the next session to make sure that all of the issues had been explored.

Case Study 4: Hiring Decisions That Reflect S/N Preferences

The way a manager interviews potential staff members may reveal his or her own sensing/intuitive preference. A sensing manager will be inclined to rely on résumés and on proven experience, but an intuitive manager will be inclined to rely more on an actual interview and on the applicant's potential. For example, an executive-employment agent who wanted to hire an HRD manager for a major bank said that he wanted someone who had already started an HRD department successfully, preferably for a bank in the same state. This specificity indicates the agent's sensing mentality. When he was unable to fill the position according to his preference, he acceded to the bank's request for someone with the creative potential to deal with new situations and enough understanding of the HRD function to be able to create new programs—a more intuitive approach.

Because a work team needs a mix of types, managers and HRD professionals must not let their own S/N preference govern hiring decisions. For example, consider the following two approaches to learning a new computer program: (1) reading the manual and following the instructions closely, and (2) plunging into the task and looking up needed information only if it does not become obvious with use. Which approach is more successful? The answer depends on the learner. Sensors would rather use skills already learned, while intuitors prefer to develop new skills. To a sensing interviewer, an intuitor may appear to have his or her head in the clouds. Conversely, the intuitive interviewer may see the sensor as being too set in his or her ways and too materialistic. Both types have strengths and weaknesses, and both can be useful. Managers and HRD professionals who have good grasps of personality typing should be able to understand and work with both types, deploying them according to their strengths.

ACTION STEPS

The theories of personality typing that have been discussed in this article must be implemented with great care and flexibility. The following checklist provides some general guidelines for managers and HRD professionals who wish to use personality-type testing to select and assign staff members:

- Read about personality-type theories.

- Contact organizations that teach or use the theories.

- Assess the existing organizational climate to determine how the theories can best be used.

- Use the Myers-Briggs Type Indicator (MBTI) or a similar instrument to type members of the organization.

- Understand that a person's own personality type affects his or her perceptions of others.

- Help employees to understand type theory and encourage them to use this understanding to reduce conflicts.

- Consider type theory as one factor in selecting employees and in making assignments.

- Use typing to understand a person's potential and best work style, not to set limits.

- Stress that all personality types have strengths and orientations that can be invaluable to the organization.

- Use type theory to explain rather than to excuse.

- Celebrate differences.

References and Suggested Readings

Keirsey, D., & Bates, M. (1984). *Please understand me.* Del Mar, CA: Gnosology Books Ltd.

Kroeger, O., & Thuesen, J.M. (1988). Type talk: How to determine your personality type and change your life. New York: Delacorte.

Pfeiffer, J.W. (Ed.). (1991). *Theories and models in applied behavioral science* (vol. 1). San Diego, CA: Pfeiffer & Company.

Sample, J.A. (1984). A bibliography of applications of the Myers-Briggs Type Indicator (MBTI) to management and organizational behavior. In J.W. Pfeiffer & L.D. Goodstein (Eds.), *The 1984 annual: Developing human resources* (pp. 145–152). San Diego, CA: Pfeiffer & Company.

Originally published in The 1992 Annual.

7

Communicating Organizational Change: Information Technology Meets the Carbon-Based Employee Unit

Joseph G. Wojtecki, Jr., and Richard G. Peters

Abstract: Change is a constant reality in today's workplace, causing substantial psychological stress within a workforce concerned about its livelihood and quality of life. Against this backdrop is the information technology (IT) explosion, bringing its unprecedented capacity for disseminating information. Many managers are embracing e-mail, intranets, and other technological innovations as efficient solutions to the high communication demands during times of change. However, simply making information available is not the same as communication. People under stress can lose as much as 80 percent of their ability to process information. Situations in which concerns are high and trust is low call for as much attention to the methods of communicating as to the messages.

This article offers insights into why human resources need more low-tech communication during times of change. The research on risk communication provides nontraditional and sometimes counterintuitive principles for avoiding some familiar pitfalls to effective internal communication.

Two powerful forces are surging through American enterprises with accelerating velocity: organizational change and information technology (IT). In the wake of organizational change often lies a workforce in turmoil, shaken by loss of employment security and loss of loyalty to seemingly uncaring employers. For all its capacity, information technology provides only limited relief for the anxieties and frustrations of human resources burdened by change.

There are costs in productivity and competitiveness, often hidden, caused by the psychological drag of constant change in the organization and uncertainty in the workforce. The question is whether effective internal communication can lessen the negative impacts of change on the workforce. If so, what part can information technology play in this?

INTERNAL COMMUNICATION: FORM AND SUBSTANCE

The constant pressure to do more with less as organizations downsize naturally drives a quest for efficiency in all processes and activities—including communication. Under such pressure, the efficiencies inherent in new information technology (IT) applications, as high-tech means for disseminating information, appear seductively attractive to busy managers. Vast amounts of information can be disseminated to most of the workforce almost instantaneously.

"This is good," the busy manager reasons, "so long as we are disseminating the right messages." The underlying premise is that simply making information available is communicating. If the substance of the message is right, and it is efficiently disseminated, then the manager assumes that he or she has communicated. However, the form of communication is critically important for meeting the needs of people experiencing the stressful effects of change. While IT capabilities have evolved exponentially, psychologists question whether the human brain has kept pace. In fact, research suggests that our minds remain hard-wired essentially as they were in the Stone Age and we cope with the world and its threats much as our early ancestors did (Nicholson, 1998).

It is in this "human" dimension that the efficiencies of IT applications become mired and fall short of meeting the workforce's crucial communication needs during change. Research by Covello (1991) and others has found that people under stress, that is, those who feel threatened or put at risk by some force beyond their control, experience "mental noise" that can cause them to lose up to 80 percent of their ability to process information. Furthermore, the remaining 20 percent of processing capacity most often will be focused on issues of high personal concern to the employee, rather than on issues deemed important by management. These principles explain why employee responses to information sometimes seem irrational.

This reality has clear implications regarding over-reliance on IT for communicating change: *Because people under stress can process a normal load of information at only 20 percent efficiency, little is gained by increasing the efficiency at which information is disseminated.* To achieve more successful outcomes during periods of change, a company's management must focus on low-tech communication—especially face-to-face dialogue—about high concern issues in order to overcome mental noise.

ADAPTING RISK COMMUNICATION TO ORGANIZATIONAL CHANGE

The Power of Perception

The foremost principle of risk communication is that "perception equals reality." In other words, what is perceived as real is real in terms of consequences. Employees react to perceived threats, rather than to "reality." Their level of stress during times of change is proportional to their perception of threat. From management's perspective, employees may appear to overreact—even to act in an irrational manner. However, from the employee's perspective the behavior is perfectly rational, given the perceived magnitude of the threat.

Thus, when workforce response to information seems irrational, management must check its own premise and seek to understand the perceptions they have somehow created. Risk communication research has identified more than twenty factors affecting perceptions of threat (Covello, 1991). Knowledge of these factors can help managers anticipate and adjust for them, especially in the way they communicate information.

Trust and Credibility

Perception of threat is a powerful source of mental noise—psychological barriers—impeding communication. Trust and credibility—the goals of all communication—can overcome these barriers. The determinants of trust are discussed in greater detail a bit later. First, it is useful to examine how organizations create credibility that leads to that employee trust.

Within every organization, as within any segment of society, there exists a credibility hierarchy. In terms of employees' preferred sources of information, that hierarchy is as follows, according to research by Foehrenback and Rosenberg (1983):

- *Supervisors:* More than 90 percent of employees surveyed named their first-line supervisor as the preferred source of information.

- *Top Executives:* Just over half of those surveyed named top executives of the organization as a preferred source of information.

- *Union Representatives:* Fewer than 30 percent named union representatives as a preferred source of information.[1]

To the extent that a preference for a particular source for information is a measure of that source's credibility, this research provides some guidance. However, only research specific to an organization can determine the actual hierarchy, so it is important to know and consider an organization's credibility hierarchy when considering which communication strategy is best. There are two reasons for this, according to Covello (1991):

- *The Rule of Credibility Transference:* A message will take on the credibility of the highest credible source that will publicly state or agree to it. (This is the basis of celebrity endorsements in advertising and marketing.)

- *The Rule of Credibility Reversal:* When a lower credible source challenges or attacks a higher credible source, the lower credible source further loses credibility. Ignoring this second rule and counter-attacking when one's position is challenged by someone with more credibility may produce a result that is exactly opposite from what is desired.

The conclusion for higher level managers, who are often perceived as less credible than first-line supervisors in high concern situations, is that they may need to bring in more credible third-party allies to communicate effectively with the workforce. Attempts to "go it alone" could well boomerang.

Within this context of trust and credibility, the dynamics of threat perception can be examined.

FACTORS IN THREAT PERCEPTION

Of the various factors of threat perception studied, three of the most powerful, trust, control, and benefit, are examined below to illustrate how they collectively impact the processing of information.

---

[1]Note that respondents were permitted more than one response.

Trust

Trust is the single most powerful factor in perception of threat. Research shows that a risk managed or communicated by a trusted source is perceived as less threatening than one represented by an untrustworthy source (Covello, 1991; Fessenden-Raden, Fitchen, & Heath, 1987; Slovic, 1993). The trust factor can alter the perception of a threat two thousand times. An example can be used to illustrate the point: A quantifiable risk, such as a health risk from poor indoor air quality, may be objectively determined to pose one chance in one million of causing cancer. When the source of information about that risk is not trusted, those who feel threatened perceive the chances as one chance in five hundred. Remember, what is perceived as real is real in its consequences.

Perceptions based on trust are similarly altered when risks cannot be so precisely quantified, for example, the risk of losing one's livelihood as the result of organizational change.

Control

Control is one tier below trust in its power over perception of threat. Research shows that when we have some control over a risk it is less threatening than if the risk is imposed involuntarily (Covello, 1991; Fischhoff et al., 1978; Slovic, 1987). The control factor can bias the perception of a risk one thousand-fold.

To continue with the same illustration: If the same indoor air quality risk of a million to one is imposed on a group that has no voice in the decision and no means of affecting the risk, the perception of this risk assumes the proportions of one in one thousand. Predictably, the group's reactions will be more consistent with the greater risk. This, in part, explains why people willingly accept a higher risk that is voluntary, such as a one in sixty-seven risk of a fatal traffic accident, yet become outraged over a much lower risk that is imposed on them, such as a one in one million increased risk of cancer.

In the same way, the perception of threat associated with management decisions during change will be skewed if these decisions are imposed and lack meaningful input from the people they impact.

Benefit

Benefit carries the same threat-perception weight as control (one thousand-fold), that is, a risk that provides some balancing benefit is less threatening than a risk with no associated benefit (Covello, 1991; Fessenden-Raden, Fitchen, &

Heath, 1987; Slovic, 1987). Using the example of indoor air quality, lack of benefit can increase the perception of a one in a million risk to an apparent one in a thousand risk, with a correspondingly intensified reaction.

To lessen the perception of risk, it is important that those who benefit from a risk be the same as those who will face its consequences. When the risks faced by some yield benefits only for others, an additional perception of threat factor is invoked—fairness—and causes further negative reactions.

Cumulative Effects

Individually, the power of these three threat-perception factors is very strong, but they are overwhelming when seen as cumulative (Fischhoff et al., 1978).

Consider again the example of indoor air quality. In two simple steps, withholding both control and benefit, a calculated risk of one in one million becomes a perceptual certainty of one in one! Add to this the effect of mistrust of the messenger, and employee reactions quickly can become extreme.

Once managers know the effects of these threat-perception factors, they should not be surprised at the workforce reactions to decisions they make over which the workforce has no control and sees no perceived benefit. What might seem irrational is very rational in a workforce that does not trust those who are communicating with them.

MANAGING THREAT PERCEPTIONS

Because *perceptions*, not reality, determine the direction and intensity of employees' reactions and behavior, organizations must learn to manage the perceptions they give. The risk communication research provides some useful principles for effective, though often nontraditional and counter-intuitive, approaches managers can follow for communicating with their workforce.

Managing the Trust Factor

To gain the advantages of trust, managers must understand the basis of trust. Research shows that when people are asked how they decide whether or not to trust someone in a high concern situation, their responses fall into these broad categories (Covello, 1993).

The Pfeiffer Book of Successful Communication Skill-Building Tools © 2004 John Wiley & Sons, Inc.

- Honesty and openness;
- Competence and expertise;
- Dedication and commitment; and
- Caring and empathy.

Most managers would wish to have these characteristics ascribed to them, but are not sure how to exhibit the characteristics for employees. Managers are often shocked to learn how the factors relate to one another in terms of earning employee trust. As Figure 1 shows, caring and empathy are equal to all the other characteristics combined for earning employee trust in high concern situations.

Trust is the most powerful threat-perception factor, and in high concern situations people seek assurance first that a manager cares about their well-being. Will Rogers once observed, "People want to know that you care, before they care what you know." Caring and empathy are best communicated by direct, face-to-face, two-way dialogue. The importance of two-way communication cannot be overemphasized in high concern situations.

The simple act of listening to an employee's concerns is one of the most compelling gestures a manager can make to demonstrate caring and empathy. Seeing employee concerns as real—that is, real in the employee's perception— further establishes the manager's caring and empathy, and in turn establishes

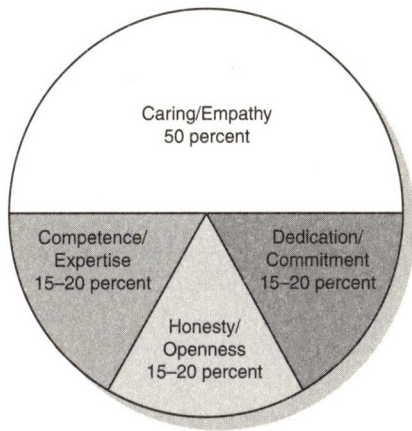

Figure 1. Relative Weight of Elements of Trust

employee trust. Generally, information technology-based channels of communication are too one-way and impersonal to allow managers the opportunity to convey empathy and caring.

Managing the Control Factor

People in a democracy generally have the right to participate in decisions that affect their lives, their property, and the things they value. By participating in the decision-making process, people gain the satisfaction of knowing that they have exerted some measure of control over what will happen to them.

Employees, as products of a democratic society, bring definite expectations to the workplace about whether or not decisions made by those in authority are acceptable to them. Their judgment often hinges on whether or not they had a voice in the decision.

Many organizations at least tacitly acknowledge the value of employee involvement in the decision process. Even the Malcolm Baldrige Award criteria recognize the value of employee involvement. However, organizations often fall short of the goal. What often substitutes for legitimate employee involvement is the more familiar model of decide-announce-defend (DAD).

In the DAD model, employee input usually is sought, if at all, during the "announce" phase—after the decision has been made. Employees are offered the opportunity to respond to a decision that has been reached, and then management defends the decision by explaining all of the compelling facts and rationale that led to the decision.

The DAD model does not qualify as employee involvement. Because the dialogue is after the fact, the decision is seen as imposed, and employees are denied an opportunity to influence it. High concern decisions reached without employee involvement trigger the threat-perception factor of control, increasing the perception of any risk associated with the decision one thousand-fold.

Management is often reluctant to accede legitimate employee involvement in the decision process because they fear the results of relinquishing control. This is not necessarily something to fear. Granting the workforce a voice in decisions, through an appropriate forum, is just that—a voice. It does not constitute a vote or a veto. All that employees need, and in most cases expect, is assurance that their point of view has been heard, reasonably considered, and responded to before the decision is made. Outrage is a common consequence of denying employees a voice in decisions that impact them in high concern situations.

The Pfeiffer Book of Successful Communication Skill-Building Tools © 2004 John Wiley & Sons, Inc.

The expectation of employees to have a voice in decisions is a reflection of our democratic society and of management trends, such as the participatory decision making stressed in total quality management (TQM) programs. The reality for managers is that this expectation has become a part of the culture, and it's very much like the genie that once out of the lamp refuses to go back inside.

Managing the Benefit Factor

Communicating the benefits associated with a perceived threat that employees are asked can be extremely difficult. In most cases, there either is an offsetting benefit to employees or there is not. Whichever is true, managers must be mindful of the impact of the perception of benefit factor (one thousand-fold) when communicating with employees. They must consider:

- If there is a benefit for accepting a risk, that benefit must be clearly defined and communicated to the employees. This is especially important for "survivors" of an organizational change, who ultimately will determine the success of the post-change organization.

- In the same way, benefits that derive to the organization (senior management, stockholders, and others), but not to the employees themselves, must be judiciously avoided. Benefits act as a positive threat-perception factor only when the same people who bear the risks gain the benefits, whereas benefits that accrue to others can increase outrage.

This second point is particularly sensitive in an era of widely reported instances of CEO bonuses linked to massive workforce reductions. In this context, some workforce cynicism is understandable.

Reducing Other Threat-Perception Factors

Although it is beyond the scope of this article to discuss in detail other prominent threat-perception factors, managers also may encounter one or more of the following points:

- *Fairness:* Are the consequences of the perceived risk fairly distributed among all members of the organization?

- *Alternatives:* Are viable alternative courses of action available? Have these been fully considered?

- *Natural:* Is the perceived risk the result of powerful, external business forces, or was it generated arbitrarily within the organization?

Recognizing and understanding these threat-perception factors can better prepare managers to communicate effectively with employees during times of change. This knowledge can help managers to understand, and even predict, workforce reactions that otherwise might seem irrational.

This may involve nothing more than respecting the employees' point of view on issues of high concern to them. Genuine caring and empathy translate to demonstrating respect and communicating one-on-one.

COMMUNICATION OF RISK DURING CHANGE

Each organization's situation is unique, and there is no one way to communicate to reduce employees' perception of risk. However, some typical methods are described below. Because two-way communication is so critical for lowering employees' perceptions of risk during change, one general option for improving upward communication and one for improving downward communication are given below.

Upward Communication

As discussed earlier, research shows that employees' most preferred source of information about an organization is their first-line supervisor. This is not surprising, because immediate supervisors have the most opportunity for direct two-way communication with employees, and they most closely understand and relate to the employees' perspective. First-line supervisors seldom are isolated or insulated from the day-to-day realities of the workplace.

Employee preference for first-line supervisors as the source of information can be interpreted at least partly as a reflection of the employees' trust and the supervisors' credibility. This has obvious implications for the downward dissemination of information, but also has important implications for credible upward communication and employee feedback.

Depending on the size of the organization, the difficulties of large spans of control can limit meaningful dialogue between the top and bottom tiers. One good way to overcome bottle necks in communication and establish an open two-way channel is to form an employee advisory forum (EAF) compris-

The Pfeiffer Book of Successful Communication Skill-Building Tools © 2004 John Wiley & Sons, Inc.

ing representative first-line supervisors. An EAF should conform closely to the following specifications:

- Forums should be established at each geographic or organizational location and, as appropriate, at headquarters.

- Membership of each EAF should be limited to twelve to eighteen people to permit quality dialogue. One or two members should be management representatives positioned high enough to make decisions on routine issues and to have influence at the highest levels for addressing larger issues. The remaining members should be first-line supervisors.

- Membership should represent a cross section of the workforce, including union members if applicable.

- Membership should be selected by the forum itself, rather than be appointed by management. This preserves the objective credibility of the forum in the view of the workforce. The membership process could begin with a selection committee made up of two initial members and then expand to involve new members.

- The forum should be self-directed, that is, it should set its own agenda and select its own issues for discussion with management. Management can place issues on the agenda, but should not be able to exclude any workforce issues.

- The forum should collaboratively explore potential resolutions to high concern workforce issues. Management should commit to listen fully to EAF concerns and recommendations and provide open, well-considered responses.

- The forum should exercise no approval authority regarding management decisions. However, management should offer full explanations of how decisions were reached, including why any forum suggestions were not adopted.

- Responsibilities of forum membership should include a commitment to ongoing dialogue with workforce "constituents" to sustain an awareness of the forum's proceedings.

Properly constituted, an EAF can build trust and increase employee involvement in addressing high concern issues. At the same time, it fully preserves management's authority and responsibility for directing the business of the organization. While an EAF might begin as an ad hoc measure for navigating a difficult period of change, its upward communication value may be sufficient to continue its function indefinitely.

Downward Communication

One mechanism for effective downward communication works particularly well in tandem with the EAF. This mechanism is the InfoEx (information exchange). An InfoEx is based on the "poster station" format and provides an effective alternative to the mass employee meeting, a familiar technique used in many organizations. These meetings fail to achieve the benefits of face-to-face dialogue. Among the limitations of mass meetings for employees are these:

■ Most attendees are too intimidated by the large group to stand up and express their personal concerns, even when invited to do so.

■ A vocal minority can dominate the meeting and not necessarily represent the majority views.

■ The necessary logistics of large group meetings impose physical barriers between the speakers and the audience (lecterns, tables, and stages). These become perceptual barriers to communication.

■ The balance of time between management presentations and open discussion commonly tips heavily in favor of the presentations, although the opposite is more appropriate.

■ Employees often leave large group meetings further frustrated that their concerns are not being addressed.

In contrast, the InfoEx format presents a greatly enhanced opportunity for two-way dialogue. The InfoEx can be conceptualized as a trade show in which the product is communication. It consists of an open-house arrangement of informational poster stations at a location convenient for employees and spanning a longer duration than most traditional meetings. (See Figure 2.) Logistically, the InfoEx consists of the following elements:

■ A general theme or message that is relevant and addresses workforce concerns about which management wants to communicate. (Themes and messages could come, for example, from the proceedings of an EAF.)

■ A convenient location large enough to accommodate numerous simultaneous small group discussions without interference.

■ Up to six exhibits or poster stations, each one addressing some aspect of the theme or message with text and graphic information on display panels. Exhibits should be simple and judiciously avoid a glitzy or expensive appearance.

The Pfeiffer Book of Successful Communication Skill-Building Tools © 2004 John Wiley & Sons, Inc.

- Tables at each station with takeaways of all information on the poster panels, plus more detailed information and background documents supporting the messages.

- A team of presenters at each station (a minimum of two) with expertise in the subject matter of that station and training in risk communication presentation skills. Presenters should include first-line supervisors active in EAFs.

- Comment cards and collection boxes at each station and other convenient locations for employees to leave comments "on the record" for later management response.

- Representatives of senior management present at all times—not attending any particular station—to circulate with employees who may engage them individually to make any comments or ask any questions they desire.

The dynamic of the InfoEx is one-on-one or small group discussions, in contrast to the large group dynamics typical of mass employee meetings. The advantages include:

- Employees have the option of coming and going at their convenience.

- They can stand back twenty feet from a properly designed poster station and obtain the key messages related to that topic.

- They can approach closer as interest warrants and obtain more detailed information on a topic.

- They can step up to the station presenters (trained in the importance of listening effectively and conveying caring and empathy) and discuss personal concerns in relative privacy.

- They can take away information for later consideration and leave comments or questions on the record for management's response.

- They can meet senior managers under less intimidating circumstances than would otherwise be possible.

An InfoEx can run for a day, from before a workday begins until after it ends, or for selected periods over several workdays. The objective is to make it as convenient as possible for employees to attend and to allow enough time that the number in attendance at any one time is likely to be relatively small. Although the InfoEx consumes more time than mass meetings for managers and presenters, it yields far more effective communication for the time invested.

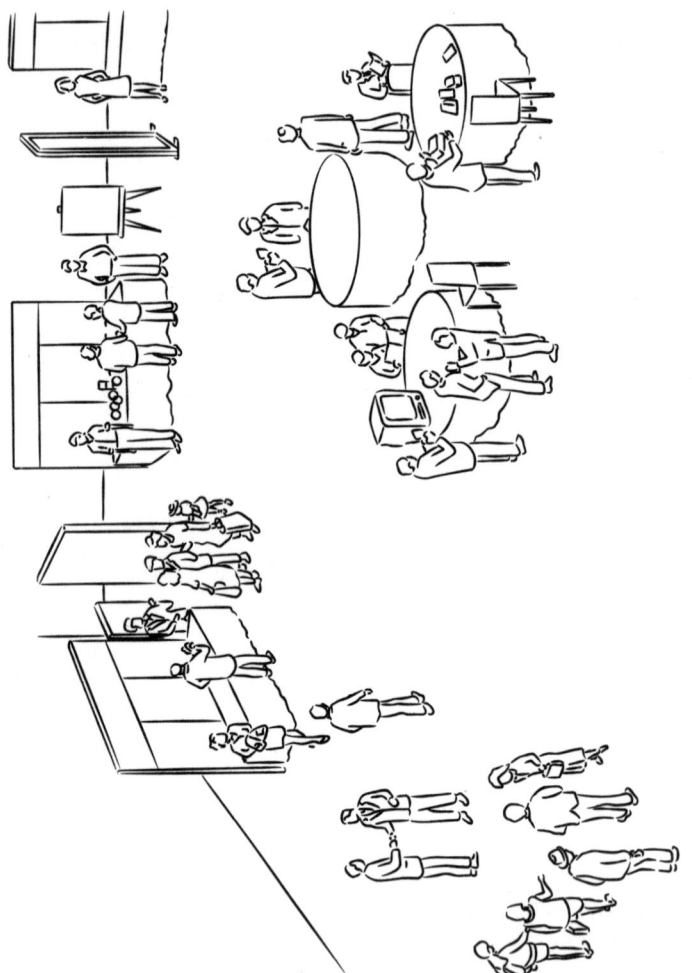

Figure 2. InfoEx Exhibit and Discussion Groups

The InfoEx is solidly rooted in the principles of risk communication, providing an excellent venue for managing important threat-perception factors and gaining trust and credibility with the workforce.

Both the EAF and the InfoEx present management with opportunities for solid return on its investment in communication. However, successful implementation requires precise application of critical risk communication principles and is best approached with a solid grounding in research.

SUMMARY

When concern is high and trust is low, conditions consistent with organizational change, a departure from the traditional communication model becomes necessary. Research studies on risk communication explain why this is so and suggest how to change the communication model for more effective results during difficult times.

In recognition of human nature, the approaches suggested by risk communication principles are low-tech rather than high-tech. They are often nontraditional and counter-intuitive, and sometimes uncomfortable to adopt. However, successful application of risk communication techniques can enhance the workforce's trust and the credibility of management and go far toward overcoming the perceptual barriers that otherwise impede communication.

Trust and credibility are the greatest assets a manager can have to lead the workforce through the throes of change, emerging intact and motivated to contribute to the success of the new organization.

Reliance on the efficient but impersonal techniques developed through information technology for disseminating information might suffice for the theoretical "carbon-based employee unit." However, human resources comprise real people, and real people require real communication—especially during times of organizational change.

References

Covello, V. (1991). Risk comparisons and risk communication: Issues and problems in comparing health and environmental risks (pp. 79–124). In R. Kasperson & P. Stallen (Eds.), *Communicating risks to the public.* Boston, MA: Kluwer Academic Publishers.

Covello, V. (1992). Trust and credibility in risk communication. *Health & Environment Digest, 6*(1), 1–3.

Covello, V. (1993). Risk communication and occupational medicine. *Journal of Occupational Medicine, 35*(1), 18–19.

Fessenden-Raden, J., Fitchen, J.M., & Heath, J.S. (1987). Providing risk information in communities: Factors influencing what is heard and accepted. *Science, Technology and Human Values, 12*(3/4), 94–101.

Fischhoff, B., Slovic, P., Lichtenstein, S., Read, S., & Combs, B. (1978). How safe is safe enough? A psychometric study of attitudes toward technological risks and benefits. *Policy Sciences, 9,* 127–152.

Foehrenbach, J., & Rosenberg, K. (1983). How are we doing? *Journal of Communication Management* (cited in Larkin & Larkin, *Communicating change: Winning employee support for new business goals.* New York: McGraw-Hill, 1994).

Nicholson, N. (1998, July/August). How hardwired is human behavior? *Harvard Business Review,* pp. 134–147.

Slovic, P. (1987, April 17). Perception of risk. *Science, 236,* 280–285.

Slovic, P. (1993). Perceived risk, trust and democracy. *Risk Analysis, 13*(6), 675–682.

Originally published in The 2000 Annual, Volume 2, Consulting.

8

Confrontational Communication

Merna L. Skinner

Abstract: Communicating with an angry person should
not be a competition or verbal volley that gathers momentum until someone "wins." Effective communicators shift the exchange from the emotional to the
rational. A person's power to disarm the emotions of
an antagonist lies in his or her initial ability to understand the nature and causes of anger. The effective
person then connects on a visceral level, as a person,
not as a corporate functionary. Next, effective communicators ask permission to provide information,
which gives the angry person perceived control over
the situation. Finally, by explaining or offering choices,
the effective communicator lays out options and further reduces emotion, replacing it with agreements.

INTRODUCTION

Communicating with an angry person is one of the most difficult business challenges a manager can face. Whether the angry person is a fellow employee, a
client, or an outside third party, being on the receiving end of heightened
emotions is stressful. The challenge of someone pounding a fist, shouting, or

making strong vocal demands forces the recipient to gather all his or her skills in order to respond.

When face-to-face with a hostile person, the natural human response is to respond in kind—to match the level of agitation in order to "stay even." In most professional situations, however, this is not an effective strategy. If you match hostility with hostility, the cycle will only perpetuate itself. The key to breaking this cycle is to establish *mutual understanding*. By finding a common ground of understanding, you can unlock the conflict and begin to build communication step by step.

In most meetings that managers attend, the content and subject matter are usually neutral in nature. Attendees typically establish a conversational rhythm that proceeds in a "give-and-take" pattern. Issues are brought up, discussed, and resolved. But when individuals come to meetings with private grievances or groups of people ban together with lists of grievances, we consider these individuals or groups as "needy." When faced with such a situation, the manager must communicate both an understanding of the grievances and a willingness to collaborate to address them.

The most extreme and challenging situation is when individuals or groups are not only needy, but also highly emotional. These situations call for a show of humanity. You must be willing to hear the other person's concerns. Once an emotionally charged person sees that you are listening and concerned, the anger will likely begin to dissipate. With the anger out of the way, you can shift the discussion to collaboration and a resolution of the issues.

To calm a hostile person and create understanding between divergent thinkers, the following four-step process is useful:

1. Inquire

2. Empathize

3. Ask permission

4. Explain or offer choices

INQUIRE

During the "inquire" phase, employ active listening skills. Focus and fully concentrate on the other person's issues and concerns. Ask open-ended questions, nod, take brief notes, and maintain eye contact as much as possible. The goal during this stage is to let the other person talk. Trying to interrupt before the person has gotten it all out is counterproductive and will only delay a resolution of the conflict.

If you are in a larger group, be sure to solicit representative opinions from as many others as possible. Although there is no way you can always poll everyone, being attuned to different points of view will build your credibility as someone committed to knowing the full extent of the issues.

EMPATHIZE

To "empathize" means to connect with someone on his or her emotional level. Empathy is not typically shown in our day-to-day business conversations; however, empathy is essential to success in an emotionally charged situation. It can best be communicated by employing a two-step process:

1. "I" to "You": This first step toward empathy simply communicates that "I" relate to how "you" feel. To do this effectively, name the emotion the person is feeling. For example:

Relate to the Person	Name of the Emotion
I appreciate	your frustration
I understand	your doubt
I share	your concern

2. "I, Too": The second step is empathizing with the person to let him or her know that you, too, feel or have in the past felt the same way. Key phrases that accomplish this are:

- "I also felt the way you do."
- "I, too, have felt that way."
- "I, too, would want to know the same thing if I were in your position."

Managing the other person's emotions at this point is about continuing to let the person calm down. Respond to high pitched or loud remarks quietly and calmly. The contrast in volume and tone will dissipate the intensity and emotionality of the situation. In the same way, if the angry person is gesturing wildly or pacing up and down, remain still and composed. Consistently applied calm responses are a powerful means of calming an antagonist down.

It may take some time to establish empathy with an angry person. He or she may at first reject what you say as "lip service." Only when you have sincerely communicated that you really see how he or she feels can you move to the next step.

Ask Permission

The natural inclination when someone has verbally attacked you is to retaliate with a quick and self-protective response. Resist this "knee jerk" reaction; instead, ask whether or not the other person would like to hear some information. By specifically requesting permission, you are putting the angry person in control—hence decreasing his or her tension. Here are some examples of appropriate language to use:

- "Would it be helpful for you to know what we have done in this area thus far?"
- "What information can I provide you?"
- "Would it be helpful to you if we . . . ?"

If your listener says "no" to all of these questions, you can then ask: "What, then, would be helpful?" All of these permission questions communicate that you are a reasonable person doing your best to reach a common ground of understanding. Once your listener says "yes," you can proceed to the final step.

Explain or Offer Choices

When you have permission to explain something, keep the explanation short and simple. You may also ask other questions to confirm your understanding. If an explanation of some sort is not appropriate, you may want to offer the angry person choices. For example:

- "Do you want to see our analysis of the situation next Tuesday or next Thursday?"
- "Would seeing the plans or the actual figures help you?"

The Pfeiffer Book of Successful Communication Skill-Building Tools © 2004 John Wiley & Sons, Inc.

The more choices you give the other person, the greater his or her sense of control will be. Knowing that there really are ways to resolve the issue will lessen the angry person's hostility. When he or she is in a more neutral and rational state, you can start to solve the problem together.

Note that this model for defusing anger does not always move in a simple and linear fashion. You may find yourself in a situation in which some residual anger surfaces just when you thought the problem had been solved. You may have to cycle through the model again or spend a longer time on an individual step. It is likely, for example, that the angry person may take quite a long time to vent his or her initial anger. Remembering that anger is essentially fear turned inside out, you must let the other person express the anger before you can move forward. In the same way, you may succeed in laying out options—but none will be acceptable. The other person's frustration may mount again, so be prepared to let him or her talk about it before attempting to lay out other options.

CONCLUSION

Remember that your success in dealing with an angry person lies in your ability to communicate with sincerity, consistency, and flexibility. He or she should know that what you are saying and how you say it are coming from the heart, not the head. Establishing a consistent pattern of responses—clear, focused, and simple—will give the angry person more security. Remember that being flexible means not being so structured or verbally disciplined that you are not prepared to address new issues that come up.

Originally published in The 2001 Annual, Volume 2, Consulting.

9

Assertion Theory

Colleen Kelley

A friend asks to borrow your new, expensive camera.
. . . Someone cuts in front of you in a line. . . . A salesperson is annoyingly persistent. . . . Someone criticizes you angrily in front of your colleagues. . . . For
many people these examples represent anxious,
stressful situations to which there is no satisfying response. One basic response theory being taught
more and more frequently in training programs is a
theory called assertiveness or assertion.

Some important aspects of assertion theory include (1) the philosophy underlying assertion, (2) the three possible response styles in an assertive situation, (3) some means of outwardly recognizing these response styles, (4)
some functional distinctions among the three styles, and (5) the six components of an assertive situation.

THE PHILOSOPHY OF ASSERTION

Assertion theory is based on the premise that every individual possesses certain basic human rights. These rights include such fundamentals as "the right
to refuse requests without having to feel guilty or selfish," "the right to have

one's own needs be as important as the needs of other people," "the right to make mistakes," and "the right to express ourselves as long as we don't violate the rights of others" (Jakubowski-Spector, 1977).

THREE RESPONSE STYLES

People relate to these basic human rights along a continuum of response styles: nonassertion, assertion, and aggression.

Assertion

The act of standing up for one's own basic human rights without violating the basic human rights of others is termed assertion (Jakubowski-Spector, 1973). It is a response style that recognizes boundaries between one's individual rights and those of others and operates to keep those boundaries stabilized.

For example, when one of her friends asked to borrow Jan's new sports car for a trip, she was able to respond assertively by saying, "I appreciate your need for some transportation, but the car is too valuable to me to lend it." Jan was able to respect both her friend's right to make the request and her own right to refuse it.

Nonassertion

The two remaining response styles, nonassertion and aggression, represent an inability to maintain adequately the boundaries between one person's rights and those of another. Nonassertion occurs when one allows one's boundaries to be restricted. In Jan's case, a nonassertive response would have been to lend the car, fearing that her friend might perceive her as petty or distrustful, and to spend the rest of the afternoon wishing she had not. Thus, Jan would not have been acting on her right to say no.

Aggression

The third response style, aggression, takes place when one person invades the other's boundaries of individual rights. Aggression, in Jan's case, might sound like this: "Certainly not!" or "You've got to be kidding!" Here, Jan would be violating the other person's right to courtesy and respect.

The Pfeiffer Book of Successful Communication Skill-Building Tools © 2004 John Wiley & Sons, Inc.

RECOGNIZING RESPONSE STYLES

Some helpful keys to recognizing nonassertive, assertive, and aggressive response styles in any given situation are (1) the type of emotion experienced, (2) the nonverbal behavior displayed, and (3) the verbal language used.

Emotion

The person responding nonassertively tends to internalize feelings and tensions and to experience such emotions as fear, anxiety, guilt, depression, fatigue, or nervousness. Outwardly, emotional "temperature" is below normal, and feelings are not verbally expressed.

With an aggressive response, the tension is turned outward. Although the aggressor may have experienced fear, guilt, or hurt at one time in the interchange, either this feeling has been masked by a "secondary" emotion such as anger, or it has built up over time to a boiling point. In an aggressive response, the person's emotional temperature is above normal and is typically expressed by inappropriate anger, rage, hate, or misplaced hostility—all loudly and sometimes explosively expressed.

In contrast to the other two response styles, an individual responding assertively is aware of and deals with feelings as they occur, neither denying himself or herself the right to the emotion nor using it to deny another's rights. Tension is kept within a normal, constructive range.

Nonverbal Behavior

Each response style is also characterized by certain nonverbal or body-language cues. A nonassertive response is self-effacing and dependent; it "moves away" from a situation. This response may be accompanied by such mannerisms as downcast eyes; the shifting of weight; a slumped body; the wringing of hands; or a whining, hesitant, or giggly tone of voice.

Aggression represents a nonverbal "moving against" a situation; it is "other-effacing" and counterdependent. This response may be expressed through glaring eyes; by leaning forward or pointing a finger; or by a raised, snickering, or haughty tone of voice.

Assertion, in contrast, is facing up to a situation; it is an approach by which one can stand up for oneself in an independent or interdependent manner. When being assertive, a person generally establishes good eye contact, stands comfortably but firmly on two feet with hands loosely at his or her sides, and talks in a strong, steady tone of voice.

Verbal Language

A third way of differentiating among assertion, nonassertion, and aggression is to pay attention to the type of verbal language being used. Certain words tend to be associated with each style.

Nonassertive words can include qualifiers ("maybe," "I guess," "I wonder if you could," "would you mind very much," "only," "just," "I can't," "don't you think"), fillers ("uh," "well," "you know," "and") and negaters ("it's not really important," "don't bother").

Aggressive words include threats ("you'd better," "if you don't watch out"), putdowns ("come on, you must be kidding"), evaluative comments ("should," "bad"), and sexist or racist terms.

Assertive words may include "I" statements ("I think," "I feel," "I want"), cooperative words ("let's," "how can we resolve this"), and empathic statements of interest in the other person ("what do you think," "what do you see").

Emotional, nonverbal, and verbal cues are helpful keys in recognizing response styles. But they should be seen as general indicators and not as a means of labeling behavior.

FUNCTIONAL DISTINCTIONS

Outwardly, the three response styles seem to form a linear continuum running from the nonassertive style, which permits a violation of one's own rights, through the assertive style, to the aggressive style, which perpetrates a violation of another's rights.

Functionally, however, as indicated in Figure 1, nonassertion and aggression appear not only very much alike but also very different from assertion. Nonassertion and aggression are dysfunctional not only because they use indirect methods of expressing wants and feelings and fail to respect the rights of all people, but also because they create an imbalance of power in which the two positions may mix or even change positions with each other. The nonassertive responder creates a power imbalance by according everyone else more rights than himself or herself, while the aggressive responder creates a power imbalance by according himself or herself more rights than everyone else.

This power imbalance is unstable. The restricted nonassertive responder may accumulate guilt, resentment, or fear until he or she becomes the ag-

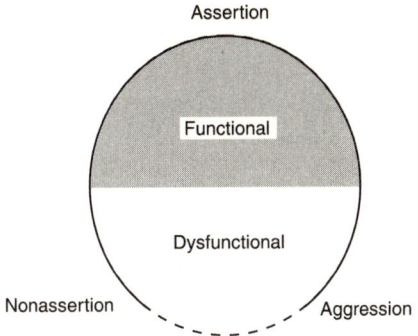

Assertion

Functional

Dysfunctional

Nonassertion   Aggression

Adapted from J. William Pfeiffer and John E. Jones, 1972, "Openness, Collusion and Feed-back," in J. William Pfeiffer and John E. Jones (Eds.), *The 1972 Annual Handbook for Group Facilitators* (p. 199), San Francisco, CA: Pfeiffer.

Figure 1. Functional and Dysfunctional Assertive

gressive responder in a burst of rage; or this person may mix a nonassertive "front" with a subversive "behind-the-scenes" attempt to "get back" at another.[1]

The assertive responder seeks a solution that equalizes the balance of power and permits all concerned to maintain their basic human rights. Thus, an imbalance of power, caused by a failure to respect the rights of all people and perpetuated by the use of indirect methods, creates a very vulnerable position for both the nonassertive and the aggressive responders, while the more functional assertive responder respects all human rights, uses direct methods, and seeks a balance of power.

COMPONENTS OF AN ASSERTIVE SITUATION

Assertion theory can be helpful in situations in which a person is anxious about standing up for his or her basic human rights. These situations include saying yes and no with conviction, giving and receiving criticism, initiating conversations, resisting interruptions, receiving compliments, demanding a fair deal as

---

[1]The mixed or indirect response can range from guilt induction to subversion in style and is represented in Figure 1 by the broken-line area.

a consumer, dealing with sexist remarks, and handling various other specific situations encountered in one's personal, social, and professional life.

A person may feel capable of being assertive in a situation but make a conscious decision not to be so, because of such things as power issues or the time or effort involved. Before making a decision to be assertive, it is helpful to examine the six components of an assertive situation:

1. The potential asserter's basic human rights and level of confidence that he or she has these rights;

2. The specific behavior to which the potential asserter is responding;

3. The potential asserter's "feeling" reactions to this specific behavior;

4. The specific behavior that the potential asserter would prefer;

5. The possible positive and negative consequences for the other person if that person behaves as the potential asserter wishes; and

6. The potential consequences of the assertive response for the potential asserter.

Once the situational assertive components have been determined, assertion-training techniques provide a means of formulating and enacting an assertive response.

CONCLUSION

Assertion theory offers a model for those who wish to stand up for their own rights without violating the human rights of others. It is a model that can be used in all types of situations—personal, professional, and social—to facilitate honest, direct, functional communication.

References and Readings

Alberti, R.E., & Emmons, M.L. (1974). *Your perfect right: A guide to assertive behavior* (2nd ed.). San Luis Obispo, CA: Impact.

Alberti, R.E., & Emmons, M.L. (1975). *Stand up, speak out, talk back!: The key to self-assertive behavior.* New York: Simon & Schuster.

Bloom, L.L., Coburn, K., & Pearlman, J. (1975). *The new assertive woman*. New York: Delacorte.

Cummings, E., et al. (1974). *Assert your self*. Seattle: Seattle-King County N.O.W.

Fensterheim, H., & Baer, J. (1975). *Don't say yes when you want to say no: How assertiveness training can change your life*. New York: McKay.

Jakubowski-Spector, P. (1973). Facilitating the growth of women through assertive training. *The Counseling Psychologist, 4*(1), 75–86.

Jakubowski-Spector, P. (1977). Self-assertive training procedures for women. In D. Carter & E. Rawlings (Eds.), *Psychotherapy with women*. Springfield, IL: Charles C. Thomas.

Lazarus, A., & Fay, A. (1975). *I can if I want to: The direct assertion therapy program to change your life*. New York: William Morrow.

Osborn, S.M., & Harris, G.G. (1975). *Assertive training for women*. Springfield, IL: Charles C. Thomas.

Pfeiffer, J.W., & Jones, J.E. (1972). Openness, collusion and feedback. In J.W. Pfeiffer & J.E. Jones (Eds.), *The 1972 annual handbook for group facilitators*. San Francisco, CA: Pfeiffer.

Phelps, S., & Austin, N. (1975). *The assertive woman*. San Luis Obispo, CA: Impact.

Smith, M.J. (1975). *When I say no, I feel guilty*. New York: McKay.

Originally published in The 1976 Annual.

10

E-Mail Basics:
Practical Tips to Improve Communication

Kristin J. Arnold

Abstract: E-mail has the enormous potential for enabling, as well as complicating, the ways we communicate. Lisa Kimball, a pioneer of the virtual team
concept, calls e-mail the "pigeon of technology. It's
everywhere." Whether you are two feet away or two
continents away, e-mail is quickly becoming the standard method for business communication. Whether
we share information, query employees, explore possibilities, bounce ideas off of others, or update action items, e-mail is emerging as the prime vehicle
for teams to communicate.

Interestingly enough, most companies have not
established common "ground rules" to ensure that
e-mail is used productively within their organizations, much less when communicating with the outside world. This article is intended to help HR
professionals and internal/external consultants set
the proper example to use and manage e-mail.

Basic Ground Rules

As you begin to set some standards within your organization, first discuss some of the ground rules for using e-mail, many of which are listed below, as a team. Your team may wholeheartedly agree, violently disagree, agree with reservations, or have its own ground rules to add. The value is in the discussion and the team members' agreement to follow its own e-mail ground rules.

Frequency.   Agree on how often team members will check messages. For example, "If in the office, we agree to check our in-box first thing in the morning, at lunch, and before we leave for the day. While traveling, we agree to check our e-mail at least once a day." Also agree on a reasonable time to respond to incoming e-mail—typically within one working day.

Technological Limitations.   Know each other's technical limitations and capabilities. Some have high-speed access and instant e-mail notification. Others, especially those e-mailing from home, may have technical limitations that affect how quickly they can receive or respond.

Tolerance.   Be tolerant of your teammates' mistakes. Some are new to using e-mail correctly, so be gracious. Coach them. Support them. Give helpful feedback and suggestions. On the other hand, don't be shy either. Ask others for help, and learn how to use e-mail to its fullest and best potential.

Keyboarding.   Increase your ease with the keyboard. Learn how to type at least fifty words per minute using inexpensive typing tutor programs such as *Mavis Beacon Teaches Typing*. Learn your software's speed keys to navigate quickly through your e-mail program.

Chat Time.   Chatting by e-mail is acceptable as long as both team members agree it's okay *and* it's not against company policies. Agree whether or not instant messaging is okay. Identify specific times to "gather," for example, between 2 and 4 p.m. EST. Otherwise, pick up the phone or go get a cup of coffee to chat.

Mix It Up.   Nurture the personal touch that fosters the spirit of teamwork. Send great e-mail along with an occasional hand-written note, a fax, a personal thanks, a phone call, etc. Mix up your media.

Traffic.   Avoid back-and-forth replies such as "thank you" and "okay." You don't have to acknowledge each and every e-mail.

Timely Response.   Get back to teammates when you say you will. Team members will assume the worst if they don't hear from you. Prevent their imaginations from conjuring up wild stories by letting them know you received the e-mail and are still working on it.

Format.   Agree on when it is appropriate to send a "paper copy" versus an e-mail. Do not send a paper copy *and* an e-mail. Agree on how to pass along critical information. Sometimes, e-mail is *not* the preferred medium. Do not hide behind e-mail to say something you should say face-to-face.

Confidential Information.   Agree on what is acceptable and unacceptable information to be passed by e-mail. If you must e-mail confidential information, agree to write "confidential" in the subject line. Otherwise, after multiple replies, the confidentiality will be long-lost or forgotten.

Flaming.   Flame wars destroy teamwork. Don't "flame" another teammate (write a strongly worded, emotionally charged opinion), and avoid *pit-bull* phrases such as "That's a stupid idea" (opinionated declarations); "I'm not about to . . ." (heated denials); and "Why is everyone . . . ?" (paranoid remarks). Don't respond to incoming flames by e-mail; otherwise, you will be entering into an "e-mail flame war" where no one emerges victorious. Instead, go face-to-face or pick up the phone.

Urban Legends.   Stop "urban legends" at your desk. These requests to forward letters to help a dying child, save the planet, or support the cause of the day are often unknowingly forwarded by kind-hearted, politically conscious team members. Don't be fooled into thinking it's safe because you know the person sending it. Check out its validity at www.urbanlegend.com.

Policies.   Review your company policy on e-mail and Internet use. Understand that e-mail is about as private as a postcard. You have no right to privacy. Your e-mail lives on long after you have hit the delete button.

Abbreviations.   Agree on common abbreviations (or acronyms), such as *as soon as possible* (ASAP), *for your information* (FYI), *close of business* (COB), *by the way* (BTW), and *in my opinion* (IMO). A good rule of thumb is to only use acronyms common to the English language, your industry, your team product/project, or your organizational culture.

Emoticons.   Emoticons or "smileys" haven't hit mainstream e-mail yet; however, they can help team members distinguish the tone of a message. Discuss the advantages and disadvantages of using emoticons and agree on when and how they should be used effectively.

Distribution Lists.   Ask your system administrator to set up a team distribution list—a "global address" that anyone can use that will automatically send a message to a predetermined list of people.

Attachments.   Agree on attachment specifications such as type and version of software. Include any compression software and settings, if applicable.

Moratoriums.   Periodically, have an "E-Mail Moratorium Day" where team members can use any other medium *except* e-mail for the day. At the end of the day, debrief the process and discuss what worked and what did not. Discover better ways to communicate with one another.

Easy Reading.   Be considerate of others when communicating by e-mail. When writing an e-mail, remember that your e-mail is *one of many other e-mails* that land in the person's in-box. Make it easy for others to read and respond to your message quickly.

CREATE COGENT MESSAGES

This section gives some pointers on drafting the text; editing the text; attaching a file; addressing the message; and sending the message.

Draft the Text

Write with your teammates in mind. Before you start typing, ask yourself, "What is the purpose of this message?" Anticipate your teammates' questions: Who needs to do what? By when? How will they do it? and Where do they need to be in order to be successful? Be clear about what you want. Be specific. Be brief and concise without being abrupt. E-mail wasn't intended for carrying on long conversations.

Multiple issues to cover? Write multiple messages. Focus on one subject per message to make it easier for your teammates to respond to each issue and to file the information when done.

Create a specific, concise subject line that will quickly identify the purpose of your e-mail, prioritize the actions needed, and motivate another to open your message. If appropriate, develop standard prefixes for the subject line, for example: *action; FYI; confidential; reply ASAP.* Develop standard subject lines for routine items such as "Team Meeting Fri 12/5 from 3 to 5 in Board Room."

Do not repeat your subject line as the first sentence of the text or anywhere else in the message. Put requests for information, deadlines, and meeting dates at the beginning of your message. Then give the details, explanations, and reasons for your request.

Be polite. Start with the person's name, as you would if you were addressing him or her in person. No need to be formal and start with Sir or Madam. If, on the other hand, you are sending a message to everyone on the team, just start the message. Alternatively, you can begin with "Hi Everyone!" "Hi Folks!" or "Hi Y'All!"

Make it easy for your teammates to answer your e-mail quickly; for example

1. Write questions and number them for ease of response and

2. Leave blanks for your teammates to respond directly on your original message.

When addressing information or action items to more than one person, start each section with the team members' names followed by the information/tasking *or* identify who is responsible for each action to be taken in boldface type or capital letters. Otherwise, teammates will assume someone else is taking care of the action.

When e-mailing an agenda for a meeting, state your purpose, desired outcomes and/or deliverables, location, and start and end times. Provide instructions on what your teammates should bring, what "homework" they should do, and the format for delivery (for example, handouts, transparencies, presentations). Enable your team to be prepared for the team meeting.

End the message with your name or signature line. Don't assume everyone knows you. Your reply address might not clearly identify you. Include the best way to contact you for immediate response or discussion. Add "Thanks" if you're asking for something or just want to say thanks! There is no need for a formal closing, such as "Sincerely."

Once you have established a working relationship, it's okay to simply sign off with your name, for example, "Kristin." No need to keep putting your signature line on every reply—it's probably already in the "thread" of the e-mail conversation.

Keep your signature line simple. Include your e-mail address and the best way to contact you. Don't clog up the system with enormous signature files with motivational quotes, commercials, cartoons, or graphics. A good rule of thumb is no more than four lines of text.

Ideally, an e-mail message should be no longer than the visible screen. If it's longer than a screen, you risk it being skimmed. Don't want to be skimmed? Then edit your message for brevity and clarity.

Edit the Text

After you have drafted your message, reread what you have written. Edit your stream of consciousness prose to make your points clear and concise. The convenience of e-mail does not give you an excuse for poor writing. Pay attention to grammar, punctuation, and spelling.

Make your e-mail easy on the eyeballs. Select a simple, universal font such as Times New Roman or Arial. Avoid cursive fonts. Use a font size everyone can read such as 12 point. UNLOCK YOUR CAPS. DON'T SHOUT AT YOUR TEAMMATES! Only use upper-case words when trying to make a point (the way I just did).

Keep your formatting simple. Just because your software can add colorful backgrounds doesn't mean you have to use them. Special formats add to the message file size and may not look as good on other computer monitors or software systems.

Divide long paragraphs into shorter ones—three to six lines of type. Leave a white space between paragraphs. When listing up to three items, consider creating a "horizontal" list: (1) point one; (2) point two; (3) point three. When listing three or more items, create a "vertical" list:

1. Use numbers (or letters) to enumerate your points.

2. Start with the same word form, such as all verbs (use, start, insert).

3. Insert white space between points.

If you must send a lengthy message, separate sections by using bold-faced or capitalized paragraph headlines or number the sections in separate paragraphs.

Condense your information. Use bullets rather than sentences. Delete irrelevant text. Use one word instead of two or three to express the same idea. Delete parenthetical comments ~~(unless you can't help yourself)~~ and exclamatory comments. ~~Can you believe people actually do that!!!!~~

Make sure the most important information is at the beginning of your message. Summarize the information that will follow in the message.

Stay away from "business speak" clichés, such as "Let's harvest the low-hanging fruit" or "We're not trying to boil the ocean here."

The Pfeiffer Book of Successful Communication Skill-Building Tools © 2004 John Wiley & Sons, Inc.

Use active voice rather than passive voice. Use positive words. Avoid *not, no, none, never*. Personalize your messages by using first names and the words *you, your, yours, our, me, my, us, I, we,* etc. When sending a message to the entire team, avoid third-person references, such as *team, them, they*.

Don't rely on your teammates' abilities to tell the difference between serious statements, satire, sarcasm, or double entendres. Avoid using satire and sarcasm altogether *or* use an "emoticon" or "smiley" to convey a specific tone of voice. Use emoticons and acronyms sparingly. Unless everyone on the team is an e-mail junkie, acronyms and smiley faces can be extremely annoying : -).

Be positive. Emphasize what you can do versus what you cannot or are unwilling to do.

Keep the overall message size to under one megabyte (1MB). Should your teammates want more information, put the details in an attachment, post it on a shared hard drive, or embed a link to a website. When sending a website address, always type in the full URL address, such as *http://qpcteam.com*. Most e-mail programs allow the user to click on the URL address and link immediately to the site.

Attach a File

Once you have written your message, you may want to put the details in an attachment or attach relevant documents. In the body of your message, let your teammates know what is in your attachments. It's their choice to open them (or not). Also, it's a nice touch to mention what type and version of software you used to create the attachment.

Try saving your document under a slightly different name. The "old" file has lots of changes, edits, pastes, and adjustments that take up space. When you "save as" to a brand new file, the "new" file is often significantly smaller and faster to send.

Send large attachments with discretion. Everyone may not have a high-speed connection. Consider making large (over 100kB) documents "small" by using alternative file formats, such as Adobe Acrobat® or WinZip®. Call your teammate before sending anything over 500kB, or, as a last resort, fax or mail lengthy documents.

Just because you sent an attachment doesn't mean your teammates were able to open it or that they actually read it. Some people either cannot (or will not) open file attachments. Consider pasting the information directly onto the message after your signature line.

Routinely and frequently scan your system for viruses, especially when receiving or downloading files from other systems. It's damaging (and embarrassing) to send a virus to a teammate.

Address the Message

You have written and edited your message and attached any necessary files. Now it is time to address your message to your teammates as well as others who need to know the information or take action.

■ Send e-mail to *(to:)* those who must take action. Courtesy/carbon copy *(cc:)* those who need to know the information, but don't need to take action or reply. Blind courtesy/carbon copy *(bcc:)* those who need to know the information, don't need to take action, and don't want (or need) anyone else to know that you shared the information with them!

■ Be careful with bcc's. Depending on your e-mail system, those who receive a bcc may not know it was supposed to be blind. On the receivers' end, it appears that the message was sent *to* them. Bcc's should not be used to "get around" others. For example, don't send an e-mail to the team leader's boss asking if you can talk to the team leader about a particular point with a bcc for the team leader!

Send the Message

When you want to send an e-mail to an expanded list (team, department, division, etc.), send the e-mail to yourself and bcc everybody else (this prevents the recipients from seeing—and having to print out—a long list of recipients) *or* consider setting up an e-mail distribution list with all your team members' addresses. Simply send the e-mail *to* the distribution list. Rather than sending bucket loads of information to everybody, ask, "I have this. Do you want it?"

If you aren't sure whether you need to keep everyone informed, add a note at the end of your message: "If you don't want to receive messages on this subject, please let me know."

Follow chain of command procedures for corresponding "up the food chain." Don't send a complaint via e-mail directly to the top just because you can.

Never assume a team member you cc'd actually read and understood your message. If you want to know whether your teammates got the message, include a personal statement asking them to let you know whether they received it or not. Or you can ask for a computerized confirmation by using the "Return Receipt Requested" option. Use this function *only* if you genuinely need to know whether the person received the message. Return receipts bug people for lots of reasons, including e-mail system compatibility and personal privacy issues. So use them sparingly.

Not everyone has e-mail. Make sure those who don't are still kept in the communications loop. Electronically fax the e-mail, or remind yourself to fax/mail them a copy.

Remember where your teammates are physically located. If you send a message, the other person might be home asleep when it arrives.

Help others triage their in-boxes by using the high, normal, low priority feature appropriately. Send messages marked "urgent" or "high priority" sparingly. You don't want to fall into the "boy who cried wolf" syndrome. If it is really urgent, pick up the phone. Most messages should be sent "normal" priority.

Before you hit the "send" button, ask yourself whether you would mind having this e-mail published in the company newsletter or your local newspaper. If your answer is yes, don't send it.

E-mail also serves as legal documentation. Say only what you mean to say. Would your attorney be able to defend you from your own words?

Use a spelling, punctuation, and grammar checker before you hit the "send" button. Set up a system default to run your "spell checker" when you hit "send." Before you blindly accept "change all," take a look at what you are accepting. Do not rely completely on your spell checker.

Before you hit the "send" button, take one last good look at your message addresses, text, and attachments.

MANAGE YOUR IN-BOX

The typical corporate e-mail user receives over thirty messages a day and spends between one and two hours dealing with these messages. Learn to manage your in-box efficiently so you can realize the benefits of e-mail: It's less formal, quicker, easier, more convenient, and more cost-effective than other forms of communication.

Quit fiddling with e-mail throughout the day. Check your e-mail regularly (perhaps first thing in the morning and right after lunch). Do not allow e-mail to interrupt your day. You don't need to know every single time you've got mail. Control your e-mail; don't let it control you!

Turn off your noisy e-mail alarm. It drives your office mates crazy.

Before you open messages, check your e-mail subject lines while in your in-box/browser. Delete the junk mail. It's the equivalent of standing by the trash can as you go through your "snail mail."

Save a tree. Only print out those e-mails for which you absolutely need to have a hard copy. When printing out e-mails for office use only, try "recycling" the unprinted side of used paper.

Handle e-mails only once. Discipline yourself to DRAFS as many messages as you can: delete; reply; act; forward; save.

Delete

Delete spam, unwanted messages, and incoming "free offers." Nothing is free. E-mail is a great way for companies to collect information and leave "cookies" (little pieces of software) on your computer.

Delete those messages you won't read or don't have time to read.

If you don't want to receive jokes, chain letters, or other types of "junk" e-mail, politely tell your teammates to delete your name from their distribution lists.

Create a "rule" or "filter" that will automatically delete unwanted e-mail from your in-box.

Reply

Reply within your agreed-on times, even if a brief acknowledgment is all you can manage. Ignoring or postponing responding to a teammate's message is downright rude. When you know your teammates are expecting a reply, but you need more time, send a short "what's happening" message to let others know when you will get back to them.

You are not expected to reply to an FYI or copy to/cc message.

Use threads (a string of responses to a single message) by setting up the "reply" function. You can set up your system to include the sender's message at the beginning or at the end of your reply—usually a matter of preference. Don't forget to edit excess forwarding information that does not relate to the content of the message.

Don't reply to a point in a prior e-mail message without quoting or paraphrasing what you're responding to and who said it. When replying to just one point of a long e-mail, clip and paste the pertinent paragraph only. ">"inserted before text means "you wrote." Try using a different color and size font so that your answers stand out from the original message. Let others know, for example, "See my response in blue."

You can use the "reply all" feature to "brainstorm" a topic, allowing everyone on the team to participate. However, be cautious about using reply all. Do all of the people from the incoming to: and cc: lines need to know?

The Pfeiffer Book of Successful Communication Skill-Building Tools © 2004 John Wiley & Sons, Inc.

Unless the matter is really urgent, don't try to reply to a message as soon as it comes in. Generally speaking, people who respond to *every* message within five or ten minutes are paying more attention to their e-mail than to their jobs.

When e-mail has been lobbed back and forth (like a tennis ball) for more than three volleys, it's time to pick up the phone or go face-to-face.

Act

Take immediate action on items that will take less than two minutes, or if they'll take longer than that but you have the time, deal with them on the spot.

Group all messages that will take longer than two minutes into an "action folder." Clean out your action folder when you have time to deal with it appropriately (usually once per day).

Flag your e-mail messages for follow-up actions.

Stop procrastinating. Just take action.

Forward

Forward misdirected e-mails to the correct address. Don't ever forward spam or chain letter e-mail. Not only are chain letters against the law, but it's tacky to perpetuate them.

When forwarding messages, put your comments at the top of the message.

E-mail gives us an illusion of privacy, but your e-mail could be forwarded to *anyone*. Do not forward your fellow teammates' mail without permission (or tacit understanding), especially if it may embarrass them. It is all too easy to forward a personal letter to the entire team, division, or company.

When forwarding e-mail, set your e-mail client character width to 70 characters. This keeps your text from getting pushed off the screen with older software that does not have a "word wrap" feature.

Fwd:Fwd:Fwd:Fwd—No one likes to scroll through the numerous names and files to get to the body of the message. More than three "forwards" and you're out!

Save

Develop an orderly filing system for those e-mail messages you wish to save. Create file folders to save your messages. Create subfolders for each process, project, or program your team works on. When saving your messages, rename them with descriptive titles under a specific subject folder so you can find them later.

Only save messages you think you will need to retrieve at a later date. After all, how many paper files have you ever gone back to?

Create a shared drive or website to post and save team information.

Keep messages remaining in your electronic mailbox to a minimum. If you don't know what to do with it, or don't have time to deal with it, save it to a "temp" folder. Clean out your temp folder at least once a week.

OTHER E-MAIL ISSUES

If you can't understand what you're reading, read it again. If you still can't understand the message, pick up the phone and call to clarify.

If a message generates emotions, look again. At first glance, the message might appear offensive. Upon rereading it, you may discover that the sender just used a poor choice of words.

Accept the fact that communication errors are inevitable. When there is a misunderstanding, take the blame. Apologize. Say what you meant more clearly. Then put the incident behind you.

Follow up important e-mail communications with a face-to-face meeting or with a telephone call/conference call with all team members. Sometimes you can explain something better verbally.

When you're away, send an "auto response" message indicating when you will return, or ask a teammate to read your mail for you and respond accordingly (give them a temporary password), or "auto forward" your e-mail to a teammate.

Never give your user ID or password to another person, and don't leave your e-mail account open when you leave your computer. Anyone could sit down at your keyboard and send out a libelous/offensive/embarrassing message under your name.

If managing your e-mail is taking up too much time, bring it up within the team. Review and/or revise your ground rules.

SUMMARY

As you put these techniques into practice, you'll find your e-mail communication will be much more crisp and meaningful. You will be able to respond promptly and with ease, as well as keep your in-box clutter-free.

Originally published in The 2002 Annual, Volume I, Training

Part 2
Experiential
Learning Activities

Experiential learning activities (ELAs) are exercises in which people learn by doing something, as opposed to just listening to a lecture or watching a demonstration. Since no substitute has yet been found for practicing the skill you're trying to learn or for witnessing directly the truth of a lesson someone is trying to impart, experiential activities have special power as a training method.[1]

The activities in this section were chosen from thirty years of the Pfeiffer *Annuals* as the best experiential exercises pertaining to communication skills. They are designed as complete packages. Each activity includes full instructions for the facilitator and participants, as well as all necessary handouts. Each also includes suggested variations the facilitator might find useful for fine-tuning the activity for a particular group or situation (you are welcome to create your own variations as well). Each recommends specific questions to be asked and discussed in order to ensure that learning takes place.

The recommended group size and time required for every activity are listed, as are the learning goals each one was designed to meet. (*Note:* You

---

[1]That special power is a double-edged sword. Experiential learning exercises also have special dangers. This is not the place for a discussion of caveats, but trainers who lack experience in the use of such activities are strongly urged to read the Introduction to the *Reference Guide to Handbooks and Annuals* (1999 Edition). It presents the theory behind the experiential-learning cycle and explains the need to complete each phase of the cycle to allow effective learning to occur.

are better positioned than any exercise's creator to determine whether it will suit the needs of your group.)

The activities adopt several different formats and processes. Some are structured practice exercises, some are role plays, and some draw their material from the participants' real-life experiences with communication in their own organizations and elsewhere.

To help speed your search for the right exercise for a given learning need, we have organized the twenty activities into two categories: Personal Communication Skills and Organizational Communication Issues.

Personal Communication Skills

These activities are designed to build skills or to increase awareness in individuals. By various means, participants practice and gain insight into such skills as speaking (or writing) clearly and concisely, listening attentively, interpreting the subtexts of body language and other forms of nonverbal communication, engaging in constructive arguments, and more.

The skills these "personal" exercises teach can be applied pretty much regardless of the culture or the management practices in place in a particular company or organization.

Organizational Communication Issues

The activities in this section have a number of objectives, but they share one common trait: all have a direct bearing on how communication works in a particular organization. Some of the exercises, such as "One-Way, Two-Way: A Communication Experiment," reveal the impact on communication of various management practices or attitudes. Others, such as "Pass It On: Simulating Organizational Communication," illustrate the relationship between communication and an organization's hierarchical structure. Some are aimed at building trust and honesty in intact work teams. Others help to shape the way a team or an organization will approach matters such as customer service, diversity, or remote working relationships.

In short, the aim of a workshop using an activity in the Organizational Issues section could be to spur changes in a company or one of its units rather than just to build skills in individual participants. And the existing culture of the organization has a more important bearing on whether these exercises will be appropriate or effective than it does for activities in the Personal Skills section.

Following are thumbnail descriptions of the activities in both categories.

1. **In Other Words: Building Oral-Communication Skills.** Exercise in speaking clearly and concisely, with built-in tips.

2. **Poor Listening Habits: Identifying and Improving Them.** The experiential activity demonstrates poor listening habits; discussions and handouts describe good ones.

3. **Mixed Messages: A Communication Experiment.** Speakers experience different reactions and attitudes from listeners, and these differences affect clear communication.

4. **Gestures: Perceptions and Responses.** Exercise using drawings to illustrate the ambiguity of nonverbal messages and the misinterpretations they can generate.

5. **Time Flies: Negotiating Personal Effectiveness Through Assertion.** Role plays teach interpersonal techniques for managing your time without alienating the people making demands on it.

6. **Resistance: A Role Play.** Illustrates and examines the effects of two different approaches to handling resistance.

7. **Seeing Ourselves As Others See Us: Using Video Equipment for Feedback.** Each learner is videotaped while making a brief presentation; the group helps analyze the tape for improvement opportunities.

8. **Your Voice, Your Self: Improving Vocal Presentations.** Practice and group feedback for public speakers, with attention to inflection, volume, speaking rate, and the like.

9. **E-Prime: Distinguishing Facts from Opinions.** Exercise demonstrating the clarity of conversations based on facts and observable behavior versus the vagueness of those based on sweeping conclusions.

10. **Speed Up! Increasing Communication Skills.** Practice exercises to encourage succinct writing and also to increase reading speed.

1. **One-Way, Two-Way: A Communication Experiment.** Exercise demonstrating a group's ability to carry out a task when members "just follow orders" versus when questions are allowed.

2. **Pass It On: Simulating Organizational Communication.** An illustration of how messages become distorted as they flow up and down an organizational hierarchy.

3. **Red Light/Green Light: From Fear to Hope.** Exercise designed to draw out honest fears, hopes, and questions from an intact work group facing an organizational change.

4. **Blivet: A Communication Experience.** Pairs try to complete a task when they can—and cannot—speak openly to each other.

5. **Analyzing and Increasing Open Behavior: The Johari Window.** Uses the classic Johari model to encourage open communication in an intact work group.

6. **Work Dialogue: Building Team Relationships.** Co-workers engage in a self-disclosure exercise focused on their working relationships.

7. **Defensive and Supportive Communication: A Paired Role Play.** Demonstrates outcomes of boss-subordinate conversations in which the boss is determined to get his way versus those in which the subject is genuinely open to discussion.

8. **Mediated Message Exchange: Exploring the Implications of Distance Communication in the Workplace.** A simulation in which group members try to accomplish a task via computer interaction with co-workers they can't see.

9. **Bugs: Improving Customer Service.** Service workers draw lessons in verbal and nonverbal communication by reflecting on their own experiences as dissatisfied customers.

10. **Enhancing Communication: Identifying Techniques to Use with Diverse Groups.** Discussions and handouts focus on ways to communicate more effectively with people of different genders, races, abilities, and backgrounds.

Personal Communication Skills

1

In Other Words:
Building Oral-Communication Skills

Editors

Goals

- To acquaint the participants with some useful tips regarding effective oral communication.

- To allow the participants to practice translating long, written messages into short but accurate and effective oral ones.

- To offer the participants an opportunity to give and receive feedback about the effectiveness of their translations and their delivery.

Group Size

A maximum of ten trios.

Time Required

Approximately one and one-half hours.

Materials

- One copy of the In Other Words Communication Handout for each participant.

- One copy each of the In Other Words Translation Sheets A, B, and C for each participant.
- A pencil for each participant.
- A clipboard or other portable writing surface for each participant.

Physical Setting

A room in which the trios can work without disturbing one another. Movable chairs should be provided for the participants.

Process

1. The facilitator explains the goals of the activity.

2. Each participant is given a copy of the In Other Words Communication Handout and is asked to read it. The facilitator leads a discussion of each of the tips presented in this handout, clarifying any points as necessary for the participants. (Twenty minutes.)

3. The facilitator instructs the participants to assemble into trios. Each participant is given one copy each of In Other Words Translation Sheets A, B, and C; a pencil; and a clipboard or other portable writing surface. The facilitator explains that one member of each trio is to concentrate on sheet A, another member is to concentrate on sheet B, and the third member is to concentrate on sheet C. Each participant is to work independently to translate the paragraph on his or her sheet into a message that is approximately half as long as the original message. This translation is to be written below the original paragraph on the sheet. (Ten minutes.)

4. The facilitator explains that within each trio all three members are to read the paragraph on sheet A silently; the member who translated this paragraph is to review his or her translation at the same time. Then the member who translated the paragraph is to turn his or her sheet face down and to deliver the translation orally. The facilitator stipulates that the oral translation need not be a word-for-word reproduction of the one that was written, but that the member delivering it should make a conscious effort to use the tips presented in the communication handout. The other two members are to listen carefully to the translation; to evaluate it for accuracy, brevity, effectiveness of statement, and use of the tips presented in the communication handout; and to provide the first member with this feedback. Then all three members are to discuss other ways in which the paragraph could

have been translated. This procedure is to be followed until all three members have translated their paragraphs, received feedback about their translations, and participated in a discussion of alternative translations. After ensuring that the participants understand the task, the facilitator asks them to begin. (Forty-five minutes.)

5. The facilitator reassembles the total group for a concluding discussion. The following questions are asked:

- What was easy or difficult about writing the translation? What was easy or difficult about delivering the translation orally?

- What common steps did each member of your trio take in translating?

- How did the translations differ with regard to member input? What might account for these differences?

- Which affected the presentations more: the writing of the translation or its delivery? How did the writing and the delivery combine in total effect?

- What are some rules for translating written messages into oral form? What other generalizations can be made about oral communication?

- What new ideas can you incorporate into your interactions with others to build your oral-communication skills further?

Variations

- The participants may be instructed to translate the paragraphs orally without writing their translations beforehand.

- The participants may be asked to translate and deliver messages that are already concise.

- If the participants share a common profession, the facilitator may replace the translation sheets with paragraphs whose content reflects issues of concern to members of that profession.

- The activity may be altered to focus on improving the participants' written-communication skills. In this case the facilitator should replace the existing communication handout with one that presents tips for effective writing.

Originally published in The Handbook, Volume X.

In Other Words Communication Handout[1]

Here are some tips to help you to communicate orally with greater effectiveness.

1. Avoid sexist language, regardless of whether your audience includes members of both sexes.

2. Use correct grammar. Never talk down to any audience.

3. Avoid slang and jargon. Clear, precise, simple language is better.

4. Avoid saying "er," "ah," and "umm."

5. Speak up. Vary your pitch, but always speak distinctly and enunciate carefully.

6. Monitor your pace as you speak. Avoid speaking too rapidly or too slowly.

7. Establish eye contact with your listeners so that they will listen and respond to what you are saying and so that you can see whether they are understanding you.

8. If you use gestures while you are speaking, make sure that they are appropriate to what you are saying.

---

[1]Adapted from T. W. Goad, *Delivering Effective Training*. Pfeiffer, 1982.

The Pfeiffer Book of Successful Communication Skill-Building Tools © 2004 John Wiley & Sons, Inc.

In Other Words Translation Sheet A[2]

Misunderstandings between persons can occur because of faulty assumptions people make about communication. Two such faulty assumptions are (1) *"you"* always know what *"I"* mean and (2) *"I"* should always know what *"you"* mean. The premise seems to be that because people live or work together, they are or should be able to read each other's minds. Some people believe that because they are transparent to themselves, they are transparent to others as well. "Because I exist, you should understand me," they seem to be saying. Persons who make this assumption often presume that they communicate clearly if they simply say what they please. In fact, they often leave the persons listening to them confused and guessing about the message being communicated. Misunderstanding is common because clarity of communication does not happen.

---

[2]From M.R. Chartier, "Clarity of Expression in Interpersonal Communication," in J.W. Pfeiffer and J.E. Jones, *The 1976 Annual Handbook for Group Facilitators,* Pfeiffer, 1976.

In Other Words Translation Sheet B[3]

Clarity of communication is influenced by the extent to which those listening and those sending are aware of their communication skills. It is possible to evaluate the assumptions one holds about his or her ability to communicate messages. Persons with careless speech-communication habits are often convinced that they are successful communicators because they are able to open their mouths and utter a stream of words. Actual skills in interpersonal communication, however, are quite different. An accurate assessment of one's own communication weaknesses and strengths is important. Often, strengths can be maximized and weaknesses improved. One person may have a charismatic personality that aids him or her in communication. Another may be very eloquent. Yet another may be able to communicate in such a way that others believe he or she understands them.

---

[3]From M.R. Chartier, "Clarity of Expression in Interpersonal Communication," in J.W. Pfeiffer and J.E. Jones, *The 1976 Annual Handbook for Group Facilitators*, Pfeiffer, 1976.

The Pfeiffer Book of Successful Communication Skill-Building Tools © 2004 John Wiley & Sons, Inc.

In Other Words Translation Sheet C[4]

The context of communication is important in determining the amount of accuracy needed or possible between persons in a given situation. How much clarity can be achieved is somewhat determined by the person's communication skills, the number of communication channels available to the person sending, how much repetition he or she can incorporate into the message, and the nature of the relationship between the persons communicating. Attempting to communicate with a person in another room presents more difficulties for the clarification process than does speaking face-to-face. In short, the speaker needs to develop a realistic expectation for the degree of clarity obtainable in a given context.

---

[4]From M.R. Chartier, "Clarity of Expression in Interpersonal Communication," in J.W. Pfeiffer and J.E. Jones, *The 1976 Annual Handbook for Group Facilitators,* Pfeiffer, 1976.

Poor Listening Habits: Identifying and Improving Them

Joseph Seltzer and Leland Howe

Goals

- To help participants to identify their poor listening habits.
- To allow participants to practice effective listening skills.

Group Size

Any number of pairs.

Time Required

Approximately one and one-half hours.

Materials

- Enough copies of the Poor Listening Habits: ABC Listening Sheet for half the participants.
- Enough copies of the Poor Listening Habits: NL Sheet for half the participants.
- One copy of the Poor Listening Habits: Theory Sheet for each participant.

- One copy of the Poor Listening Habits: Effective Listening Sheet for each participant.
- A pencil for each participant.
- A writing surface for each participant.
- A newsprint flip chart and a felt-tipped marker.
- Masking tape for posting newsprint.

Physical Setting

A room that is large enough to allow pairs to converse without disturbing one another.

Process

1. The facilitator explains the goals of the activity and tells the participants they will be involved in several activities that will require them to exaggerate poor listening habits.

2. The group is divided into pairs.

3. A copy of the ABC listening sheet and a pencil are distributed to one person in each pair. The participants who do not have the ABC listening sheet are designated "speaker number one" and are instructed to start talking to their partners about any subject they wish. (Five minutes.)

4. The facilitator stops the conversations and asks how it felt to be the speaker. The facilitator explains that the listeners were asked to count the speakers' words that began with "a," "b," and "c." The listeners are asked, "How did this scorekeeping affect your ability to listen?" (Five minutes.)

5. A copy of the NL sheet and a pencil are distributed to each number-one speaker, and the other participants are designated "speaker number two." The number-two speakers are instructed to start talking to their partners about any subject other than that discussed previously by their partners. (Five minutes.)

6. The facilitator interrupts the conversation and asks the number-two speakers how it felt to be the speaker. The facilitator explains that the listeners were instructed not to listen. The number-one speakers are asked what methods they used to keep from listening. They are also asked to recall some of the things the number-two speakers said. The facilitator leads a

discussion on which methods seemed to interfere most with listening and how a habit of using such methods can be broken. (Ten minutes.)

7. The facilitator gives the following instructions:

   The number-one speakers will try to talk to their partners about the topics they previously chose, and the number-two speakers will respond by talking about the topics they previously chose. Continue the conversation until you are told to stop.

8. After a couple of minutes, the facilitator interrupts the conversations and asks, "What was the biggest listening problem with these conversations?"

9. The facilitator announces that the number-one speakers should select new topics and that as they talk, the number-two speakers should interrupt repeatedly by asking "why" questions (e.g., "Why did he do that?" or "Why is that important?"). The number-one speakers must begin their responses with the word "because."

10. After a couple of minutes, the facilitator interrupts the conversations and asks, "What were the listening problems in this why-because conversation?"

11. The facilitator asks the number-two speakers to choose topics about which they feel positively and strongly. The facilitator then announces that each number-one speaker will attempt to argue forcefully against the number-two speaker's position.

12. After a couple of minutes, the facilitator asks participants how this conversation felt and what the listening problems were.

13. The total group is reassembled. Each participant is given a copy of the theory sheet and a copy of the effective listening sheet and is asked to read both handouts and to identify his or her own poor listening habits.

14. The facilitator elicits comparisons between the items listed on the theory sheet with the listening methods that were used in each of the activities. The participants' responses are recorded on newsprint. (Ten minutes.)

15. The facilitator leads a discussion on how to break each habit listed on the theory sheet and how to acquire the skills listed on the effective listening sheet. (Ten minutes.)

16. The participants are instructed to resume conversations with their partners. This time one member of each pair relates a personal experience while his or her partner attempts to use effective listening skills; then the roles are reversed. (Five minutes.)

17. The facilitator leads a discussion on the following questions:

- How did it feel to be a speaker this time? A listener?

- How was this last experience similar to and different from the previous experiences in this activity? What poor listening skills did you continue to use?

- How can you improve your listening skills? With whom do you need to practice more effective listening?

- What can you conclude about effective listening and its benefits?

(Fifteen minutes.)

Variations

- The activity also can be used as an icebreaker by rotating partners for each new conversation.

- Subgroups can be formed for identifying and discussing poor listening habits.

- The activity can be shortened by eliminating some of the conversations.

Originally published in The 1987 Annual.

Poor Listening Habits: ABC Listening Sheet

Do not allow your partner to read this sheet.

As your partner is talking, keep track of the total number of words he or she uses that begin with "a," "b," and "c." Do not count the articles "a" and "an" and do not count the conjunction "and." Do not tell your partner what you are doing.

You can take part in the conversation, but be sure to keep an accurate score while your partner is talking.

A   **B**   **C**

Poor Listening Habits: NL Sheet

Do not allow your partner to read this sheet.

The "NL" in the title stands for "Not Listening." While your partner is talking, your task is to not listen. You may attempt to not listen in any way you like, as long as you stay in your seat. You may occasionally say something, but it need not relate to what your partner has been saying. Although your partner may realize you are not being attentive, do not tell him or her that you are deliberately not listening.

POOR LISTENING HABITS THEORY SHEET

Most people spend more time listening than they spend on any other communication activity, yet a large percentage of people never learn to listen well. One reason is that they develop poor listening habits that continue with them throughout life. The following list contains some of the most common poor listening habits.

1. *Not Paying Attention.* Listeners may allow themselves to be distracted or to think of something else. Also, not wanting to listen often contributes to lack of attention.

2. *"Pseudolistening."* Often people who are thinking about something else deliberately try to look as though they were listening. Such pretense may leave the speaker with the impression that the listener has heard some important information or instructions offered by the speaker.

3. *Listening but Not Hearing.* Sometimes a person listens only to facts or details or to the way they were presented and misses the real meaning.

4. *Rehearsing.* Some people listen until they want to say something; then they quit listening, start rehearsing what they will say, and wait for an opportunity to respond.

5. *Interrupting.* The listener does not wait until the complete meaning can be determined, but interrupts so forcefully that the speaker stops in midsentence.

6. *Hearing What Is Expected.* People frequently think they heard speakers say what they expected them to say. Alternatively, they refuse to hear what they do not want to hear.

7. *Feeling Defensive.* The listeners assume that they know the speaker's intention or why something was said, or for various other reasons, they expect to be attacked.

8. *Listening for a Point of Disagreement.* Some listeners seem to wait for the chance to attack someone. They listen intently for points on which they can disagree.

POOR LISTENING HABITS: EFFECTIVE LISTENING SHEET

One way people can improve their listening is to identify their own poor listening habits and make an effort to change them. The list on the Poor Listening Habits Theory Sheet will help people to identify some of their own listening patterns. If the listeners will then pay special attention to the circumstances that seem to invite such behavior, they can consciously attempt to change their habits. For example, if you realize that you are "pseudo-listening" to someone, you can stop and ask that person to repeat his or her last idea. You can even say, "I'm sorry; my mind was wandering." The more you become conscious of poor listening behavior, the more likely you are to change your poor listening habits.

Besides ridding themselves of bad listening habits, people can acquire positive listening habits. Listed below are a few descriptions of behavior that can lead to effective listening:

1. *Paying Attention.* If people really want to be good listeners, they must, on occasion, force themselves to pay attention to the speakers. When speakers are dull conversationalists, a listener must sometimes use effort to keep from being distracted by other things. It is important not only to focus on the speakers, but to use nonverbal cues (such as eye contact, head nods, and smiles) to let them know they are being heard.

2. *Listening for the Whole Message.* This includes looking for meaning and consistency or congruence in both the verbal and nonverbal messages and listening for ideas, feelings, and intentions as well as facts. It also includes hearing things that are unpleasant or unwelcome.

3. *Hearing Before Evaluating.* Listening to what someone says without drawing premature conclusions is a valuable aid to listening. By questioning the speaker in a nonaccusing manner, rather than giving advice or judging, a listener can often discover exactly what the speaker has in mind—which many times is quite different from what the listener had assumed.

4. *Paraphrasing What Was Heard.* If the listener nonjudgmentally paraphrases the words of the speaker and asks if that is what was meant, many misunderstandings and misinterpretations can be avoided.

3

Mixed Messages: A Communication Experiment

Branton K. Holmberg and Daniel W. Mullene

Goals

- To explore the dynamics of receiving verbal and nonverbal communication cues that are in conflict with one another.

- To examine how nonverbal cues can convey listener attitudes that can affect the communication process.

- To develop an understanding of the importance and impact of being direct and congruent in all forms of interpersonal communication.

Group Size

A minimum of four trios is most effective. (One or two extra members can join trios to serve as additional process observers.)

Time Required

Approximately forty-five minutes to one hour.

Materials

- A copy of the Mixed Messages Communicator Instruction Sheet for one member of each trio.

- A copy of the Mixed Messages Observer Instruction Sheet and a pencil for the second member in each trio.

- One of four different Mixed Messages Listener Instruction Sheets ("Anything You Can Do, I Can Do Better," "Who Gives a Damn?," "How Sweet It Is," or "This Is How It Ought to Be") for the third member in each trio. If there are more than four trios, one or more listener roles can be duplicated.

- Newsprint and a felt-tipped marker (optional).

Physical Setting

Enough room for the trios to work without disturbing one another. The observer in each trio should be seated slightly away from the communicator and listener.

Process

1. The facilitator divides the group into trios, disperses them about the room, and tells them to talk about whatever they wish.

2. After five minutes, the facilitator gives a copy of the Mixed Messages Communicator Instruction Sheet to one member of each trio, a copy of the Mixed Messages Observer Instruction Sheet and a pencil to another member of each trio, and a copy of one of the four Mixed Messages Listener Instruction Sheets to the remaining member of each trio. Members are told only that one person in each trio is a communicator, one a listener, and one an observer.

3. Participants are then told to read their instruction sheets, but not to discuss the information on them with other members. When all members have read their instruction sheets, the facilitator tells them to begin the activity.

4. After ten minutes, the facilitator stops the communicator/listener phase and instructs the members to share their role instructions. Observers are told to report their observations (to give feedback) to communicators and listeners.

5. After ten minutes of observer reports, the large group reassembles for a discussion of the effects the different listener roles had on the feelings and perceptions of the communicators. The facilitator briefly explains each listener role, and members discuss:

- How it felt to play the different listener roles;

- How it felt to try to communicate with the different types of listeners (including frustrations and satisfactions);

- The level of communication achieved by each trio and each type of listener.

- The facilitator may list or chart major points on newsprint.

6. The facilitator examines and develops the importance of congruence, clarity, and openness in communication, at both verbal and nonverbal levels. He or she then solicits comments from participants on how these learnings can best be applied in their various back-home situations.

Variations

- The facilitator can direct the members of each trio to exchange cards with another trio after the observer report in order to give members an opportunity to try out new roles.

- Observers can become communicators, communicators listeners, and listeners observers in the second round.

- There can be four rounds, with all trios simultaneously using the same listener role and a different role being used during each round.

- If there is only one round, each listener role can be demonstrated to the total group before the discussion phase.[1]

Originally published in The Handbook, Volume VII.

MIXED MESSAGES COMMUNICATOR INSTRUCTION SHEET

You and your listener are simply to carry on the conversation that your trio has already started. Try your best to communicate your message to your partner. It is your responsibility to keep the conversation going. Do not discuss or share these instructions at this time.

MIXED MESSAGES OBSERVER INSTRUCTION SHEET

Your task is simply to collect data on what the communicator and listener are doing during their conversation. Do not concern yourself with the content of the conversation, but write down your observations about the *processes* they are using to communicate. Pay attention to what the listener and communicator do (eye contact, gestures, body positions, and other nonverbal behavior).

Describe what you observe as accurately as possible without judging it. You will be asked later to give feedback to the communicator and listener. Do not discuss or share these instructions at this time.

MIXED MESSAGES LISTENER INSTRUCTION SHEET

"Anything You Can Do, I Can Do Better"

You and your communicator are to continue the conversation that your trio started a few minutes ago. You are to appear attentive and to listen carefully to your partner, but you are to challenge everything your partner says. You may interrupt while he or she is talking, anticipate what would have been said next, and disagree or present your own point of view. You may point your finger, lean forward as if about to pounce, and engage in other nonverbal behaviors that accent your verbal behavior. You are the critic.

After you have made your criticism or statement, wait and allow your partner to begin the conversation again. Your task is not to take over the conversation but merely to interrupt, disagree, or challenge whatever is said. If your partner hesitates, remain silent until he or she begins to talk again and then resume your role. Do not discuss or share these instructions at this time.

MIXED MESSAGES LISTENER INSTRUCTION SHEET

"Who Gives a Damn?"

You and your communicator are to continue the conversation that your trio started a few minutes ago. You are to listen carefully to what your partner is saying, but are to send your partner nonverbal signals that indicate your boredom (i.e., look away, doodle, slump in your chair or sprawl on the floor, twist and fidget, clean your fingernails, fiddle with your clothing, or such). If your partner accuses you of being uninterested, insist that you are interested—you may even review what has been said—but continue to send nonverbal signs of boredom. Do not discuss or share these instructions at this time.

MIXED MESSAGES LISTENER INSTRUCTION SHEET

"How Sweet It Is"

You and your communicator are to continue the conversation that your trio started a few minutes ago. You are to appear attentive, listen carefully, and agree with everything your partner says, regardless of your own opinions on the subject. When your real opinion is opposite of what your partner is saying, smile as you indicate agreement. You may make comments such as "That's a good (great) way of putting that," "That's very insightful of you," "Oh, wow," and so on. Resist any invitation from your partner to share your ideas ("Oh, I agree with you") or to criticize or evaluate the ideas being communicated. Do not discuss or share these instructions at this time.

MIXED MESSAGES LISTENER INSTRUCTION SHEET

"This Is How It Ought to Be"

You and your communicator are to continue the conversation that your trio started a few minutes ago. You are to listen carefully to your partner and actively pursue the ideas your partner is sharing with you. Indicate that you understand his or her ideas by paraphrasing (restating) them. If you disagree, simply state your ideas calmly and logically. Ask for clarification or examples if these would be helpful. You also can indicate that you are interested in the conversation by the use of nonverbal cues such as establishing eye contact and leaning toward the speaker. Do not attempt to lead the conversation or change its direction. Although your partner is the "communicator," you are to play an active part in making the communication process as clear and mutual as possible. Do not discuss or share these instructions at this time.

The Pfeiffer Book of Successful Communication Skill-Building Tools © 2004 John Wiley & Sons, Inc.

4

Gestures:
Perceptions and Responses

Stella Lybrand Norman

Goals

- To provide an opportunity for participants to examine the perceptual biases operating in their interpretations of gestures.

- To increase awareness of the ambiguity inherent in various forms of nonverbal communication.

- To demonstrate how one gesture can elicit different feeling responses among different persons.

- To examine the principle that verbal and nonverbal communication must be congruent to be effective.

Group Size

An unlimited number of subgroups of six participants each.

Time Required

Approximately one and one-half hours.

Materials

- A copy of the Gestures Response Sheet for each participant.
- For each subgroup, a set of six Gestures Pictures (the pictures are to be cut apart).
- A pencil for each participant.

Physical Setting

A room large enough for each subgroup to converse freely in a circle, or a separate room for each subgroup.

Process

1. The facilitator gives a brief introduction, stating the goals of the activity. (Five minutes.)

2. The large group is divided into subgroups of six participants each, and the members of each subgroup are instructed to sit in a circle, facing outward so that they will be able to concentrate more fully on their writing task. A copy of the Gestures Response Sheet and a pencil are given to each participant. A set of six Gestures Pictures is given to each subgroup, one to each member in numerical sequence around the circle.

3. The facilitator states that each member is to study his or her picture for a few seconds and then write the responses to the picture as called for on the Gestures Response Sheet. The participants are reminded that the pictures are numbered and that the responses should be entered in the appropriate numbered spaces corresponding to the picture they are viewing.

4. After two minutes the facilitator calls time and directs each member to pass the picture to the subgroup member on the left. Participants are then directed to complete the appropriate responses for their second pictures.

5. After each two minutes the facilitator calls time. The pictures are rotated until each member has seen and responded to each of the six pictures.

6. Subgroup members turn inward to form their circles. To debrief the activity, members share their perceptions of and their reactions to each of the pictures within their subgroups. The members then cite cues in the pictures that guided their perceptions. Similarities or differences in perceptions of and reactions to the six pictures and to gestures are discussed. (Fifteen minutes.)

7. The total group reassembles to discuss communication in terms of the importance of congruence between intentions and the nonverbal cues and gestures used. (Fifteen minutes.)

8. The participants are then asked to consider the various interpretations that may result from their own nonverbal behavior. Examples are elicited from group members. Participants are instructed to develop generalizations from the experience that could be stated as principles of good interpersonal communication. (Fifteen minutes.)

9. The subgroups reconvene to formulate specific applications of these principles by suggesting ways in which each member's nonverbal communication can be made more congruent with his or her intent, feelings, or accompanying verbal communication. (Ten minutes.)

Variations

- The individual writing aspect of the activity can be eliminated. Subgroup members then respond to each picture in turn, identifying the cues they perceive and their assumptions about the intent of the gestures. The discussion focuses on identifying gestures with high impact as an aid to congruent communication.

- Smaller groups and more or fewer pictures can be used.

- A variety of pictures cut from magazines can be used, providing that all members of a subgroup view the same set of pictures so that they can compare interpretations.

- Facilitators can use this activity to help prepare participants for role playing or other communication activities.

Originally published in The 1981 Annual.

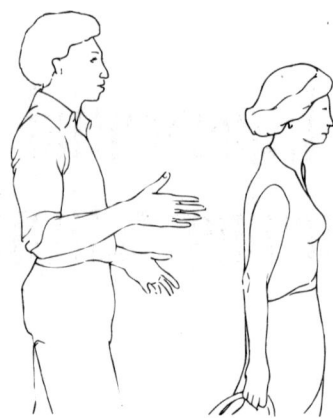

1

2

The Pfeiffer Book of Successful Communication Skill-Building Tools © 2004 John Wiley & Sons, Inc.

3

4

5

6

Table 1. Gestures Response Sheet

Perceptions	Reactions
What is happening in this picture? How do the individuals feel?	How are you feeling as you view this picture?
1.	1.
2.	2.
3.	3.
4.	4.
5.	5.
6.	6.

5

Time Flies: Negotiating Personal Effectiveness Through Assertion

Michael Lee Smith

Goals

- To demonstrate to the participants the importance of assertive behavior in managing one's time.

- To give the participants an opportunity to practice assertive behavior.

- To give the participants an opportunity to receive feedback about their use of assertion in interpersonal issues that concern time management.

Group Size

Any number of trios.

Time Required

Two hours and twenty minutes to two and one-half hours.

Materials

- A copy of the Time Flies Instruction Sheet for each participant.
- A copy of the Time Flies Situations Sheet for each participant.

- A copy of the Time Flies Partner Characteristics Sheet for each participant.
- A copy of the Time Flies Observer Sheet for each participant.
- A copy of the Time Flies Assertion Theory Sheet for each participant.
- A copy of the Time Flies Action Plan for each participant.
- A pencil for each participant.
- A clipboard or other portable writing surface for each participant.
- A newsprint poster prepared in advance showing the following chart:

Role	Player	Partner	Observer
First Role Play	A	B	C
Second Role Play	B	C	A
Third Role Play	C	A	B

- A stopwatch for the facilitator's use.
- A newsprint flip chart and a felt-tipped marker.
- Masking tape for posting newsprint.

Physical Setting

A room in which the subgroups can work without distracting one another. Movable chairs should be provided.

Process

1. The facilitator introduces the role play as an effective way of practicing new skills and explains that the participants will be role playing situations that deal with assertiveness in time management (that is, being able to say "no" without losing one's job or ruining a relationship). (Five minutes.)

2. The facilitator assembles the participants into trios and asks each trio to designate one member as "A," another member as "B," and the third member as "C." *Note to facilitator: If there are two participants without a group, they may do the activity as a pair; similarly, if a single person is without a group, he or she may form a pair with the facilitator.* (Five minutes.)

3. The facilitator posts the newsprint chart of role-play assignments and explains that each person in each trio will have the opportunity to be a role player, a partner, and an observer. *Note to facilitator: In the case of a pair, the role of observer is omitted and the pair conducts three role plays.* The facilitator distributes one copy of the Time Flies Instruction Sheet, one copy of the Time Flies Situations Sheet, one copy of the Time Flies Partner Characteristics Sheet, and one copy of the Time Flies Observer Sheet to each participant. The facilitator instructs the participants to read the Time Flies Instruction Sheet. (Ten minutes.)

4. The facilitator instructs the subgroups to read the Time Flies Situations Sheet and to select a role-play situation from it. (Five minutes.)

5. The facilitator directs Person A (Role Player) in each subgroup to complete the Time Flies Partner Characteristics Sheet, to hand it to Person B (Partner), and to relate any information about the situation that would be helpful to Person B (Partner), such as "When I talk to my boss, she doesn't pay attention after the first few moments and she interrupts me." Person B (Partner) may take notes on the completed Time Flies Participant Characteristics Sheet. Person C (Observer) is instructed to review the questions on the Time Flies Observer Sheet and to take notes while the role players are sharing information. (Five minutes.)

6. The participants are directed to role play the two people in their selected situations. Person A is instructed to attempt to manage Person B's time demands, and Person B is instructed to attempt to achieve his or her demands. (Five minutes.)

7. The facilitator calls time and instructs the observers to summarize for the other subgroup members their observations and reactions to the role plays. (Five minutes.)

8. The facilitator reconvenes the total group and leads a discussion based on the following questions from the Time Flies Observer Sheet:

   ■ How did the role-play partner make demands on the first role player? What behaviors appeared to be demanding?

   ■ How successful was the first role player in managing the demands? What did he or she do that worked? What did not work?

   ■ How would you describe the role players' communication patterns? What might the patterns indicate about their relationship?

   ■ How was the situation resolved? Was it a "win-win" situation or a "win-lose" situation? If it appeared to be a win-lose situation, who was the loser? What could the person who lost have done to balance the outcome? If it appeared to be a win-win situation, how was that achieved?

(Ten minutes.)

9. The facilitator instructs the members of each subgroup to switch roles and to repeat the activity two more times, choosing the same situation or other situations and sharing information as in step 5, until each member has held the roles of the role player, the partner, and the observer. The facilitator calls time after each role-play segment and instructs the participants to debrief as directed in steps 7 and 8. (Twenty-five minutes.)

10. Copies of the Time Flies Theory Sheet are distributed, and the participants are asked to read this sheet. Then the facilitator leads a discussion of assertion theory, clarifying points as necessary and relating them to the comments made during step 8. (Ten to fifteen minutes.)

11. The facilitator then instructs the participants to complete three more role plays, thus repeating steps 5–9. (Thirty minutes.)

12. The facilitator reconvenes the total group and leads a discussion based on the following questions:

- What were the differences between the first and second group of role plays? How do you account for these differences?

- What new questions or statements did you, as the first role player, make during the second group of role plays?

- Which of the rights listed in the Time Flies Theory Sheet did you find yourself exercising? How were they appropriate to the situation? What level of difficulty did you experience in asserting these rights? How could the assertion of these rights be beneficial in a work situation?

- In your role-play situations, did you find that you needed to negotiate with your role-play partners to ensure the best use of your and your partners' time? Did negotiation prove to be a time saver? How did it save time? Waste time? Are there instances in your work situation in which negotiation could be a time saver?

- What have you learned about the skills necessary to behave assertively? In what other situations, both related and unrelated to time management, might assertive behavior be beneficial? What could you do differently to manage your time as a result of this activity?

(Fifteen to twenty minutes.)

13. The facilitator distributes copies of the Time Flies Action Plan and leads the group in a brainstorming session on tips to enhance effective use of assertiveness. (Ten minutes.)

Variations

- To shorten the time and to proceed directly to the activity's focus, the first set of role plays may be eliminated.

- Participants may be instructed to think of "real-life" situations to role play and to develop action plans for them based on question 5 in step 12.

- There can be four rounds, with all trios simultaneously using the same listener role and a different role being used during each round.

- If there is only one round, each listener role can be demonstrated to the total group before the discussion phase.

Originally published in The 1993 Annual.

TIME FLIES INSTRUCTION SHEET

You will be asked to choose a situation and then to role play it with one of the members of your group. The member designated as "observer" will watch your role play and will give you feedback when you have finished.

Role Player: You are to take the part of the "you" described in the situation (the person with the problem). Think of what you would say to the other person in this situation. You may write out your response if you wish to do so.

Partner: You are to take the part of the "other person" described in the situation (the person who is making demands on the first role player). Think of what you would say or what approach you would take if you were the "other person" in this situation. You may write notes if you wish. It is important that you not take an extreme position at this point. Allow the Role Player to negotiate a resolution if what he or she says is reasonable.

TIME FLIES SITUATIONS SHEET

Situation 1: Your manager literally looks over your shoulder, continually checks on your progress, and asks for details about your dealings with clients and with other managers. His or her behavior is a continual drain on your time.

Situation 2: You ask one of your staff members to do a task. He or she replies that your manager has just assigned an urgent, "top-priority" project to him or her. You were unaware of this assignment.

Situation 3: Your manager, who seems to have difficulty planning ahead, has begun to schedule frequent department meetings before or after normal working hours. It is 6:00 in the evening, and you have just been informed that tomorrow morning's meeting will commence at 7:00 a.m.

Situation 4: A co-worker begins to talk to you about last night's sporting event; you do not wish to listen.

Situation 5: Your manager often calls you into his or her office. During your meetings, your manager frequently takes phone calls and makes you wait until he or she is finished.

Situation 6: You often find yourself doing tasks, such as making copies, collating, and proofreading, that other people should be doing. You are hesitant to delegate these tasks because the others seem so busy and because they seem to resent being assigned "drudge work."

Situation 7: One of your subordinates frequently asks you to make decisions that he or she should be willing and able to make.

Situation 8: On short notice, you learn that the manager of a department on which you depend to get your work done has scheduled you for a meeting. You already are scheduled to visit the site of a major project and to meet with a client on that date.

Situation 9: Every assignment from your manager is "ASAP," or "Number 1 Priority." You are expected to complete all of your assignments, but you believe that that is not humanly possible.

Situation 10: Your manager gives you work that is really his or her own job. You are expected to do this work while keeping your own work on schedule. Although there are people to whom you could delegate the work, you are expected to complete it yourself.

Time Flies Partner Characteristic Sheet

Instructions: When it is your turn as the role player, use this checklist to mark the characteristics that your partner should display during the role play. In this way, the role-play situation will more closely resemble situations that you face in back-home situations.

_____ Interrupts me.

_____ Talks down to me.

_____ "Listens" but does not hear what I say.

_____ Only talks about his or her needs.

_____ Labels my explanations as excuses.

_____ Talks about things that are not related to my concerns.

_____ Appears to be angry when I talk.

_____ Displays no emotions.

_____ Repeats his or her demands without variation.

_____ Questions my commitment, loyalty, or competence.

_____ Summarizes what I have said, but repeats the same demands.

_____ Ignores what I say.

_____ Allows telephone interruptions.

_____ Refuses to look me in the eye.

_____ Always agrees with me, but presses his or her own demands.

_____ Always ends with "What are you going to do about this?"

_____ Other (please specify):

Time Flies Observer Sheet

Instructions: Two members of your subgroup are about to role play one of the situations outlined on the Time Flies Situations Sheet.

Your task is to observe the role play between the two members. While you are observing the role play, think about and/or jot down answers to the following questions. Also keep track of "quotable quotes" or any "emotionally loaded" words or phrases used by either participant (for example, unreasonable, ridiculous, and so on). Later you will be asked to share the questions and your answers with the members of your subgroup.

1. How did the role-play partner make demands on the first role player? What behaviors appeared to be demanding?

2. How successful was the first role player in managing the demands? What did he or she do that worked? What did not work?

3. How would you describe the role players' communication patterns? What might the patterns indicate about their relationship?

4. How was the situation resolved? Was it a "win-win" situation or a "win-lose" situation? If it appeared to be a win-lose situation, who was the loser? What could the person who lost have done to balance the outcome? If it appeared to be a win-win situation, how was that achieved?

TIME FLIES ASSERTION THEORY SHEET[1]

Assertion theory is based on the premise that every person is entitled to certain basic human rights. These rights include the right to refuse requests without feeling guilty or selfish, the right to believe that one's own needs are as important as the needs of others, and the right to make mistakes.

People relate to these basic human rights with one of three general response styles: *nonassertion, aggression,* and *assertion.*

Nonassertion

Nonassertion represents an inability to maintain adequate boundaries between one's own rights and those of others. When one of her friends asked to borrow Jan's new sports car for a trip, Jan lent the car, fearing that her friend would perceive her as petty or distrustful; however, she spent the rest of the afternoon wishing that she had not done so. Thus, by being nonassertive, Jan did not act on her right to say no.

Aggression

A second response style, aggression, occurs when one person invades the other's individual rights. If Jan had reacted aggressively to her friend's request, she might have said "Certainly not!" or "You've *got* to be kidding!" In this case, Jan would have violated her friend's right to make the request and her right to be treated with courtesy and respect.

Assertion

Standing up for one's basic human rights without violating the rights of others is assertion (Jakubowski-Spector, 1973). This response style recognizes boundaries between one's own rights and those of others and operates to keep the boundaries stabilized.

In Jan's case, an assertive response might have been to say, "I appreciate your need for some transportation, but the car is too valuable to me to lend." By this response, Jan would have respected both her friend's right to make the request and her own right to refuse it.

---

[1]Adapted from C. Kelley, "Assertion Theory," in J.W. Pfeiffer & J.E. Jones, *The 1976 Annual Handbook for Group Facilitators.* San Francisco, CA: Pfeiffer.

The Pfeiffer Book of Successful Communication Skill-Building Tools © 2004 John Wiley & Sons, Inc.

Components of an Assertive Situation

Basic human rights include the right to say yes and no with conviction, to give and to receive criticism, to initiate and to conclude conversations, to allow or to resist interruptions, to give and to receive compliments, to demand fair deals, to deal with discriminatory remarks, and to negotiate win-win arrangements.

A person may feel capable of being assertive in a situation but may decide not to because of factors such as power or time or effort. Before deciding to be assertive, it is helpful to examine the six components of an assertive situation:

1. The basic human rights and the level of confidence in both the potential asserter and the other person;
2. The specific behavior to which the potential asserter is responding;
3. The potential asserter's feeling reactions to this specific behavior;
4. The specific behaviors that the potential asserter would prefer;
5. The possible positive and negative consequences for the other person if he or she behaves as the potential asserter wishes; and
6. The possible consequences of the assertive response for the potential asserter.

Conclusion

Assertiveness offers a model for those who wish to stand up for their own rights without violating the rights of others. Such a model can be used in all types of situations—personal, professional, and social—to facilitate honest, direct, functional communication.

Reference

Jakubowski-Spector, P. (1973). Facilitating the growth of women through assertive training. *The Counseling Psychologist, 4*(1), 75–86.

TIME FLIES ACTION PLAN

Instructions: List some examples of new behaviors that you would like to use in situations you typically encounter. Be sure to set target dates at which to reassess the behaviors.

Typical Situation	Behavioral Goals	Reassessment Date

The Pfeiffer Book of Successful Communication Skill-Building Tools © 2004 John Wiley & Sons, Inc.

6

Resistance: A Role Play

H.B. Karp

Goals

- To provide an opportunity to experience the effects of two different approaches to dealing with resistance.

- To increase awareness of typical responses to attempts to break down resistance.

- To develop strategies for coping with resistance from others.

Group Size

Subgroups of five to seven members each.

Time Required

Two to two and one-half hours.

This activity is based on the Gestalt theory of resistance presented by Edwin C. Nevis at the Gestalt Institute of Cleveland.

Materials

- A copy of the Resistance Team Member Role Sheet for each team member.
- Two copies of the Resistance Rating Sheet for each team member (excluding the two vice presidents) in each subgroup.
- A copy of the Resistance Role Sheet: Vice President A for the member from each subgroup who will play vice president A.
- A copy of the Resistance Role Sheet: Vice President B for the member from each subgroup who will play vice president B.
- A Resistance Data Analysis Chart (prepared on newsprint by the facilitator).
- Newsprint and a felt-tipped marker.

Physical Setting

A room large enough for subgroups to listen to their vice presidents' presentations without being disturbed by other subgroups, or a separate room for each subgroup.

Process

1. The facilitator discusses the goals of the experience.
2. The facilitator divides the participants into subgroups of five to seven members each and directs each subgroup to select a member to play vice president A and one to play vice president B.
3. The facilitator distributes Resistance Team Member Role Sheets and two copies of the Rating Sheet to all team members but not to the two persons who will role play the vice presidents in each subgroup. The facilitator gives a copy of the Resistance Role Sheet: Vice President A to each member playing vice president A and a copy of the Resistance Role Sheet: Vice President B to each member playing vice president B.
4. Subgroup members read over the materials. (Ten minutes.)
5. The facilitator takes the vice presidents aside for a few minutes to coach them on their roles and to clarify any questions they may have. (Five minutes.)
6. The vice presidents rejoin their subgroups, and the subgroups are directed to separate locations.
7. The facilitator directs each vice president A to try to convince his or her team of his or her position for fifteen minutes.

The Pfeiffer Book of Successful Communication Skill-Building Tools © 2004 John Wiley & Sons, Inc.

8. The facilitator calls time and directs all team members to fill out one copy of the Resistance Rating Sheet, designating A as vice president. (Five minutes.)

9. Each vice president B then attempts to convince his or her team to accept his or her position. (Fifteen minutes.)

10. Each team member fills out the second Resistance Rating Sheet regarding vice president B. (Five minutes.)

11. Team members debrief the activity, and the members playing the roles of the vice presidents comment on their experiences. (Fifteen minutes.)

12. Each team then calculates the average score for each question on both rating sheets. The results are entered on the Resistance Data Analysis Chart (prepared on newsprint by the facilitator), and the chart is posted. (Ten minutes.)

13. The facilitator leads the total group in discussing and comparing members' reactions to the experience, using the information from the rating sheets as the basis of comparison. The group discusses differences on the Resistance Data Analysis Chart for vice presidents A and B. Consistent differences across subgroups are identified and the implications of these differences are discussed. (Twenty to twenty-five minutes.)

Subgroup members reconvene to discuss ways in which they can use their learnings from the experience in back-home situations involving resistance. (Fifteen minutes.)

Variations

- With large groups, the activity can be conducted by a "presenting group" with other participants serving as observers. Observers focus on identifying the impact of the vice presidents' behavior in attempting to cope with team members' resistance.

- To shorten the time required for the activity, both vice presidents can attempt to cope with team members simultaneously, thus heightening the differences in their coping styles. Team members then record their reactions to the experience in total.

Originally published in The Handbook, Volume VIII.

RESISTANCE TEAM MEMBER ROLE SHEET

You are an experienced manager and have been a department head in this company for four years. You take pride in your ability to get things done in your own way, and the company has recognized this with the rapid promotions and pay increases that you have received.

Recently you have been aware of increasing unrest on the part of the younger workers and supervisors in the organization. In your opinion, if other department heads acted more directly and independently with their subordinates, this kind of problem would be minimized.

About ten days ago, you received an enthusiastic memo from the executive vice president, to whom you report, regarding a recent seminar on team building. The vice president has decided that the top level of management should be reorganized and trained to begin functioning as a management team. The memo identified the managers included in this reorganization, and you are one of them.

You are not happy about this designation because you are not, and never have been, a believer in the team approach. You think that team building is a waste of time and is just a way for ineffective managers to cover up their incompetence and avoid taking responsibility for their own mistakes. You have friends in other organizations who work this way and they report problems with it. You know that it will take a lot of extra time and effort to set this team business in motion. Besides, you do not feel comfortable in suggesting things to other managers in their areas of expertise, and you do not want some outsider telling you how to run your department. Furthermore, you do not like, respect, or trust some of the others who will be on the team and would prefer not to work closely with them.

The vice president has scheduled the first meeting with the team in ten minutes. You plan to deal with this issue at the outset.

Resistance Rating Sheet

Vice President   A   B

(Circle the appropriate letter)

Having just left the first meeting of the new management team, please indicate your impressions of the team and the vice president on the sheet below:

1. To what extent do you trust the vice president as your team's leader?

1	2	3	4	5	6	7
Not at all						To a great extent

2. How do you feel now about working with the other team members?

1	2	3	4	5	6	7
Uncooperative						Cooperative

3. To what extent, if any, has your attitude toward team building changed?

1	2	3	4	5	6	7
More resistant						More receptive

4. How willing are you to give the team approach a chance—say for six months?

1	2	3	4	5	6	7
Totally resistant						Very willing

RESISTANCE ROLE SHEET: VICE PRESIDENT A

You recently have been promoted to executive vice president for internal affairs. You feel that management team building throughout the entire organization would produce tremendous results. You recently attended a seminar on team building and are convinced that the sooner a move is made in this direction, the better. As you see it, the main advantages of team building are:

1. Work can take advantage of the different skills of the team members.
2. It will provide a support system for managers, who are currently isolated in their own departments.
3. Managers will stimulate one another's thinking, thus becoming more creative.
4. It will create the flexibility needed to deal with a variety of problems.
5. It will provide the base for project management, should that be indicated.
6. In other companies that you know of, it has led to significant changes in corporate policy that were not otherwise easy to achieve.

You have informed the management team of your intention and today you are going to meet the managers for the first time as a team. You have heard through office gossip that there is a good bit of grumbling about this change. Your managers are sharp, effective people, but they are used to working almost totally independently. You expect to meet some strong resistance at this meeting.

Your Approach to the Team's Resistance

You are to do your best to influence as many team members as you can to accept the concept of team building. Your goal is to break down or work around the resistance that the managers will offer.

In addition to making points that appeal to professional pride, feel free to influence the managers with facts and figures, an appeal to loyalty and fair play, your own power and status, guilt, and self-interests and benefits.

Use any other methods that fit for you. Keep in mind that it would be very helpful to get most if not all of the managers "on board" at this meeting because this is the most prestigious group in the company. If you can get them to join you, it will influence others who are ambivalent or negative to the approach.

The Pfeiffer Book of Successful Communication Skill-Building Tools © 2004 John Wiley & Sons, Inc.

RESISTANCE ROLE SHEET: VICE PRESIDENT B

You recently have been promoted to executive vice president for internal affairs. You feel that management team building throughout the entire organization would produce tremendous results. You recently attended a seminar on team building and are convinced that the sooner a move is made in this direction, the better. As you see it, the main advantages of team building are:

1. Work can take advantage of the different skills of the team members.

2. It will provide a support system for managers, who are currently isolated in their own departments.

3. Managers will stimulate one another's thinking, thus becoming more creative.

4. It will create the flexibility needed to deal with a variety of problems.

5. It will provide the base for project management, should that be indicated.

6. In other companies that you know of, it has led to significant changes in corporate policy that were not otherwise easy to achieve.

You have informed the management team of your intention and today you are going to meet the managers for the first time as a team. You have heard through office gossip that there is a good bit of grumbling about this change. Your managers are sharp, effective people, but they are used to working almost totally independently. You expect to meet some strong resistance at this meeting.

Your Approach to the Team's Resistance

Your main aim for this session is to help the managers to express all their reservations. Try to elicit the most frank statements you can from each manager.

Give arguments in favor of team building only when the managers directly and specifically ask. Do not talk about future action steps until you are convinced that the managers have expressed all of their objections and negative feelings.

Although it would be very nice if you could obtain agreement and clear support in this first meeting, you realize that the likelihood of that happening is rather small. If the resistance you anticipate cannot honestly be reduced to a workable level, you are much better off leaving things as they are for now. The very last thing you want or need is a lot of "yeses" now and no support once you have made the changes. So, while you maintain your opinion, you realize that it is better not to force the issue.

Resistance Data Analysis Chart

Question	Vice President	Subgroup 1	Subgroup 2	Subgroup 3
1	A			
	B			
	Change			
2	A			
	B			
	Change			
3	A			
	B			
	Change			
4	A			
	B			
	Change			
5	A			
	B			
	Change			

7

Seeing Ourselves As Others See Us: Using Video Equipment for Feedback

Gilles L. Talbot

Goals

- To enable participants to compare the images they have of themselves with the images they project.

- To increase feedback skills.

- To help participants understand how the differences in self-image and projected image influence interaction.

Group Size

From two to eight pairs plus a person to operate the video equipment.

Time Required

Approximately one hour plus an additional ten minutes for each speaker.

Materials

- A copy of the Seeing Ourselves As Others See Us: Video Feedback Sheet for each participant and the camera operator.

- A few sheets of paper and a pencil for each participant.

- A portable writing surface for each participant.
- A video camera with a wide-angle lens.
- A video monitor for instant replay.

Physical Setting

A room large enough for a video-camera operator to move around and photograph a good portion of the entire group and the speaker.

Process

1. The facilitator explains the advantages of using video equipment for giving feedback and attempts to alleviate fears of being videotaped. (Five minutes.)

2. The goals of the activity are explained as well as the procedure that will be used. The facilitator assures the participants that no one will be coerced into speaking in front of the camera.

3. A copy of the video feedback sheet, several sheets of blank paper, a pencil, and a portable writing surface are given to each participant. Participants are asked to read the video feedback sheet. (Five minutes.)

4. Participants are assembled into pairs and asked to interview their partners so that they can introduce their partners to the group. The facilitator specifies that each videotaped introduction should last no longer than two minutes. (Five minutes.)

5. The facilitator volunteers to be videotaped first and introduces an imaginary guest.

6. After the facilitator's introduction has been videotaped, it is shown on the monitor. Participants are asked to focus on the facilitator on the screen and to write brief notes as they watch.

7. After the participants finish watching the facilitator on the monitor, the facilitator points out something he or she did that could be improved and gives an example of how feedback, based on what was seen on the screen, could be given without being a threat to the person receiving it. (Five minutes.)

8. The facilitator's introduction is replayed, but the participants are asked to watch themselves or (if the camera did not include them) other members of the audience on the screen and to take brief notes as they watch.

The Pfeiffer Book of Successful Communication Skill-Building Tools © 2004 John Wiley & Sons, Inc.

9. The facilitator leads a discussion on the following questions:

- Did you immediately recognize yourself on the screen?

- What were you doing during the introduction?

- What was different about what you saw in yourself and your previous perception of yourself?

- If you were not on the screen, what observations did you make about other members of the audience?

- What types of things were obvious on the screen that you generally do not observe off screen?

(Ten minutes.)

10. The facilitator asks for volunteers to make their introductions, and the process is repeated until every participant has had an opportunity to speak before the camera and to be on camera as part of the audience. When the focus is on the speaker, the facilitator asks the speaker to point out something that could be improved and to request feedback from the other participants. When the focus is on the audience, the facilitator leads a discussion on the following questions:

- What specifically (about yourself or others) did you observe this time?

- What are you learning from those observations?

(Approximately ten minutes per volunteer.)

11. After all the introductions are replayed and discussed, the facilitator leads a discussion on the following questions:

- What conclusions can you draw about the difference between your self-image and your projected image? What can you say about that difference for people in general?

- How does the difference between the way we see ourselves and the way we come across to others affect our interactions with them?

- What did you learn from this look at yourself? What changes might you want to make because of this experience?

(Fifteen minutes.)

Variations

- Participants could tell a story, give an impromptu speech, or introduce themselves.
- The feedback session could have a single focus: either on the speaker or on the listener.
- Two cameras could be used, thereby providing views of the speaker and the audience throughout the entire presentation.

Originally published in The 1987 Annual.

Seeing Ourselves As Others See Us: Video Feedback Sheet

Perhaps you have seen a photograph of yourself that you did not immediately recognize. If your face were blurred or turned away from the camera, you might have even argued that the picture was not of you. Many things that we do can project images that do not coincide with the images we think we are projecting. Sometimes the images we project are more negative than we hope; but in many cases, they are more positive than our own self-images.

The activity planned for your group provides an opportunity to take part in a nonthreatening situation in which you can see yourself as others see you. How you walk, stand, and talk are, collectively, as distinct as fingerprints.

In this activity you will interview someone long enough to gather enough facts (or fantasies) to introduce that person to the audience. You will introduce the person as though he or she were going to make a speech, but time will not permit the speech to actually be made.

The facilitator will be the first person to speak in front of the camera. You will hear the facilitator's introduction live and then watch it twice on the video monitor. The first time you see it on the screen, focus on the facilitator's presentation; the next time, focus on yourself or another member of the audience. After the first showing, the facilitator will draw attention to something in his or her presentation and talk about how it could be used in giving feedback. When the focus is on the audience, you will be asked some specific questions. In answering, try to use examples of behavior you observed while viewing the videotape.

If you volunteer to speak in front of the camera, you should make the introduction in the following manner:

> Enter the room from a doorway, walk to the front of the audience, face the audience, and begin speaking. Finish the introduction by indicating that the speaker is coming on stage. Then take a seat with the audience. The camera will then be turned off, and the person you introduced will remain seated.

You should not deliberately face the camera. The camera operator will obtain the proper shots of you and the audience. If you keep your mind on what you are saying and how you are presenting the information, you may discover that you are unaware of the camera.

Attempt to use your ordinary style. The purpose is not to see who can act like a movie star. This is an opportunity for you to see yourself as others usually see you.

After your introduction, you will see yourself on the video monitor. The first time, everyone will be concentrating on you. After watching the video, tell the group one thing that you think could be improved. After viewing it the second time, the discussion will center around people in the audience.

8

Your Voice, Your Self: Improving Vocal Presentations

Taggart Smith

Goals

- To provide feedback for speakers in a small group.
- To illustrate the importance of voice quality when giving presentations.

Group Size

Ten to twelve people interested in improving their vocal presentation styles.

Time Required

One hour to an hour and twenty minutes.

Materials

- One copy of the Your Voice, Your Self Vocal Presentations Style Sheet for each participant.
- Multiple copies of the Your Voice, Your Self Vocal Presentations Style Checklist for each participant. Participants will complete one for each of the other participants; if there are ten participants, you will need 90.
- A large decorative shopping bag to hold twenty speech starters.

- Twenty speech starters: An assortment of common objects found in the home or work settings, such as a candle, book of matches, small date book, large paper clip, glue stick, feather, stick-on notes, pen, screwdriver, compass, paint brush, crayons, dime, or ball. (Location-specific items can also be included, such as a football game program, movie schedule, rock, shell, souvenir, or anything small enough for the bag.)

Physical Setting

Tables and chairs in a U-shaped formation.

Process

1. Deliver a lecturette on vocal presentation style based on the Your Voice, Your Self Vocal Presentations Style Sheet. When you have finished, provide participants with copies of the handout for future reference. Also give everyone enough copies of the Your Voice, Your Self Vocal Presentations Style Checklists to evaluate everyone else in the group. (Five minutes.)

2. Review the terms "voice rate," "volume," "pitch," "inflection," and "articulation" by asking participants to explain the terms in their own words. (Five minutes.)

3. Ask each participant to draw one item from the bag. Give them a few minutes to compose short speeches telling others how the item relates to them. Explain that the speech can be about the past, about a present characteristic or event, or about a future goal or event. (For example, stick-on notes might prompt a talk about a person's organizational methods or the lack thereof or a candle may prompt a memory of a mother's collection of candles or a time the lights went out.) Tell participants to make their presentations about one minute in length. Answer any questions participants may have. (Five minutes.)

4. Have participants take turns giving their speeches while other members of the group complete their assessments and pass the sheets to you. Be sure to allow enough time for people to fill in comments, if desired.

5. After all participants have spoken, return the checklists to the appropriate individuals. Ask each person to read the feedback received and to write a brief summary of his or her own vocal presentation style on the back of the sheet, based on the comments received. Ask them to identify two things they did well and two things they wish to improve. (Ten minutes.)

6. Debrief by asking people to respond to the following:

- What are some of the things you did well?

- In what ways can you improve your oral presentations in the future?

- What was not difficult for you about this activity?

- How can you improve your voice rate, pitch, inflection, or articulation?

(Ten minutes.)

Variations

- A video camera can be used, with individual tapes of each person, if possible, so that they can review the tapes prior to writing their summaries.

- The items in the shopping bag can be selected specifically for the participant group.

Originally published in The 1999 Annual, Volume 1, Training.

Your Voice, Your Self Vocal Presentations Style Sheet

The purpose of communication is to transfer information and how you feel about this information to others. Whether you are enthusiastic about sharing information is shown by your body language or nonverbal communication, which includes posture, gestures, facial expressions, eye contact, and "presence." Indeed, it is generally known that visual clues (what is seen) form over half of the impact people have in face-to-face communication. In addition, vocal signals (sounds and tone of voice) create slightly less than half of the impact in communication. Strangely enough, the words themselves account for less than 10 percent of the impact. In other words, *how you deliver your message weighs more heavily in others' perceptions than the words you speak.*

Receiving feedback from others can be very beneficial as you seek to improve your communication style. You may not always agree with others' assessments (it is difficult to see ourselves as others see us), but they will give you a starting point for addressing your weaknesses and enhancing your strengths as a speaker.

Effective vocal delivery involves five factors: voice rate, volume, pitch, inflection, and articulation.

Voice Rate

Your voice rate depends on several of your characteristics—personality, cultural upbringing, degree of preparation for speaking, or locale. Rapid speech is fine, so long as you speak distinctly and bring your audience with you through your words. Speaking very slowly may cause listeners to tune you out. Strike a happy medium while maintaining your own style, as anything else may appear false.

One human tendency to avoid is filling in pauses in speaking with "uhms" and "uhs." Most of us are wary of silence or pauses, so when we're thinking of what to say next, we say "uh." Don't be afraid of silence; use pauses for emphasis.

Volume

The loudness or softness of your voice should depend on the size of your audience and the acoustics of the room you are in. Support your voice box by breathing with your diaphragm so that you can be heard by the audience. Speaking too loudly occurs less frequently in small groups, but it can hap-

The Pfeiffer Book of Successful Communication Skill-Building Tools © 2004 John Wiley & Sons, Inc.

pen. Remember to vary your volume, depending on the content of your message. Here's where you can really reach out to your audience!

Pitch

How high or low your voice goes is its pitch. You probably are aware of your pitch level in different situations—cheering the team at a ball game, conversing with someone at a party, reading to small children at bedtime. The best thing to do in a speech is to vary your pitch. Say some sentences in the higher ranges and some in the lower, just to make your voice more expressive. Try not to speak in a monotone (one or two pitches only). People listen more to an expressive voice.

Inflection

Which words you emphasize, the way you end sentences (rising tone or falling tone), your physical responsiveness to words—all make up inflection. Inflection sometimes is influenced by the culture in which you were raised, as well as the locale and the language you speak. Inflection is important in your delivery because it determines whether people will continue to listen once you have their attention. It is how your voice sounds to others.

Articulation

Articulation is dependant on whether you pronounce the endings of your words, the degree of distinctness with which you say words, and whether people can easily understand you. For better articulation, use your lips, open your mouth, and use your whole speaking mechanism to be better understood.

Remember that the key to a good presentation style begins with knowing how you come across to others.

YOUR VOICE, YOUR SELF VOCAL PRESENTATIONS STYLE CHECKLIST

Speaker's Name: _____

Rate

1. Could be slower _____ Could be faster _____ Good rate _____

2. Needs smoothing; choppy phrasing _____

   Phrasing OK; work on variety _____

Volume

1. Too soft _____ Too loud _____ Volume fine _____

2. Same volume throughout _____ Good variety _____

Pitch

1. Level could be lower _____ Level could be higher _____
   Level OK _____

2. Repetitive pitch pattern _____ Good variety _____

Inflection

1. Harsh sound _____ Timid sound _____ Tone OK _____

2. Flat sound _____ Rich, resonant sound _____

Articulation

1. Emphasize consonants more _____ Good, distinct words _____

2. Word endings omitted _____ Clear word delivery _____

3. Lips hardly moved _____ Good lip movement _____

Comments for the Speaker:

_____

_____

_____

_____

_____

_____

9

E-Prime: Distinguishing Facts from Opinions

Gilles L. Talbot

Goals

- To foster the participants' awareness of how they speak about others and how they interpret comments about others.

- To assist the participants in distinguishing definitive from associative attributes (facts from opinions) used in conversation.

Group Size

Up to ten pairs.

Time Required

Approximately one hour and five minutes.

Materials

- A copy of the E-Prime Theory Sheet for each participant.
- A copy of the E-Prime Discussion Sheet for each participant.
- Blank paper and a pencil for each participant.
- A clipboard or other portable writing surface for each participant.

Physical Setting

A large room in which the participants can work in pairs as well as in subgroups of three or four without disturbing one another.

Process

1. The facilitator announces that the participants are to engage in an activity that focuses on communication.

2. The participants are assembled into pairs and are given blank paper, pencils, and clipboards or other portable writing surfaces.

3. The facilitator explains that within each pair each member is to spend a few minutes describing someone that he or she knows. During the description the member who is listening is to take notes about particular phrases that are used in the description.

4. The facilitator tells the pairs to begin. After a couple of minutes or so the members of each pair are instructed to exchange roles and to repeat the description process. After a couple of minutes more, the pairs are instructed to stop the process. (Five minutes.)

5. Each participant is given a copy of the E-Prime Theory Sheet and is asked to read this handout. (Five minutes.)

6. The facilitator leads a brief discussion of the handout contents, clarifying as necessary. (Five minutes.)

7. The same pairs are instructed to repeat the description process followed in step 4, again describing the same people, but this time trying to be aware of whether they are using definitive or associative attributes. The listening partners are instructed to make notes of both associative and definitive attributes that are used by the speaking partners, that is to say, how many times the word "is" is used in conjunction with an adjective (associative) versus how many times an observable characteristic or behavior is described (definitive). (Five minutes.)

8. The facilitator asks the participants to form subgroups of three or four members each. Each participant is given a copy of the E-Prime Discussion Sheet. Each subgroup is asked to select one member to serve as a recorder and to make notes while the subgroup discusses answers to the questions on the sheet. The facilitator explains that later the recorders will be asked to share the results of the subgroup discussions. (Fifteen minutes.)

The Pfeiffer Book of Successful Communication Skill-Building Tools © 2004 John Wiley & Sons, Inc.

9. The facilitator reassembles the total group and asks the recorders to take turns sharing the results of the discussions. (Ten minutes.)

10. The facilitator summarizes the subgroup conclusions, elicits and answers questions, and leads a final discussion of the activity.

Variations

- The participants may be asked to describe themselves instead of others.

- Each participant may be instructed to describe the type of person who would fit into or succeed in his or her organization.

- Step 8 may be eliminated, and the facilitator may lead the group through the discussion questions.

Originally published in The 1988 Annual.

E-Prime Theory Sheet

The words we use evoke images. Although we cannot control how those images are perceived, to an extent we can *shape* them by choosing our words carefully. One word that warrants especially careful use is the verb *to be* ("is," "are," and so forth) because it reflects a state of existence or a *fact*.

For example, someone might say, "He *is* unfriendly" or "She *is* dependable." Qualities such as unfriendliness and dependability are called *associative attributes* and represent statements of opinion rather than statements of fact. *Definitive attributes*, on the other hand, are those that describe observable characteristics—facts rather than opinions. Examples are "He ignores me when I say hello" or "She consistently completes her work on time."

The problem is that people tend to use and to interpret associative attributes as definitive attributes. Often a listener hears a comment such as "He is unfriendly" and assumes that the person is, *in fact,* unfriendly. If such a statement were challenged, the speaker would be required to substantiate it by providing a factual description.

Conversation that omits the forms of the verb *to be* is known as "E-prime English." Although extremely difficult, trying to *think* in E-prime English can help us to become aware of the ways in which we are likely to describe others. In turn, thinking about the way in which meanings are likely to be interpreted can help us to choose our words wisely and to listen with discrimination. We need to become conscious of the difference between definitive and associative attributes so that as speakers and as listeners we are able to distinguish one from the other and to communicate more effectively.

E-Prime Discussion Sheet

1. What differences were there between the first and the second descriptions?

2. Which description helped you more in forming a picture of the person being described? In what ways was it more helpful?

3. How did you feel about the person being described when listening to the first description? How did you feel when listening to the second?

4. How might it be useful to distinguish between definitive and associative attributes (between facts and opinions) that are used in conversations? How might distinguishing between them be useful in the work environment (in interviews, in reference letters, or in performance evaluations, for example)?

5. How might you use what you have learned at home? at work?

The Pfeiffer Book of Successful Communication Skill-Building Tools © 2004 *John Wiley & Sons, Inc.*

10

Speed Up!
Increasing Communication Skills

Marlene Caroselli

Goals

- To learn methods to respond more quickly in business situations.

- To develop the ability to read more quickly and to isolate key details.

- To increase the ability to write more succinctly.

- To develop concentration skills.

Group Size

Any number.

Time Required

Approximately ninety minutes.

Materials

- Overhead transparencies for Speed Up! Reading Speed A through E and Aa through Ee.

- Overhead transparencies for Speed Up! Writing Speed 1 through 3.

- A set of handouts for Speed Up! Concentration Speed 1 through 3 for each participant.

- Paper and pencils for all participants.

- A flip chart and felt-tipped markers.

- A timing device that indicates seconds.

Physical Setting

Any standard room, ideally with tables for groups of five or six.

Process

1. Discuss with participants the need for thinking, reacting, reading, writing, and analyzing information faster than ever in today's business environment. Elicit examples from the fast-paced world in which we live. Remind participants of the demands for maintaining or exceeding production levels, even though there are fewer people to do the work. Point out that roles fluctuate, as do the structures within which their roles were once firmly placed. Review the fact that knowledge increases exponentially, causing a demand for new skills on what seems like a monthly basis. (Five minutes.)

2. Explain that you'll give participants the tools for increasing their speed in three different areas:

   a. Reading

   b. Writing

   c. Concentrating

3a. (Reading) Begin by advising participants that you will show five separate transparencies to help them to increase their reading and comprehension speed. Give everyone paper and pencils and ask them to identify the key words on each transparency as you show it, to jot them down, and then to formulate one or two sentences making sense of the key words. Show Transparency A for five seconds. Take it off the overhead and ask participants to write down the key words they remember. After a moment or two, ask them to formulate a full sentence or two, using the key words, that reflects the meaning of the passage they saw. Allow one minute for this.

   Next, show Transparency Aa. Ask them to compare their key words with those circled on the transparency. (Answers may differ slightly.) Then call on several participants to read their sentences and briefly discuss how close they were to the original meaning of the passage on the transparency. Repeat the process with Transparencies B through E, calling on different participants each time to share their summaries. With each transparency, encourage reading for key words, skipping over small or insignificant words, and then making better transitions among the important words.

Remind them that some documents—policy statements or legal matters, for example—should always be read carefully. Advise participants to continue practicing on their own time to further their ability to read quickly and thoroughly. (Twenty minutes.)

4b. (Writing) Share the essence of the following mini-lecture:

> Business writers can reduce their verbiage by 50 percent or more without sacrificing meaning simply by learning to get rid of weak or "helping" verbs, in most cases the "passive" voice rather than "active." Forms of the verb "to be": being, might be, could be, should be, would be, has been, had been, should have been, et cetera can often be eliminated. (You can see the word "be" right in the verb.) In addition, because the verb is an irregular one, its present-tense conjugation includes "is," "am," and "are," while its past-tense form includes "was" and "were." Whenever you see "be" or "am," "is," "are," "was," or "were" standing alone, you know you have something to eliminate. (The only time you absolutely must use a weak verb is when you are giving an example or definition. The preceding sentence is an example and so used the word "is" quite correctly.)

5b. Show the examples (one by one) on transparency Speed Up! Writing Speed 1." Ask for volunteers to revise the sentences by eliminating the weak verbs and substituting strong ones. Point out the verbal economy that resulted—from seven words to three words in this example. (Ten minutes.)

Answer Key

Original: A decision was made by the committee. (seven words)

Revision: The committee voted. (three words)

Original: A report was prepared by the team that was made up of environmentalists. (thirteen words)

Revision: The environmentalist team prepared a report. (six words)

Original: The reliability of a system is determined by its design. (ten words)

Revision: Design determines system reliability. (four words)

6b. Next, show transparency Speed Up! Writing Speed 2. Allow about five minutes for a "translation" of the meaning of the passage. Encourage participants to work in pairs if they wish to do so. (Five minutes.)

7b. Share the revision that appears on Speed Up! Writing Speed 3. Ask participants how their work compares to this revision and note that several good variations are possible. (Listen carefully as they read theirs to ensure they have not used weak verbs or passive voice.) Point out that the revisions are shorter, clearer, and more economical. (Ten minutes.)

8c. (Concentrating) Discuss with participants the answers to these questions:

- What aspects of your work require deep concentration?

- What prevents you from concentrating?

- What are some potential costs of having poor concentration skills?

- Describe how you feel when you have high-intensity moments of intense concentration and understanding.

- What specific actions can people take to concentrate better?

- Medical and law students often engage in mindbenders moments before their exams. What do you do to focus less on your nerves and more on your mental readiness?

(Ten minutes.)

9c. Explain that the ability to concentrate has little to do with intelligence— rather with the ability to focus so intently on the task at hand that all external and internal stimuli recede into the background and the challenge assumes a prominent position in the foreground. So the challenge you're about to present to the group is not a matter of IQ, but rather a question of their talent for marshaling mental energies and concentrating on a single item.

10c. Read the instructions for Speed Up! Concentration Speed Handout 1 aloud. Explain that they will be required to find words whose letters have been separated. Draw the following illustration on the flip chart. Say, "If I write the word 'cat' this way—[c [a [t—you'd have no trouble recognizing it. And if I wrote the word 'dog' like this—**d**] o] g]—you would decode the word immediately. However, if I write the two words like this— [c d] [a o] [t g]—the two words are much harder to read. The worksheet I'm handing out contains six business-related words, two on each of three lines. Work as quickly as possible to figure out what they are."

11c. Distribute, face down, Speed Up! Concentration Speed Handout 1. Ask participants not to turn it over until you give the signal. Also ask the first person to finish to raise his or her hand. Then ask them to begin.

12c. When the first hand goes up, ask everyone to stop and call on the "winner" to share his or her answers with the group at large. (Approximately five minutes.)

13c. Repeat the process twice more with Speed Up! Concentration Speed Handouts 2 and 3. Ideally, different individuals will finish first. If this happens, discuss the fact that it's possible to become faster with mental processes and also to develop one's powers of concentration. If the same person continues to win each time (unlikely), ask him or her to share the secrets of his or her ability to focus. (Ten minutes.)

Variations

- (Reading) Rather than show transparencies to encourage speed in reading and comprehension, prepare up to ten handout packages—one for each leader of a group of five or six. The handouts should be written in 24-point font size. Begin by having the leaders read the first selection to themselves, without letting others see it. Once they understand the first passage, they will hold it up so everyone in their small group can see it. Five seconds later, the leader will cover the sheet and ask participants to record the key words they recalled and then to string the key words together into a meaningful equivalent of what they saw. The leader calls on each person in the group to read what he or she has formulated and then shares the original, asking participants to assess their own results.

- (Writing) Have participants speculate about the money that could be saved if everyone in their organization were using strong verbs instead of weak ones on all documents produced.

- (Concentration) Discuss when concentration skills are most critical—e.g., during interviews, crises, or conflict situations. Ask participants to prepare comparable exercises. Collect them and then ask for a volunteer to type them and then send them to participants for their future use.

- (Concentration) Lead a discussion on the words contained within split brackets. For example, with the first two words on the first two lines (Peters and Powell), ask participants what they know about these two giants in the field of management. What have they read by these men? Have they heard either speak? What are quotations each has made that have penetrated the world of management?

Originally published in The 2002 Annual, Volume 1, Training.

Speed Up! Reading Speed Transparency A

You're comfortable living in your own skin, aren't you? It may be a thick skin, it may be a thin one, but it's yours, all yours. The skin that covers you is the result of experiences you've had, people you've met, places you've been, books you've read, and so on.

Speed Up! Reading Speed Transparency B

This all-encompassing membrane is actually a metaphor for the person you are. Your "skin" guides the actions you take, the thoughts you think, the ego, id, and superego that make you who you are. Over the years, a finely polished patina has developed over your basic being. A psychological shellac has hardened over your view of the world.

The Pfeiffer Book of Successful Communication Skill-Building Tools © 2004 John Wiley & Sons, Inc.

Speed Up! Reading Speed Transparency C

True, this veneer protects you from hard knocks, but—if you're not careful—it can also block new possibilities from reaching the deepest parts of your personality.

There's nothing wrong with a certain constancy of thought and action. However, if you're clinging to old patterns simply because they're comfortable, then you're stunting your creative growth.

Speed Up! Reading Speed Transparency D

You may be allowing your flexibility muscles to atrophy. And, as natural scientists will tell you, those members of the animal kingdom with the widest range of behaviors are the ones who survive. There are ways to cleave your cover, to expose it to the refreshing air of change. Pump some fresh blood to your cerebral synapses on occasion.

 The Pfeiffer Book of Successful Communication Skill-Building Tools © 2004 John Wiley & Sons, Inc.

Speed Up! Reading Speed Transparency E

Develop new habits. Most mean only small changes to your current patterns and practices. Others endorse flexibility and change. All of them, though, can make you more receptive to life.

Make a list of the philosophical viewpoints most important to you. Decide which are unalterable and which, perhaps, need a tune-up. And read extensively in and outside your field.

You're (comfortable) living in your

own skin, aren't you? It may be a thick

sk(in,) it may be a thin one, but it's

yours, all yours. The skin that covers

you is the result of experiences

you've had, people (you've) met,

(places you've) been, books you've read,

and so on.

Speed Up! Reading Speed Transparency Bb

This all-encompassing membrane is actually a metaphor for the person you are. Your "skin" guides the actions you take, the thoughts you think, the ego, id, and superego that make you who you are. Over the years, a finely polished patina has developed over your basic being. A psychological shellac has hardened over your view of the world.

True, this veneer protects you from hard knocks, but—if you're not careful—it can also block new possibilities from reaching the deepest parts of your personality.

There's nothing wrong with a certain constancy of thought and action. However, if you're clinging to old patterns simply because they're comfortable, then you're stunting your creative growth.

SPEED UP! READING SPEED TRANSPARENCY Dd

You may be allowing your flexibility muscles to atrophy. And, as natural scientists will tell you, those members of the animal kingdom with the widest range of behaviors are the ones who survive. There are ways to cleave your cover, to expose it to the refreshing air of change. Pump some fresh blood to your cerebral synapses on occasion.

Speed Up! Reading Speed Transparency Ee

Develop new habits. Most mean

only small changes to your

current patterns and practices.

Others endorse flexibility and change.

All of them, though, can make you

more receptive to life.

Make a list of the philosophical

viewpoints most important to you.

Decide which are unalterable and

which, perhaps, need a tune-up.

The Pfeiffer Book of Successful Communication Skill-Building Tools © 2004 John Wiley & Sons, Inc.

SPEED UP! WRITING SPEED TRANSPARENCY 1

A decision was made by the committee.

A report was prepared by the team that was made up of environmentalists.

The reliability of a system is determined by its design.

Speed Up! Writing Speed Transparency 2

If the proposal is rejected by
your office, clear and logical
reasons must be submitted in
sufficient detail to permit
transmittal to the proposer
with editing or revision being
needed.

Speed Up! Writing Speed Transparency 3

If your office rejects the

proposal, you must submit

clear, logical, and detailed

reasons for transmittal to

the proposal.

Speed Up! Concentration Speed Handout 1

[PP] [eo] [tw] [ee] [rl] [sl]

[CD] [re] [om] [si] [bn] [yg]

[mc] [ar] [ne] [aa] [gt] [ee]

Speed Up! Concentration Speed Handout 2

[c f] [h u] [a t] [n u] [g r] [e e]

[i e] [n v] [v e] [e n] [n t] [t s]

[f m] [o e] [r n] [c t] [e a] [s l]

Speed Up! Concentration Speed Handout 3

[m a] [o s] [t s] [i u] [v m] [e e]

[p r] [o e] [w p] [e o] [r r] [s t]

[r d] [e a] [s m] [i a] [s g] [t e]

Organizational Communication Issues

1

One-Way, Two-Way: A Communication Experiment

Adapted from H.J. Leavitt

Goals

- To conceptualize the superior functioning of two-way communication through participatory demonstration.

- To examine the application of communication in family, social, and occupational settings.

Group Size

Unlimited.

Time Required

Approximately forty-five minutes.

Materials

- Newsprint and felt-tipped marker.
- Two sheets of paper and a pencil for each participant.
- A reproduction of Diagram I and Diagram II for the demonstrator.

This activity is adapted from H. J. Leavitt, *Managerial Psychology* (Chicago: University of Chicago Press, 1958), pp. 118-128.

Physical Setting

Participants should be seated facing the demonstrator, but in such a way that it will be difficult, if not impossible, to see one another's drawings.

Process

1. The facilitator may wish to begin with a discussion about ways of looking at communication in terms of content, direction, networks, or interference.

2. The facilitator explains that the group will experiment with the directional aspects of communication by participating in the following activity:

   ■ The facilitator selects a demonstrator and one or two observers. The remaining participants each are supplied with a pencil and two sheets of paper. They are instructed to label one sheet Diagram I and the other Diagram II.

   ■ The facilitator tells the group that the demonstrator will give them directions for drawing a series of squares. Participants are instructed to draw the squares exactly as the demonstrator tells them, on the paper labeled Diagram I. Participants may neither ask questions nor give audible responses.

   ■ The demonstrator is asked to study the arrangement of the squares in Diagram I for two minutes.

   ■ The facilitator instructs the observers to take notes on the behavior and reactions of the demonstrator and/or the participants.

   ■ The facilitator prepares the following three tables on newsprint.

Table 1 (for Diagram I)

Number Correct	Estimate	Actual
5		
4		
3		
2		
1		
0		

The Pfeiffer Book of Successful Communication Skill-Building Tools © *2004 John Wiley & Sons, Inc.*

Table 2 (for Diagram II)

Number Correct	Estimate	Actual
5		
4		
3		
2		
1		
0		

Table 3 (Summary)

	Diagram I	Diagram II
Time Elapsed		
Estimated Median		
Actual Median		

- The facilitator asks the demonstrator to turn his or her back to the group or to stand behind a screen. The facilitator then asks the demonstrator to proceed and to tell the group what to draw as quickly and as accurately as possible. The facilitator again cautions the group not to ask questions.

- The time it takes the demonstrator to complete the instructions is recorded in the summary Table 3 under Diagram I.

- Each participant is asked to estimate the number of squares he or she has drawn correctly in relation to the other squares. The facilitator then tabulates the participants' estimates in Table 1.

- The first phase of the experience is repeated with the following modifications: The demonstrator uses Diagram II, faces the group, and is allowed to respond to questions from the group. The participants should use the papers labeled Diagram II.

- The facilitator has each of the participants estimate the number of squares he or she has drawn correctly in the second phase of the activity and tabulates the estimates on Table 2. The facilitator then uses

Tables 1 and 2 to calculate the median (or average) estimated accuracy for both Diagram I and Diagram II. These medians are posted in Table 3.

- The group is then shown the actual diagrams for the two sets of squares. Each participant counts the number of squares he or she has drawn correctly on each diagram.

- In the last columns of Tables 1 and 2, the facilitator tabulates the number of squares the participants have drawn correctly for each diagram. From the data, the facilitator determines the medians for Diagrams I and II and enters these in Table 3.

3. The facilitator leads a discussion of the results in terms of time, accuracy, and level of confidence, calling upon "back-home" experience and application.

4. The observers report their process observations. The group discusses these in relation to the data generated during the first phase of the discussion.

Variations

- Instead of medians, means (arithmetic averages) may be computed.
- Additional phases such as the following can be included:
  - Two-way, with demonstrator facing participants, who are permitted to react nonverbally.
  - Two-way, with demonstrator not facing participants.
  - Two or more participants can be selected to work together as a demonstration team.
  - Teams of participants can be formed to draw the diagrams on newsprint cooperatively.
- The content can be changed to include data relevant to the objectives of the training and/or a more complex type of problem.
  - Physical models, such as those made of dominoes or blocks, can be described by the demonstrator.

Originally published in The Handbook, Volume I.

DIAGRAM I: ONE-WAY COMMUNICATION

Instructions: Study the series of squares below. With your back to the group, you are to direct the participants in how they are to draw the figures. Begin with the top square and describe each in succession, taking particular note of the relationship of each to the preceding one. No questions are allowed.

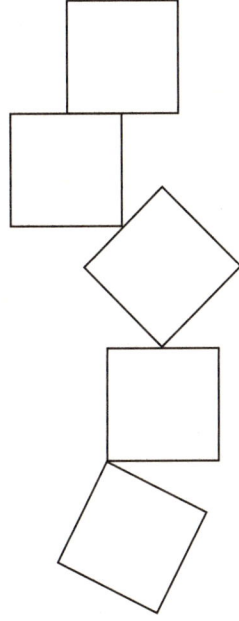

DIAGRAM II: TWO-WAY COMMUNICATION

Instructions: Study the series of squares below. Facing the group, you are to direct the participants in how they are to draw the figures. Begin with the top square and describe each in succession, taking particular note of the relation of each to the preceding one. Answer all questions from participants and repeat if necessary.

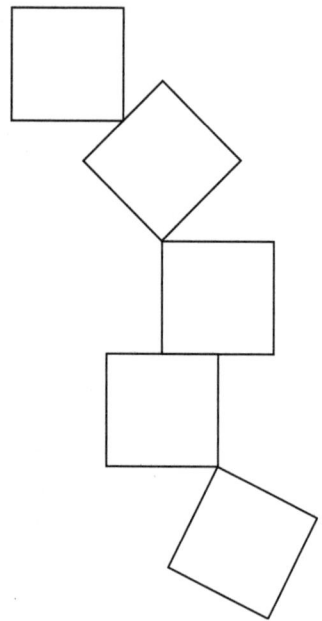

2

Pass It On: Simulating Organizational Communication

Linda Costigan Lederman and Lea P. Stewart

Goals

- To enhance the participants' understanding of the complexity of oral communication patterns within an organization.

- To illustrate what happens to messages that are transmitted orally through several different channels within an organization.

- To explore ways to improve oral communication within an organization.

Group Size

Twenty to thirty-two participants.

Time Required

One hour and forty-five minutes.

A different version of this structured experience appeared in L. C. Lederman and L. P. Stewart, "One Day in an Organization," in SIMCORP *Participants' Manual*, Total Research Corporation, 1983. Adapted with the permission of the authors.

Materials

- One copy of the Pass It On Instruction Sheet for each participant.
- One copy of the Pass It On Observer Sheet for each observer.
- A pencil for each observer.
- A clipboard or other portable writing surface for each observer.
- One copy of the Pass It On Messages (to be used only by the facilitator).
- A name tag for each participant. Prior to conducting the activity, the facilitator labels these tags as follows:
- One tag labeled "President";
- Three to five tags labeled "Executive Vice President";
- Three to five tags labeled "Vice President";
- Three to five tags labeled "Manager";
- Three to five tags labeled "Production Worker";
- Three to five tags labeled "Operations Worker";
- Two to four tags labeled "Observer"; and
- Two tags labeled "Recorder."
- Six newsprint signs designating the areas of the room assigned to the various subgroups. Prior to conducting the activity, the facilitator prepares these signs with the following labels (one label per sign): "President," "Executive Vice Presidents," "Vice Presidents," "Managers," "Production Workers," and "Operations Workers."
- A newsprint reproduction of the organizational hierarchy illustrated on the instruction sheet. The facilitator prepares this reproduction prior to conducting the activity.
- Masking tape for posting newsprint.
- Two newsprint flip charts and two felt-tipped markers (one chart and marker placed at the president's station and another chart and marker placed at the operations workers' station).

Physical Setting

A large room that will allow the participants to move back and forth freely. The signs designating the stations for the organizational subgroups should be taped to the wall in different areas of the room. One flip chart and felt-tipped marker should be placed at the president's station, and the other flip chart and marker should be placed at the operations workers' station. The newsprint reproduction of the organizational hierarchy should be taped to the wall in such a way that it can be viewed by all participants.

Process

1. The facilitator explains the goals of the activity.

2. The participants are assigned roles for the simulation: one president, three to five executive vice presidents, three to five vice presidents, three to five managers, three to five production workers, three to five operations workers, two to four observers, and two recorders. Name tags are distributed. The subgroups that comprise the organizational hierarchy are stationed at different areas within the room; one recorder is stationed near the president, and one is stationed near the operations workers; and the observers are stationed in different places so that they can observe the activity from different vantage points.

3. Each participant is given a copy of the Pass It On Instruction Sheet and is asked to read this sheet. Each observer is also given a copy of the observer sheet, a pencil, and a clipboard or other portable writing surface and is asked to read the observer sheet. The facilitator elicits and answers questions about the activity. (Fifteen minutes.)

4. The facilitator gives the organizational subgroups their assigned messages one by one, each time reciting the subgroup's message carefully but so that the other subgroups cannot hear the content; no participant is allowed to see his or her subgroup's written message or to write the recited message. In addition, each recorder is instructed to receive messages from the appropriate participant(s) and to record these messages on newsprint; the facilitator emphasizes to each recorder that the received messages must not be translated into the recorder's own words.

5. The participants are instructed to begin the simulation. The facilitator monitors their actions to ensure that the flow of communication is as described on the instruction sheet.

6. The facilitator stops the simulation when all messages have been recorded on newsprint. (The recorder stationed near the president will have recorded three messages, and the recorder stationed near the operations workers will have recorded four messages.)

7. The total group is reassembled, and the observers are asked to share the content of their observer sheets.

8. The facilitator leads a discussion of the activity. The following questions are asked:

   ■ What reactions did you have to the conveying and receiving of messages? What difficulties did you experience? How did you compensate for these difficulties? What surprises did you experience?

   ■ What are some words you would use to describe the oral communication within the organization portrayed in this simulation? How does your description compare with the way in which oral communication occurs in your own organization?

   ■ What can you generalize about oral communication among hierarchies within an organization?

   ■ How might oral communication within an organization be improved? What would have to happen in order to generate this improvement?

   ■ What could you personally do to simplify the oral-communication process in your own organization? How might you increase clarity and reduce distortion in communication?

Variations

■ After step 8 the participants may be asked to use the improvements they have suggested to convey different messages.

■ If the participants share a common profession, the facilitator may devise different messages that reflect that profession.

■ To shorten the activity, the number of organizational levels may be reduced.

Originally published in The Handbook, Volume X.

Pass It On Instruction Sheet

Instructions: During the upcoming activity, you and your fellow participants will take part in a simulation of the flow of organizational communication. If you have been assigned a role within the organizational hierarchy, you will be conveying and receiving certain messages. To begin the activity, the facilitator will instruct each subgroup separately about the message that it is to convey, and one of the members of this subgroup will deliver the message *orally* to one of the members of the subgroup that is to receive the message. Consult the organizational hierarchy illustrated below and the copy that follows to determine the flow of messages.

Organizational Hierarchy

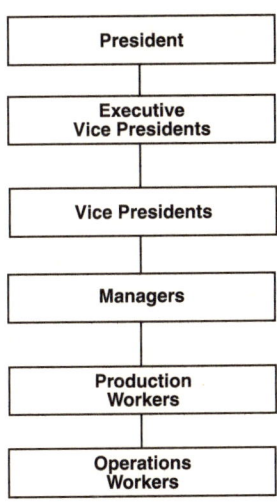

President

The president conveys his or her assigned message to and receives messages from the *executive vice presidents*. Each time the president receives a message, he or she recites this message to the recorder standing nearby, who then records the message *word for word* on newsprint.

Executive Vice Presidents

The executive vice presidents convey their assigned message to the *vice presidents*. They receive a message from the president and convey it to the vice presidents, and they receive messages from the vice presidents and convey these to the president.

Vice Presidents

The vice presidents convey their assigned message to the *managers*. They receive messages from the executive vice presidents and convey them to the managers, and they receive messages from the managers and convey them to the executive vice presidents.

Managers

The managers convey their assigned message to the *vice presidents and the production workers*. They receive messages from the vice presidents and convey them to the production workers, and they receive messages from the production workers and convey them to the vice presidents.

Production Workers

The production workers convey their assigned message to the *managers*. They receive messages from the managers and convey them to the operations workers, and they receive a message from the operations workers and convey it to the managers.

Operations Workers

The operations workers convey their assigned message to and receive messages from the *production workers*. Each time a message is received, the operations worker who received it recites the message to the recorder standing nearby, who then records the message *word for word* on newsprint.

Pass It On Observer Sheet

Instructions: During the upcoming activity, you are to observe the participants' interactions carefully and write answers to the following questions. Later you will be asked to share these questions and your answers with the total group. If you need clarification of this assignment, consult the facilitator in private; do not share the content of this sheet with the participants who are involved in the simulation.

1. How are the participants choosing to convey and receive messages?

2. What types of feelings and reactions are the participants displaying?

3. What distortions of messages are occurring in the exchange? What are the participants doing to reduce distortion and/or increase clarity?

4. What similarities and differences are becoming apparent among subgroups as the participants convey and receive messages? What patterns are developing within and among subgroups? What significance do these patterns have?

PASS IT ON MESSAGES

President's Message

This year's company picnic will be held on Saturday, May 1. All employees and their families are cordially invited.

Executive Vice Presidents' Message

Because extra cash is available at present, it has been decided to make some improvements to the company's building. The exterior of the building will be painted in April, and the interior will be painted in June.

Vice Presidents' Message

The company is instituting a system to reward employees whose performance is exceptional. Each month one employee will be chosen as the recipient, and this individual will be given $250 during a special award ceremony.

Managers' Message

All production and operations workers are being asked to work an extra two hours per shift for the next two weeks so that the company can fill a large customer order.

Production Workers' Message

The production workers would like a company-paid policy of disability insurance to be added to the employee-benefits package.

Operations Workers' Message

The operations workers would like to have four more vending machines installed: two machines that dispense soft drinks and two that dispense snacks.

3

Red Light/Green Light: From Fear to Hope

Niki Nichols

Goals

- To help individuals or groups to discuss upcoming changes openly.
- To identify and address fears, doubts, questions, and hopes about an impending organizational change.
- To learn to see the positive aspects of change.

Group Size

Fifteen to twenty-five participants from a department in an organization undergoing reorganization or other change.

Time Required

One to one and one-half hours.

Materials

- One of each (red, yellow, and green) index cards for each participant.
- Pens or pencils for each participant.

- Newsprint felt-tipped markers (or whiteboard markers) for the facilitator.
- A newsprint flip chart (or whiteboard) with a "traffic signal" drawn in red, yellow, and green.

Physical Setting

A writing surface, desk, table, or clipboard for each participant.

Process

1. The facilitator introduces the goals of the activity, then asks participants to list some of the changes taking place in the organization at the present time. He or she lists these on newsprint. (Five minutes.)

2. The facilitator explains that most people look at how any change will impact or change them personally. Some personal reactions to change could include that they feel successful with what they are doing now, they recall a past change that caused problems, they do not wish to learn new ways of doing things, or they fear failure in the new environment.

3. The facilitator shows the traffic signal drawn on newsprint and labels the lights as Fears (red) Questions or Reservations (yellow), and Hopes (green).

4. He or she then distributes one of each color (red, yellow, and green) index card and a pen or pencil to participants and instructs them to write a Fear they have about the upcoming change on the red card, a Question or Reservation on the yellow card, and a Hope on the green card. (Five minutes.)

5. After five minutes the facilitator collects all cards, shuffles them and redistributes the cards, three per participant without regard to color. (Five minutes.)

6. The facilitator asks for eight or ten items that have been written on red cards and posts them on the newsprint, then what has been written on eight or ten yellow cards, and what has been written on eight or ten green cards, posting the items in each case. The facilitator continues until all cards have been posted. [*Note:* There will be duplicates, which can be dealt with by using check marks.] (Ten to fifteen minutes.)

7. The facilitator forms three subgroups to identify patterns and themes for red, yellow, or green cards. (Ten minutes.)

The Pfeiffer Book of Successful Communication Skill-Building Tools © 2004 John Wiley & Sons, Inc.

8. Subgroups report their results to the total groups. The facilitator leads a discussion of ways to deal with the fears and discusses the reasons for fear, acknowledging that it can be legitimate and giving some ways to deal with it directly, rather than allowing it to fester. (Ten to fifteen minutes.)

9. The facilitator leads a discussion of the themes found on the green cards and ways to make some of the hopes expressed come true. (Ten to fifteen minutes.)

10. The facilitator ends with the following questions:

   - How do you feel now about the organizational change? How is the way you feel now different from when you began this activity?

   - What have you learned about the way change affects you?

   - What have you learned about the nature of change in general?

   - What will you do to assist yourself and others in adjusting to this change?

   (Ten to fifteen minutes.)

Variations

- The trainer may ask representatives from management to address the themes and answer the questions (yellow cards) that surface, although this step must be undertaken very carefully.

- A task force could be formed to bring the fears and concerns to senior management.

- Participants can pair off to discuss their concerns and doubts with one another, with an emphasis on seeking solutions.

- Self-stick notes may be used instead of index cards, with participants placing the notes directly on the flip chart.

- Participants can be asked to pick three of the following statements that they identify the most with. Subgroups can be formed by statement to discuss ways to overcome the fear or concern.

   - "I know how to do my job the way it is now."
   - "I do my job well."
   - "We have always done it this way."
   - "The last change caused more problems than it fixed."
   - "I will not know what to do."
   - "I will have to do things differently."
   - "I do not understand why this is happening or how it will work."

- "I will not be able to learn new skills."
- "I have too much to do now, and this will add more."
- "I do my job very well now, but I may only be average at something new."
- "Just how different is this, anyway?"

■ The activity can be extended by giving participants more than one of each color card.

Originally published in The 1998 Annual, Volume 1, Training.

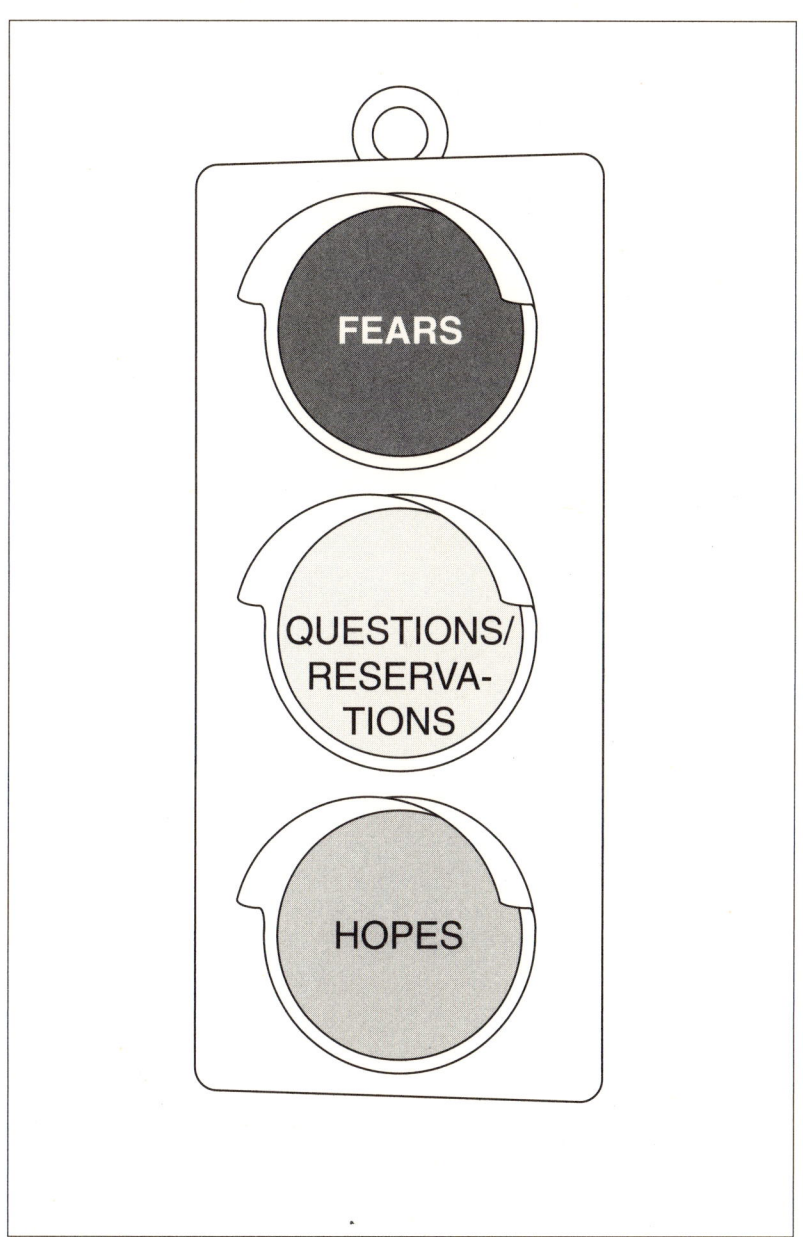

4

Blivet: A Communication Experience

Ken Myers, Rajesh Tandon, and Howard Bowens, Jr.

Goals

- To demonstrate and experience one-way and two-way verbal communication.
- To demonstrate and experience barriers and aids to verbal communication.
- To explore how different status positions affect interpersonal communication.

Group Size

Nine to thirty participants, in numbers divisible by three.

Time Required

Approximately one and one-half hours.

Materials

- A copy of the Blivet Manager Briefing Sheet for each manager.
- A copy of the Blivet Assistant Manager Briefing Sheet and a copy of the Blivet Assembly Sheet for each assistant manager.
- A copy of the Blivet Manager Briefing Sheet, a copy of the Blivet Assistant Manager Briefing Sheet, a copy of the Blivet Observer Guide, and a pencil for each observer.

- One unassembled Blivet for each manager.
- One assembled Blivet (See Directions for Manufacturing Blivets) for each assistant manager.
- One table blind for each trio (see Directions for Assembling a Blivet Table Blind).
- Newsprint and a felt-tipped marker.

Physical Setting

A room large enough to accommodate one table and two chairs for each trio, with space between the groupings. Additional rooms for initial briefings are desirable. The physical arrangement may be laid out in a variety of ways as room availability, size, and general convenience dictate. Four criteria are important:

- Some minimal separation of participating trios is necessary.
- Spatial relationships of trios must be such that participants with unassembled Blivets cannot see the finished solutions on adjacent tables.
- There must be room for observers to stand adjoining the participant pairs they are to observe.
- There must be room for the facilitator to move among the trios to observe the process.

An example of a workable physical arrangement is as follows:

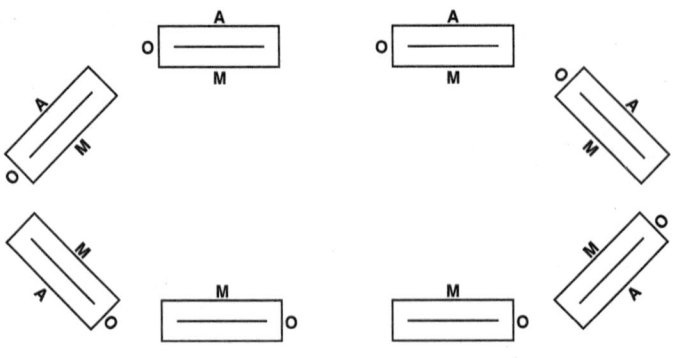

— = Table blind
O = Observer
M = Participants (managers) with unassembled Blivets
A = Participants (assistant managers) with assembled Blivets

The Pfeiffer Book of Successful Communication Skill-Building Tools © 2004 John Wiley & Sons, Inc.

Process

1. The facilitator prepares the tables prior to the experience: Each table contains two Blivets, separated by a blind (see Directions for Assembling a Blivet Table Blind). One Blivet is assembled and is *hidden* under a Blivet Assembly Sheet, which is placed upside down; the Blivet across the table is unassembled.

2. The facilitator briefly introduces the activity by explaining its goals.

3. The participants are divided into three equal subgroups, subgroup one being "managers," subgroup two being "assistant managers," and subgroup three being "observers.

4. The facilitator gives each manager a copy of the Blivet Manager Briefing Sheet and each assistant manager a copy of the Blivet Assistant Manager Briefing Sheet. The manager and assistant manager subgroups are then sent to separate locations. The facilitator briefs the observers in the activity area and gives them each a pencil, a copy of the Blivet Manager Briefing Sheet, a copy of the Blivet Assistant Manager Briefing Sheet, and a copy of the Blivet Observer Guide. He or she stresses that they are not to participate in the assembly process, that they may speak to participants only to caution them about rule observation, that they are to observe and record events, and that they will report later on their observations.

5. The facilitator reviews the task with the manager and assistant manager subgroups separately. He or she reminds the managers that they will have *unassembled* Blivets and reminds the assistant managers that they will have assembled Blivets, all Blivets being of the same size and shape. (He or she makes no mention of color.) The facilitator tells both subgroups that they are not to touch anything on the tables until they have been instructed to begin the activity.

6. All participants are assembled in the large room and are directed to their appropriate locations. The facilitator announces that he or she will play the role of the company president during the twenty minutes they have to complete the task. He or she then tells them that the operator has just announced trouble on the line and that they are to begin the activity from that point.

7. During the course of the activity, the facilitator rotates between the subgroups, playing the role of the president by "intimidating the managers," obviously impatient, and consistently reminding them of the time remaining. (This adds realistic noise, distraction, frustration, and even anger to the task.)

8. After five minutes or so, when frustration has obviously set in, the facilitator announces that the operator has opened up two-way communication. After a few more minutes, if the manager and assistant manager are still assuming that their Blivet pieces are the same color, the facilitator mentions that nothing was said about colors being the same. He or she continues periodically to remind participants of the time deadline.

9. If a substantial number of Blivets remain unassembled within two minutes of the activity completion deadline, the facilitator removes the blinds from the tables, announcing that the phone company has installed "videophones."

10. The facilitator calls a halt to the activity. He or she assembles the participants and briefly goes over the goals of the experience. Each observer then reports on the communication processes of the pair he or she observed and on the elements that affected or hindered one-way and two-way communication between the manager and the assistant manager.

11. The participants comment on their feelings during and reactions to the experience. The focus is particularly on frustration in communicating, the differences between effective and ineffective communication processes, and how effectiveness is influenced by one-way or two-way communication. The facilitator also may direct the discussion to the effects of the different status positions on the communication within the pairs. The facilitator lists the major discussion points on newsprint. He or she keeps the discussion focused on personal reactions and on *communication* issues, rather than on the task or whether some pairs completed it "successfully."

12. The facilitator gives a lecturette on helping and hindering behaviors that affect interpersonal communication. Participants are then encouraged to equate these learnings to real-life situations.

Variations

- The facilitator can devise briefing sheets appropriate to the subgroup's setting and circumstances; i.e., titles or positions need not necessarily be "supervisor-subordinate"; the Blivet could be a shredded report, a piece of machinery, a surgical instrument, etc.; the separation of the participants could represent different cities or sites such as the bridge and the engine room. The initial communication breakdown requiring one-way communication can be portrayed as being over any nonvisual communication device that offers the opportunity for resumption of normal communication.

- The goals and learnings can focus on helping behavior, interpersonal perceptions, leadership style, or problem solving.
- The lecturette can precede the activity.
- The videophone can be introduced as a structured portion of the activity.

Originally published in The 1979 Annual.

BLIVET MANAGER BRIEFING SHEET

You are a sales manager. You were in the office of the president of your company demonstrating a new automated wastebasket opener (called a Blivet) when it fell apart in your hands. The only other assembled Blivet is with your assistant sales manager in Chicago at a trade show. You are now on the phone with your assistant and have said that you think you can get your disassembled Blivet together again if the assistant will describe the assembled one. You have just mentioned that the president is angry and wants the demonstration to resume immediately when the operator cuts in and says that there is trouble on the line. You can continue to hear your assistant, but you cannot talk back because the other person cannot hear you.

The problem: You must get the Blivet assembled to continue the demonstration to the president. You must utilize such communication opportunities as are available to you, given the present situation.

BLIVET ASSISTANT MANAGER BRIEFING SHEET

You are an assistant sales manager. You are in Chicago at a trade show where you are displaying a new automated wastebasket opener (called a Blivet). You have just received an urgent page to call your supervisor, the sales manager, back in Cleveland. You return the call, and your supervisor explains the problem. He was demonstrating the only other assembled Blivet to the company president when it fell completely apart. The president is angry and is intimidating your supervisor to get the Blivet assembled and continue the demonstration. Your supervisor thinks it may be possible to reassemble the broken Blivet if you will explain how to do it, based on your assembled one. At this point, the operator cuts in to say that there is trouble on the line. You can continue to talk to the sales manager, who can hear you, but you cannot hear anything on your end of the line.

The problem: You must explain how to get the Blivet together so that your supervisor's demonstration to the company president can be completed. You must communicate with your supervisor, using such communication opportunities as are available to you in this situation.

The Pfeiffer Book of Successful Communication Skill-Building Tools © 2004 John Wiley & Sons, Inc.

BLIVET OBSERVER GUIDE

Your task is to observe and record the interaction between the participants as they try to construct a second Blivet identical to the first (in size and shape but not in color). The Blivets are in the form of a large block "T." Try to remain inconspicuous. Do not interfere as the participants go about their task or respond to any of their questions. However, do not let the person with the unassembled Blivet talk during the one-way-communication portion of the activity. At the conclusion of the activity, be prepared to comment briefly on what you saw taking place.

Here are some things to look for:

1. Communication aids or blocks that occurred between the two participants:

   - Assumptions of varying color, perceptions of the Blivet, etc.

   - Use of technical or geometric terms.

   - Actions that are independent of instructions or preconceived notions about how the Blivet is to go together.

2. Awareness and sharing of the overall picture:

   - Did one communicate that the Blivet is in the shape of a capital "T"?

   - Did either participant question whether the two Blivets were made of the same colors?

3. Did the participants take time, when two-way communication was opened up, to appraise where they were and to plan or talk about where to go from there or what help might be needed?

4. To what extent did emotions (such as frustration or anger) become involved? Was it a rational step-by-step process? What was each member's response to pressure? How did the roles affect these responses?

5. Did either participant abdicate the situation and stop trying?

Use the other side of this sheet for additional comments. Do not be limited by these suggestions. Rather, try to think of other things that are aiding or blocking communication. Make some notes as the activity proceeds, because it is difficult to recall key events and issues later.

Directions for Manufacturing Blivets

Blivets should be made from heavy colored construction paper or similar material. The manager and assistant manager each receive a Blivet with pieces of the same size and shape, but not of the same color. The easiest way to handle this is to choose as many different colors of construction paper as there are trios (or at least five), cut an entire Blivet from each color, and then assemble a packet for each trio containing the following:

1. one complete Blivet, with each piece of a different color;
2. a second Blivet with each piece of a different color, these colors to be different from piece "1" above;
3. one Blivet Assembly Sheet.

Cut each Blivet along solid and dotted lines. Each Blivet has five parts.

Blivet Assembly Sheet

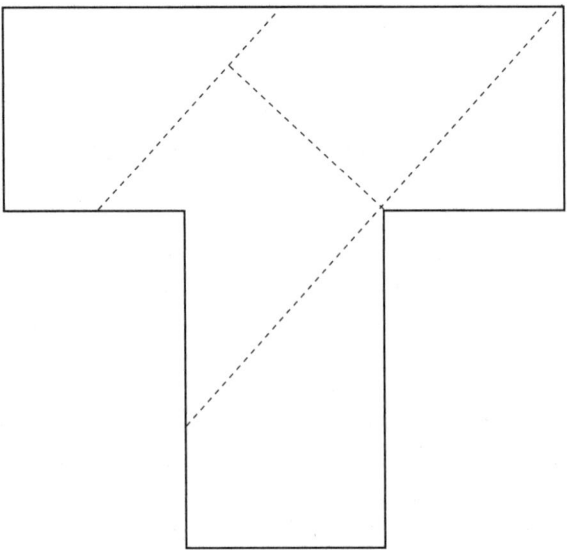

Directions for Assembling a Blivet Table Blind

1. Manufacture one blind for each trio's table.

2. Use heavy cardboard and cut as follows:

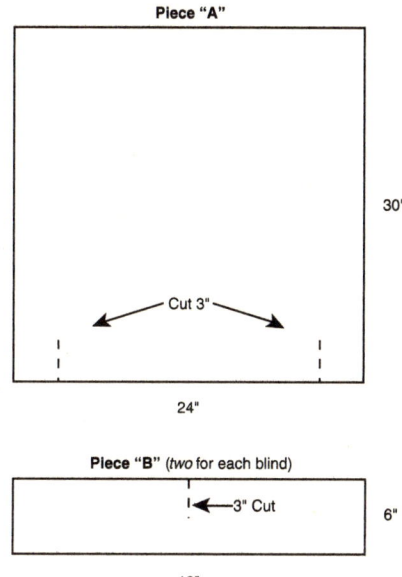

Piece "A"

30"

Cut 3"

24"

Piece "B" (*two* for each blind)

3" Cut

6"

12"

3. Assembly:

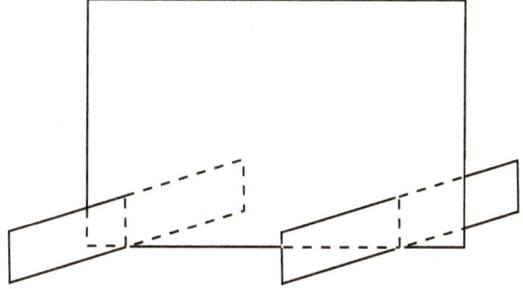

5

Analyzing and Increasing Open Behavior: The Johari Window

Philip G. Hanson

Goals

- To describe open and closed behavior in terms of the Johari Window.

- To identify facilitating and inhibiting forces which may affect the exchange of feedback.

- To encourage the development of increased open behavior in the group through facilitated feedback.

Group Size

Eight to twelve participants. Several subgroups may be directed simultaneously.

Time Required

Approximately two and one-half hours.

Materials

- A copy of the Johari Window Self-Rating Sheet for each participant.

- A pencil for each participant.

- A copy of the Johari Window Model Theory Sheet for the facilitator.
- Newsprint and felt-tipped markers for each subgroup.
- A newsprint flip chart and a felt-tipped marker for the facilitator's use.
- Masking tape for posting newsprint.
- A copy of the Johari Window Model (optional).

Physical Setting

A room large enough to accommodate the group or subgroups and to allow subgroups to work comfortably and with minimal noise distraction.

Process

1. The facilitator begins with a lecturette to the total group on giving and receiving feedback, based on the Johari Window Model Theory Sheet. Central to the lecturette, the facilitator will emphasize how decreasing the "Blind Spot" (the area unknown to self) and decreasing the "Facade" (the area unknown to others) will increase the "Arena" (the area known to everyone), thereby fostering openness. The facilitator will also emphasize the role of meaningful feedback in this process.

2. Each participant is given a copy of the Johari Window Self-Rating Sheet and a pencil.

3. The facilitator suggests that one goal participants may have is to discover data about themselves that they were previously unaware of, i.e., "decreasing the Blind Spot." The only way they can do this is to solicit feedback and to be receptive to it. In terms of the Johari Window Model, the vertical line will move to the right as the "Blind Spot" is decreased.

4. The facilitator illustrates the decreasing "Blind Spot" on newsprint using the following model:

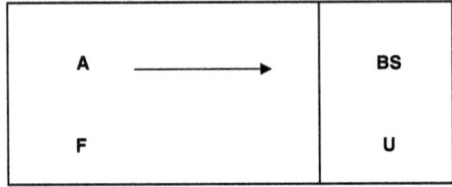

5. The facilitator explains that a scale from one to nine runs across the top of the Self-Rating Sheets, describing the extent to which a person solicits feedback. The participants are asked to think about their last group meeting and about times when they wondered how they were being perceived by other group members.

6. Participants then are asked to look at the scale across the top of the blank window and to find a point on that scale that describes the extent to which they actually solicited feedback in that group session. The facilitator emphasizes that the participants are not rating how many times they felt the need for feedback but how many times they actually asked for it. The participants then are instructed to draw a vertical line to the bottom of the window from the point they have identified on the top scale.

7. The facilitator suggests that another goal they may have in the group setting is that of becoming more open by disclosing some of the data that they have kept from the group or by giving feedback to others, i.e., decreasing the "facade." The facilitator illustrates how the horizontal line drops when the "facade" is decreased:

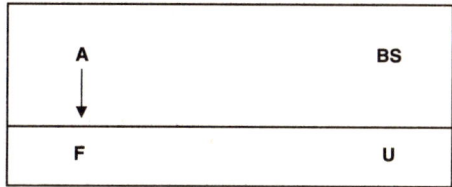

8. The facilitator tells the group to notice how as the "Blind Spot" and "Facade" decrease, the "Arena," or openness to others, increases. He or she then asks them to look at their Johari Window Self-Rating Sheets again and to notice on the left-hand margin a scale running from one to nine, measuring the extent to which a person discloses himself or herself, or gives feedback to the group. The facilitator asks the participants to think back again on their last group meeting(s) and remember how many times during that group session they felt the need to give feedback to other group members, express their own feelings and perceptions about themselves, or take a stand on group issues.

9. The participants are asked to locate on the scale at the left-hand margin the extent to which they actually gave feedback or disclosed themselves to the group. The facilitator emphasizes that they are to rate only the extent to which they actually gave feedback, not how many times they felt

like doing so. When they have located the position on the scale they are to draw a horizontal line across the window pane.

10. At this point, the facilitator will illustrate the use of the Johari window by interpreting variously constructed windows.

11. The group or groups are divided into subgroups of three or four, depending upon the size of the group.

12. The facilitator asks the participants to take twenty to thirty minutes to share their windows with the members of their subgroups. They are to ask for feedback as to how they would have been rated in terms of soliciting and giving feedback, thus comparing self-ratings with others' perceptions. When this exchange is complete, they are to begin to identify the forces in their groups that make it easy or difficult to solicit or give feedback. As a subgroup they are to make a list of these facilitating and inhibiting forces, taking about fifteen minutes to accomplish this task. The facilitator supplies newsprint and felt-tipped markers to each subgroup.

13. After approximately forty-five minutes, the facilitator asks the participants to reassemble and to share the information generated by the subgroups. The subgroups are asked to integrate their lists into a final list of forces and in this process discuss what steps the group wants to take in order to increase facilitating forces and decrease inhibiting forces affecting the feedback process. The facilitator may wish to suggest that participants make contracts with one another as a method of increasing the exchange of feedback.

Originally published in The 1973 Annual.

Johari Window Model Theory Sheet

The process of giving and receiving feedback can be illustrated through a model called the Johari window. The window was originally developed by two psychologists, Joseph Luft and Harry Ingham, for their program in group process. The model can be looked upon as a communication window through which you give and receive information about yourself and others.

Looking at the four panes in terms of columns and rows, the two columns represent the *self* and the two rows represent the *group*. Column one contains "things that I know about myself;" column two contains "things that I do not know about myself." Row one contains "things that the group knows about me"; row two contains "things that the group does not know about me." The information contained in these rows and columns is not static but moves from one pane to another as the level of mutual trust and the exchange of feedback varies in the group. As a consequence of this movement, the size and shape of the panes within the window will vary.

The first pane, called the Arena, contains things that I know about myself and about which the group knows. It is an area characterized by free and open exchange of information between myself and others. The behavior here is public and available to everyone. The Arena increases in size as the level of trust increases between individuals or between the individual and his or her group and more information, particularly personally relevant information, is shared.

The second pane, the Blind Spot, contains information that I do not know about myself but of which the group may know. As I begin to participate in the group, I communicate all kinds of information of which I am not aware, but which is being picked up by other people. This information may be in the form of verbal cues, mannerisms, the way I say things, or the style in which I relate to others. The extent to which we are insensitive to much of our own behavior and what it may communicate to others can be quite surprising and disconcerting. For example, a group member once commented that every time their facilitator was asked to comment on some personal or group issue, the facilitator always coughed before answering.

In pane three are things that I know about myself but of which the group is unaware. For one reason or another I keep this information hidden from them. My fear may be that if the group knew of my feelings, perceptions, and opinions about the group or individuals in the group, they might reject, attack, or hurt me in some way. As a consequence, I withhold this information. This pane is called the "Facade" or "Hidden Area." One of the reasons I may keep this information to myself is that I do not see the supportive elements in the group. My assumption is that if I start revealing my feelings, thoughts, and reactions, group members might judge me negatively. I cannot find out, however, how members will really react unless I test these assumptions and reveal something of myself. In other words, if I do not take some risks, I will never learn the reality or unreality of my assumptions. On the other hand, I may keep certain kinds of information to myself when my motives for doing so are to control or manipulate others.

The last pane contains things that neither I nor the group knows about me. Some of this material may be so far below the surface that I may never become aware of it. Other material, however, may be below the surface of awareness to both myself and the group but can be made public through an exchange of feedback. This area is called the "Unknown" and may represent such things as intrapersonal dynamics, early childhood memories, latent potentialities, and unrecognized resources. Because the internal boundaries can move backward and forward or up and down as a consequence of soliciting or giving feedback, it would be possible to have a window in which there would be no Unknown. Because knowing all about oneself is extremely unlikely, the Unknown in the model illustrated is extended so that part of it will always remain unknown. If you are inclined to think in Freudian terms, you can call this extension the "Unconscious."

One goal we may set for ourselves in the group setting is to decrease our Blind Spots, i.e., move the vertical line to the right. How can I reduce my Blind Spot? Because this area contains information that the group members know about me but of which I am unaware, the only way I can increase my awareness of this material is to get feedback from the group. As a consequence, I need to develop a receptive attitude to encourage group members to give me feedback. That is, I need to actively solicit feedback from group members in such a way that they will feel comfortable in giving it to me. The more I do this, the more the vertical line will move to the right.

Another goal we may set for ourselves, in terms of our model, is to reduce the Facade, i.e., move the horizontal line down. How can I reduce my Facade? Because this area contains information that I have been keeping from the group, I can reduce my Facade by giving feedback to the group or group members concerning my reactions to what is going on in the group and inside of me. In this instance, I am giving feedback or disclosing myself in terms of my perceptions, feelings, and opinions about things in myself and in others. Through this process the group knows where I stand and does not need to

The Pfeiffer Book of Successful Communication Skill-Building Tools © 2004 John Wiley & Sons, Inc.

guess about or interpret what my behavior means. The more self-disclosure and feedback I give, the farther down I push the horizontal line.

You will notice that while we are reducing our Blind Spots and Facades through the process of giving and soliciting feedback, we are, at the same time, increasing the size of our Arena or public area.

Johari Window Self-Rating Sheet

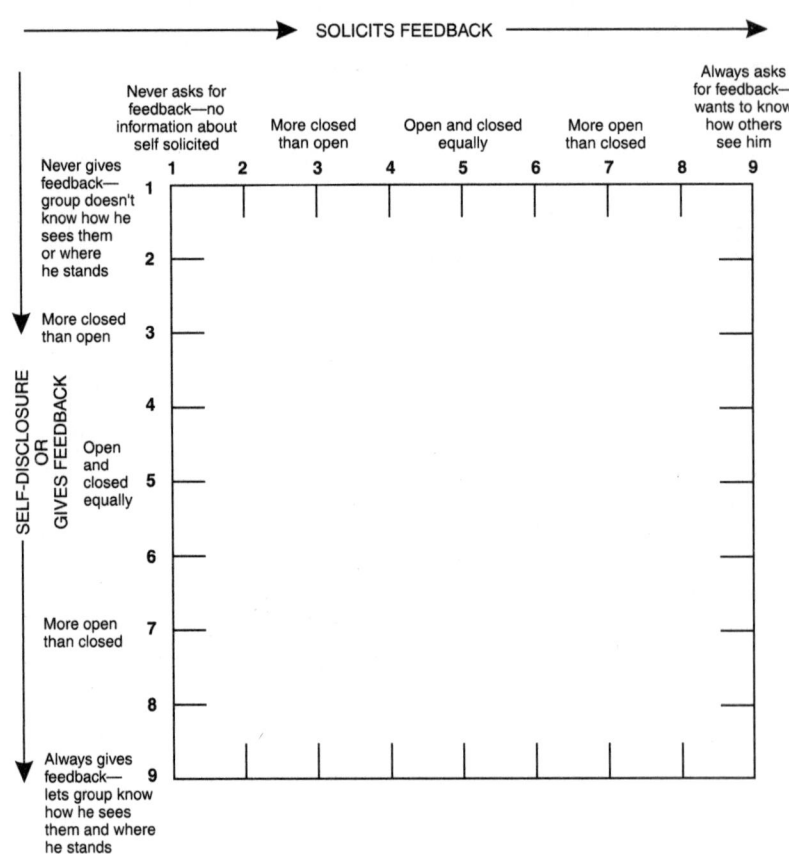

The Pfeiffer Book of Successful Communication Skill-Building Tools © 2004 John Wiley & Sons, Inc.

Johari Window Model

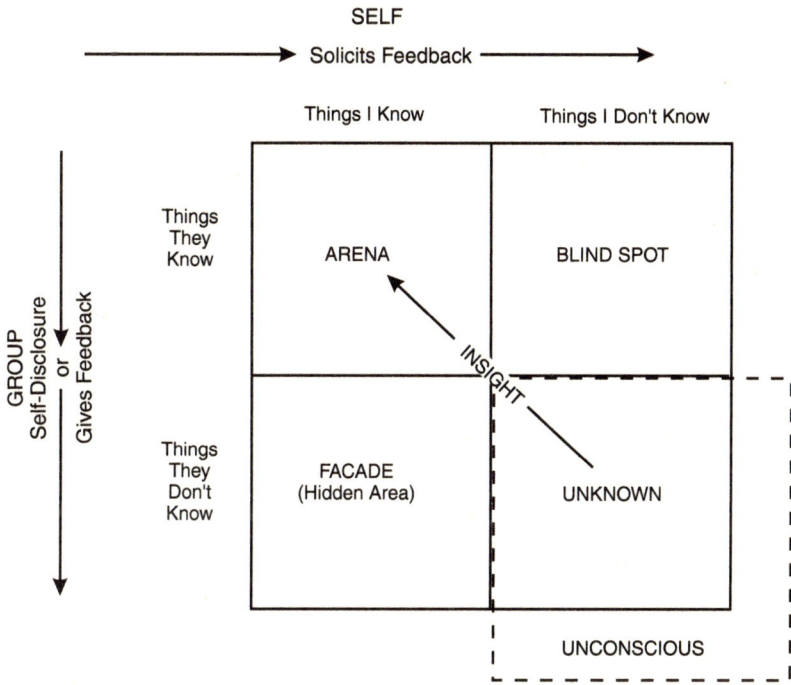

SELF

Solicits Feedback

Things I Know   Things I Don't Know

GROUP
Self-Disclosure
or
Gives Feedback

Things They Know

Things They Don't Know

ARENA

BLIND SPOT

INSIGHT

FACADE (Hidden Area)

UNKNOWN

UNCONSCIOUS

Requests to reprint the Johari Window Model should be addressed to Mayfield Publishing Company in Mountain View, California.

6

Work Dialogue: Building Team Relationships

Judith F. Vogt and Karen L. Williams

Goals

- To explore the sequence of building from interpersonal to team relationships.

- To provide an opportunity to enhance work relationships through mutual openness and disclosure.

- To allow the participants to practice interpersonal skills related to sharing personal information, taking risks, listening, and giving and receiving feedback.

Group Size

Up to ten pairs of participants. Participants should know one another and have worked together, either as members of an ongoing team or from having worked together in cross-functional teams.

Time Required

Approximately two and one-half hours.

Materials

- A copy of the Work Dialogue Instructions for each participant.
- A copy of Work Dialogue Booklet for each participant. (*Note to the facilitator:* Prepare each Work Dialogue Booklet by cutting along the dashed lines. Assemble the pages in order and staple them along the left side to form a booklet.)
- Newsprint flip-chart paper and felt-tipped markers for each subgroup.
- Masking tape for posting newsprint.

Physical Setting

- A room, series of rooms, or outdoor area in which the pairs can communicate in relative privacy. Also, a space in which all participants can work in groups of three to five members each, with wall space for posting flip-chart "products."

Process

1. The facilitator introduces the activity by discussing the following points:

   - Today's organizations have shifted (or are shifting) to work relationships based on employee empowerment and participation, teams and groups, interdependence, process orientation, continuous learning, and quality.

   - For example, work relationships occur in self-managed work teams, temporary (or project) teams, total quality management teams, etc.

   - Such relationships require that people be able to deal productively with others in face-to-face situations. Whether working in short- or long-term work groups, individuals need interpersonal skills, understanding of group dynamics, the ability to work creatively with others for extended periods, and the ability to handle ambiguity in both relationships and tasks.

   - To meet the demands of team and group work, people need to have experience and confidence in the skills of relationship building, including being open, taking risks, giving and receiving feedback, listening, and clarifying expectations.

   (Five minutes.)

The Pfeiffer Book of Successful Communication Skill-Building Tools © 2004 John Wiley & Sons, Inc.

2. The facilitator has the participants form pairs by any convenient method, asking them to pair up with persons whom they do not know as well as others. (Five minutes.)

3. One copy of the Work Dialogue Instructions and one Work Dialogue Booklet are distributed to each participant. The facilitator reviews the instructions with the participants. (Five minutes.)

4. Each pair is directed to proceed to a private area and to follow the instructions. The participants are told what time to return to the common meeting room. (One and one-half hours.)

5. When the total group has reassembled, the facilitator helps the participants to process the experience by encouraging them to share what they have learned about themselves. [*Note:* One of the guidelines is confidentiality. It is imperative to ensure that this norm is maintained by permitting each person to talk only about himself or herself, not about his or her partner.] The processing questions may include the following:

   ■ What was this experience like for you? How did it change as the time progressed?

   ■ What did you discover about yourself by engaging in this dialogue? What did you discover about the relationship with your partner?

   ■ What did you learn from this process about building work relationships? What skills are important in building relationships?

   (Ten to fifteen minutes.)

6. After the experience has been processed for individual learnings, the facilitator shifts the focus to implications of the experience for group and team work. The participants are instructed to form groups of three to five members each, depending on the size of the total group (threes if the total group is small and fives if it is large). Dialogue partners should not be in the same group. Each group is given two sheets of flip-chart paper and felt-tipped markers. The discussion groups are asked to extract and list implications for teams resulting from the dialogue experience. The facilitator encourages the participants to focus on the *process* of the dialogue experience. [Once again, participants are reminded not to discuss their dialogue partners' reactions or comments.] (Twenty minutes.)

7. Masking tape is distributed. Each group, in turn, is asked to post its list of implications and briefly to describe the highlights of its discussion. (Ten to twenty minutes.)

8. The facilitator leads a concluding discussion based on the following questions:

- What are some ways to build team relationships? What things would inhibit building team relationships?

- What can you apply immediately to a team in which you are a member?

Variations

- If this activity is being used as a team-building activity or with an ongoing work group, the group can then establish norms or expectations for itself for the future based on its members' learnings. The norms can be posted and used periodically as a process check for the group's progress. It is important to emphasize here that relationships are dynamic and that norms and expectations are likely to change over time to accommodate new conditions.

- The participants might want to develop a matrix listing various types of teams and the group-relationship factors that they perceive as particularly salient for those teams. This would help facilitators, leaders, and group members to focus future relationship and team-building activities.

- Pertinent lecturettes (e.g., on group development, the Johari Window, the concept of a "psychological contract," or group norms) can provide team members with a greater understanding of the potential of groups that recognize interpersonal competence in group development and group work.

- Dialogue partners can maintain their relationship throughout a workshop or back on the job as "helping pairs." Periodically, they can get together to explore experiences or concerns relevant to their earlier discussions. It is important to clarify that group-based issues should be brought back to the group for resolution. However, the pair discussions can provide support or insight to members prior to their taking personal observations to the group.

- Self- and/or group-assessment tools can be used as a follow-up to the dialogue. These can help to strengthen each person's self-learning and/or the group's functioning.

- The dialogue can be utilized in team settings. Two options are possible. First, if members have minimal interpersonal or group skills, it is suggested that dialogue partners complete the booklet first. After Step 5, each dialogue pair selects two sentence stems that they think are essential for the team to discuss. Each pair describes why it selected the items. Once the team has had an opportunity to discuss at least one item from each pair, it can return to Step 6 and continue.

The Pfeiffer Book of Successful Communication Skill-Building Tools © 2004 John Wiley & Sons, Inc.

A second option for utilizing the dialogue as a team activity requires that group members have good interpersonal skills, especially in terms of openness and trust. Steps 2, 3, and 4 can be replaced by a team dialogue (a group of sixteen is the maximum size). First, the group discusses the introductory comments for clarity and implications. Then each member starts the discussion of an item by completing the stem. Others follow if they want to. Once discussion slows down for that item, another group member starts discussion of the next item by completing the stem; again other members participate if they choose to. This process continues through all the items or until the allocated time has expired. All members should have an opportunity to initiate an item and to participate in the open discussion. If this is not happening, the facilitator may want to break the group into smaller groups or even pairs, so that each person can participate and learn from the process.

- The activity can be ended after Step 5, after adding a concluding discussion question such as "What have you learned from this experience that you can apply to the team as a whole?"

Originally published in The 1995 Annual, Volume 1, Training.

WORK DIALOGUE INSTRUCTIONS

About This Dialogue

The conversation that you are about to begin is intended to help you develop more effective work relationships. Tasks are accomplished more effectively if people who work together have the ability to exchange expertise, ideas, points of view, feelings, and attitudes.

It is also important that you be able to clarify expectations and assumptions that you make about one another in relation to the work to be done. Furthermore, the system's (team, group, division, or organization) culture emerges from interactions that members have with one another.

One purpose of this discussion is to foster greater understanding of others at work. By telling about yourself and by sharing perceptions with another person, you will be working toward a higher level of trust. Trust is the foundation for effective group work, especially in settings that demand coordination, teamwork, creativity, and quality.

Guidelines for This Dialogue

1. The booklet consists of a series of open-ended statements. You and your partner will take turns, each completing the next statement orally. Focus your discussion around work-related issues.
2. All of this discussion is confidential. Do not repeat later what your partner has said during the dialogue.
3. Do not look ahead in the booklet.
4. Do not skip items. Consider each statement in the order in which it is presented.
5. You may decline to respond to any statement.
6. When you and your partner have finished reading this introduction, turn the page and begin.

Following Up

The items are intended to open a dialogue that can be carried on in your work relationship. You may wish to make definite plans to continue this exchange in the future. Some activities that you may consider follow:

- Go through this dialogue booklet again after about six months.
- Schedule meetings to discuss items and your relationship.
- Contract with each other for support in changing your behavior at work.

The Pfeiffer Book of Successful Communication Skill-Building Tools © 2004 John Wiley & Sons, Inc.

Work Dialogue Booklet

Work Dialogue: Building Team Relationships

Usually, I am the kind of person who . . .   1

I want to become the kind of person who . . .   2

When I am feeling anxious in a new work situation, I usually . . .   3

I am happiest at work when . . .   4

My greatest area of growth at work is . . .   5

I am resistant when . . .   6

I usually react to negative criticism by . . .   7

I usually react to supportive remarks by . . .   8

To me, belonging to a team means . . .   9

When I am in a new work group, I . . .   10

Briefly discuss how the dialogue is going.   11

When things aren't going well at work, I . . .   12

Basically, the way I feel about my work is . . .   13

When I think about your responsibilities, I think that . . .   14

The most important skill in developing work relationships is listening.   15
To improve your ability to hear each other, follow these steps: the person whose
turn it is completes the following item in two or three sentences; the listener then
paraphrases in his or her own words what the speaker has said; then the listener
completes the same item, and the other partner paraphrases what he or she has heard.

As a member of a team, I expect . . .   16

When each of you has had a turn, share what you may have learned about   17
listening. During this dialogue, you may wish to continue the development of
your listening capabilities by paraphrasing what your partner has said.

At work, I'm best at . . .   18

In conflict situations between people at work, I usually . . .   19

The thing I like best about you is . . .   20

I prefer to receive feedback about myself and my work . . .   21

The ways I prefer to receive information are . . .   22

The kinds of task information I value are . . .   23

The next thing I'm going to try to accomplish at work is . . .   30

The next step in my career development seems to be . . .   31

Faced with a conflict between the goals of the organization (division)   32
and your own welfare, I predict that you would . . .

My own personal goals are to . . .   33

The worst co-worker I ever had . . .   34

When I ask for help at work, I . . .   35

When someone helps me at work, I . . .   36

Have a brief discussion of how this dialogue is going so far. How open are you being? How do you feel about your participation up to this point?   37

The emotion I find most difficult to control at work is . . .   38

When I offer help at work, I . . .   39

Your work seems to be . . .   40

The best colleague I ever had . . .   41

Have a brief discussion of what your responses to the last few items say   48
about what you believe to be valuable in work relationships and teams.

I think our personal goals and our organization's goals can be   49
mutually achieved if . . .

I think of terms such as "boss," "supervisor," and "manager" as . . .   50

The best leader I ever worked with . . .   51

When I see you work with others, I . . .   52

In a work group, I am most comfortable when my colleagues . . .   53

In a work group, I feel most comfortable when leadership . . .   54

My impression of you now is . . .   55

In a work group, I usually get most involved when . . .   56

Listening check: Paraphrase your partner.   57

In ambiguous, unstructured situations, I . . .   58

I like to be a follower when . . .   59

When I have to work with others to accomplish goals, I . . .   60

My position in this organization . . .   61

I would like my role in the organization/team to . . .   62

Together we can . . .   63

Have a brief discussion of your participation in and reactions   64
to this conversation.

7

Defensive and Supportive Communication: A Paired Role Play

Gary W. Combs

Goals

- To examine the dynamics of defensive and supportive communication in supervisor/subordinate relationships.

- To develop skills in listening to and understanding a contrasting point of view.

- To explore the concept of synergy in paired communication.

- To examine the expectations that defensive communication creates for a continuing relationship.

Group Size

Any number of pairs, preferably with an equal balance between the sexes.

Time Required

Approximately one and one-half hours.

Materials

- A copy of the appropriate Defensive and Supportive Communication Background and Role-Description Sheet for each participant.
- Two copies of the Defensive and Supportive Communication Discussion Guide for each participant.
- A pencil for each participant.

Physical Setting

A room large enough to allow pairs to interact without disturbing one another.

Process

1. The facilitator introduces the experience by presenting a lecturette on defensive and supportive communication, covering the following points:

    - Communication becomes defensive when the sender's goal is to persuade the receiver to agree with his or her opinions, ideas, facts, or information.[1]

    - Defensive communication is characterized by evaluation, control, strategy, superiority, and certainty.[2]

    - Communication becomes supportive when the goal is to actively hear and understand the other's opinions, thoughts, or feelings.

    - Supportive communication is characterized by empathy and spontaneity; it promotes problem solving and synergy.

2. The facilitator divides the participants into pairs and announces that there will be four rounds of paired role play to enable participants to experience the two forms of communication and to understand how the dynamics of each form emerge. He or she explains that during rounds 1 and 2, one member of the pair will role play a supervisor and the other a subordinate and that their roles will be reversed during rounds 3 and 4. Pairs are instructed to determine who will role play the supervisor and subordinate for rounds 1 and 2.

---

[1]See C. R. Rogers and F. J. Roethlisberger, "Barriers and Gateways to Communications," *Harvard Business Review*, 1952, 30, 46-52.

[2]See J.R. Gibb, "Defensive Communication," *Journal of Communications*, 1961, 11, 141–148.

3. A Defensive and Supportive Communication Background and Role-Description Sheet is given to each participant (Case 1, 2, or 3 may be used). The facilitator notes that specific instructions for each round are described on the role-description sheet. Players are given time to study their roles.

4. The facilitator initiates round 1. He or she allows five to seven minutes for the interaction.

5. After stopping the role play, the facilitator distributes one copy of the Defensive and Supportive Communication Discussion Guide and a pencil to each participant. Each participant fills out the form by placing a "1" in the spaces provided to indicate his or her feelings about round 1 (three minutes). The round is then discussed by the partners (five minutes).

6. The facilitator initiates round 2. At the conclusion of round 2, participants once again fill out the same Defensive and Supportive Communication Discussion Guide, this time by placing a "2" in the appropriate places. They then discuss round 2 with their partners. They are told to focus on the differences between rounds 1 and 2.

7. For rounds 3 and 4, the pairs of participants reverse roles. The facilitator distributes different versions of the Defensive and Supportive Communication Background and Role-Description Sheet, and steps 4 through 6 are repeated with new role-play situations. Following round 3, another copy of the Defensive and Supportive Communication Discussion Guide is distributed to each participant. It is filled out (three minutes) and discussed (five minutes) as before.

8. At the conclusion of round 4, participants once again fill out their discussion guides and briefly discuss the differences between rounds 3 and 4. They then are instructed to think about the differences between their two different role-playing situations.

9. The facilitator assembles the total group and leads a discussion of the different modes of communication. He or she may ask the group:

   ■ What were the differences between the defensive and supportive modes of communication? (Reactions to questions on the Defensive and Supportive Communication Discussion Guide can be reviewed at this point.)

   ■ What were the differences between *sending* and *receiving* the two types of communication?

   ■ How did the power relationship of the supervisor and subordinate roles affect the communication processes?

- How were the outcomes of rounds 1 and 2 different? To what degree were the outcomes of round 2 synergistic? (The facilitator explains the concept of synergy.)

- What are the implications of the two modes of communication in real-life settings?

Variations

- Role-play situations can be invented by the facilitator, the total group, or individual pairs.

- A demonstration role play in front of the total group can precede the paired role play.

- Rounds 3 and 4 can be eliminated.

- A group discussion of rounds 1 and 2 can precede rounds 3 and 4.

- Participants can change partners for rounds 3 and 4.

- Supportive communication can be used first in round 1. Differences between rounds 1–2 and 3–4 (in which defensive is used first) can be processed in terms of different expectations for the next communication.

Originally published in The 1979 Annual.

Defensive and Supportive Communication Background and Role-Description Sheet

Case 1: The Performance Appraisal System

Background: This case focuses on the development of a system to appraise employee performance. Dale Clark, personnel director, has asked to meet this afternoon with Robin Smith, director of administrative services, to discuss Robin's proposal for such a system. They are meeting at 2 p.m.

Role-Description Sheet 1 (Supervisor)

Robin Smith: You are director of administrative services for an organization that has tripled its size since its creation two years ago. This rapid growth has led to a need to develop an appraisal system that will foster the development of employees for managerial positions and furnish data for maintaining an inventory of employee talent and for making promotion and transfer decisions.

Early last week, you wrote a memo to the company personnel director, Dale Clark—who is your subordinate—describing the need for such a system and outlining your thoughts for its design. As soon as a design is agreed on, you expect Clark to implement and administer the system.

Under your plan, supervisors would use a standard form to appraise employees every twelve months. The appraisal would be discussed with the employee and signed by both the supervisor and employee. Copies of the appraisal would be retained by the personnel department and the appraising supervisor, as well as the employee.

Your proposed system is based on the assumption that it is important for supervisors to let employees know those areas in which they need to develop. For purposes of record keeping, you also feel that it is important that a standardized form be used for performance appraisal. Two days ago, Dale Clark requested a meeting to discuss your proposal and, you think, probably to raise some questions about your design.

Round 1: Your goal is to get Dale Clark to agree with the tenets of your design. You should explain as best you can the rationale supporting the design. You are determined that your way shall prevail.

Round 2: Your goal is to create a climate to explore the differences between yourself and your personnel director. You should encourage Clark to express his or her position and search for a resolution that achieves your objectives as well as those of the personnel director.

Defensive and Supportive Communication Background and Role-Description Sheet

Case 1: The Performance Appraisal System

Background: This case focuses on the development of a system to appraise employee performance. Dale Clark, personnel director, has asked to meet this afternoon with Robin Smith, director of administrative services, to discuss Robin's proposal for such a system. They are meeting at 2 p.m.

Role-Description Sheet 2 (Subordinate)[3]

Dale Clark: You are the personnel director for an organization that has tripled its activity since its creation two years ago. Last week you received a memo from your boss, Robin Smith, director of administrative services, noting that the organization's growth has led to a need to develop a performance-appraisal system. The purpose of the system is to foster the development of employees for managerial positions, furnish data for maintaining an inventory of employee talent, and aid in making promotion and transfer decisions.

Under the plan outlined in Smith's memo, supervisors would use a standardized form to appraise employees once a year. The appraisal would be discussed with the employee and signed by both the supervisor and employee. Copies of the appraisal would be retained by the personnel department, the supervisor, and the employee.

You believe that this approach is detrimental to employee development. It places the supervisor in the role of judge and tends to bring about a defensive reaction from the subordinate. You favor a problem-solving approach in which the supervisor initiates an interview with the employee and elicits ideas for job improvement. The supervisor stimulates employees to self-diagnose their needs for development; the interview is not initiated by a written appraisal. Problems not addressed by the subordinate can be brought up by the supervisor after the employee has voiced his or her concerns. Such problems can be introduced by asking for the subordinate's help.

You feel that this method of appraisal is superior to the traditional one suggested by Smith because it develops a climate of mutual interest and al-

---

[3]The approach to appraisal expressed in this role is drawn from N.R.F. Maier, *The Appraisal Interview: Three Basic Approaches.* San Diego, CA: Pfeiffer & Company, 1976.

most always leads to new ideas and improved performance. The employee is motivated to think constructively rather than defensively.

Two days ago, you requested a meeting with Robin Smith to discuss your ideas. You hope to achieve some modifications in your supervisor's design.

Both Rounds: You are to interact with Smith, explaining your approach and its rationale.

Defensive and Supportive Communication Background and Role-Description Sheet

Case 2: Management and Organizational Behavior

Background: Gerry Thompson is a student in Professor Reilly's management and organizational behavior class. The class is an introductory, graduate-level seminar that meets from 1 p.m. to 4 p.m. on Wednesday afternoons. Each student is required to complete midterm and final examinations and a library-research paper on a topic of his or her own choosing. Each student is expected to submit a brief proposal (one-half to one page) noting his or her topic and objectives for research. The proposals are returned with comments and suggested bibliographic sources. When a proposal is deficient, Professor Reilly asks to meet with the student.

Role-Description Sheet 1 (Supervisor)

Professor Reilly: You are an associate professor of organizational behavior in a major university. You have been teaching for six years and have published several articles reporting your research. You teach a seminar in management and organizational behavior once a year; most of the people in the class are full-time students pursuing a master's degree in administration.

Because this is an introductory seminar, you believe that it is important for students to become familiar with the research literature in organizational behavior. Students should develop their capacities to critically examine and compare major theories and ideas in the field and be able to present their analysis in a logical and coherent fashion. Because of these beliefs, you require students to complete a major paper based on library research. Gerry Thompson, a student in the seminar who works full time for a major organization in the area, wrote a proposal for a paper on organizational change. It would be a case study of the reorganization that recently occurred in the administrative-services division of Gerry's organization. Because it is not based on library research, the paper, as far as you are concerned, is unacceptable. You have asked Gerry to meet you after class so that you can explain the proposal's deficiencies.

Round 1: Your goal is to have Gerry revise the proposal so that it is based solely on library research. You should be friendly, patient, and explain as best you

The Pfeiffer Book of Successful Communication Skill-Building Tools © 2004 John Wiley & Sons, Inc.

can your rationale for requiring a paper based on a survey of appropriate literature. You are determined that your way shall prevail.

Round 2: Your goal is to create a climate in which to explore the differences between your ideas and Gerry's. You should encourage Gerry to express his or her position and search for a resolution that achieves both of your objectives.

Defensive and Supportive Communication Background and Role-Description Sheet

Case 2: Management and Organizational Behavior

Background: Gerry Thompson is a student in Professor Reilly's management and organizational behavior class. The class is an introductory, graduate-level seminar that meets from 1 p.m. to 4 p.m. on Wednesday afternoons. Each student is required to complete midterm and final examinations and a library-research paper on a topic of his or her own choosing. Each student is expected to submit a brief proposal (one-half to one page) noting his or her topic and objectives for research. The proposals are returned with comments and suggested bibliographic sources. When a proposal is deficient, Professor Reilly asks to meet with the student.

Role-Description Sheet 2 (Subordinate)

Gerry Thompson: You are a middle manager in the data-processing section of your organization. Your college degree is in mathematics. Your organization's flexible time program enables you to go to school two afternoons a week to obtain your master's degree in administration. By returning to school you hope to become a better manager and improve your chances for promotion.

For your term project, you wrote a proposal for a paper on organizational change. The paper will be based on an analysis of the reorganization that recently occurred in the administrative-services division of your organization. From the analysis you intend to extract a number of principles regarding organizational change. You feel that this approach will be of more benefit to you than a paper based on a review of research studies.

Professor Reilly has asked to meet with you after class. You assume that the professor wants to make some suggestions about your proposed project.

Both Rounds: You are to interact with Professor Reilly to explain your rationale for doing an analytical case study instead of a paper based on library research.

The Pfeiffer Book of Successful Communication Skill-Building Tools © 2004 John Wiley & Sons, Inc.

Defensive and Supportive Communication Background and Role-Description Sheet

Case 3: Internal Auditing

Background: The setting is the internal auditing division of a large governmental insurance organization. Lee Black is the administrator of the division; it includes five units charged with reviewing the work of field claims examiners. Black has asked Pat Fisher, one of the unit supervisors, to meet to discuss a specific problem.

Role-Description Sheet 1 (Supervisor)

Lee Black: You have worked for this organization for twelve years, seven of them at the administrative level. You have been the division administrator for three years. Your bachelor's degree is in psychology; in addition, you have completed several courses in administration.

The problem concerning you is that total work production in the unit that Pat Fisher supervises is lower than that of other units. Fisher's unit completes approximately fifty audits a week; the other units average eighty audits a week, with some completing as many as one hundred a week. The quality of work completed in Fisher's unit, however, is superior to that completed in the other units.

You have thoroughly evaluated the situation and its implications for the divisions. Because of pressures for production from your boss and complaints from the other unit supervisors that Fisher's unit is giving the division a bad reputation, you feel that you must insist on higher production. You have decided to impose a quota on the unit of seventy-five audits per week, even though there might be a temporary decline in the quality of work produced. This seems to you to be more than fair, since it is still below the average production of the other units.

You are meeting with Pat Fisher this morning at 10 a.m. to explain your plan and its rationale.

Round 1: Your goal is to have Fisher implement a quota of seventy-five audits per week. You should be friendly, patient, and explain as best you can the rationale supporting your decision. You are determined that your way shall prevail.

Round 2: Your goal is to create a climate for exploring the problem of low production; Fisher should be encouraged to express his or her position. You should discuss your idea for a quota system, but be open to other ways of resolving the problem.

DEFENSIVE AND SUPPORTIVE COMMUNICATION BACKGROUND AND ROLE-DESCRIPTION SHEET

Case 3: Internal Auditing

Background: The setting is the internal auditing division of a large governmental insurance organization. Lee Black is the administrator of the division; it includes five units charged with reviewing the work of field claims examiners. Black has asked Pat Fisher, one of the unit supervisors, to meet to discuss a specific problem.

Role-Description Sheet 2 (Subordinate)

Pat Fisher: You have worked for this organization for sixteen years. You have had supervisory responsibilities for ten years and have had your present position of unit supervisor for three years. You have a B.S. degree in accounting and have had several in-service training classes in supervision.

You believe that quality work is important and take pride in the fact that your unit's work is generally of a higher quality than that of other units. To achieve high quality, you insist that each case be fully examined regardless of the size or importance of the claim. This frequently entails researching the latest interpretation of government regulations and consulting with others outside the division. You encourage those who work for you to help each other and frequently hold staff meetings to discuss problem cases. Lee Black, your supervisor, has asked you to meet this morning at 10 a.m. One of your subordinates has informed you that, according to rumor, Black is going to impose a quota on your unit. Although you are aware of the fact that your unit's production is somewhat lower than that of the other units, you feel that this is compensated for by the higher quality of work within your unit.

You are willing to listen to Black's arguments, but you are dead set against quotas. It has been your experience that quota systems are easily subverted and inevitably lead to a lower quality of work.

Both Rounds: You are to interact with Black, expressing your position and its rationale.

DEFENSIVE AND SUPPORTIVE COMMUNICATION DISCUSSION GUIDE

Use these scales to guide your discussion after each round of interaction. Place a "1" on each of the scales to indicate your experience in round 1, a "2" on each scale at the end of round 2, etc.

1. How well did you listen to the other person's point of view?

Not Well ___ ___ ___ ___ ___ ___ ___ ___ ___ Very Well

2. What kind of feeling climate was stimulated by the interaction?

Competitive ___ ___ ___ ___ ___ ___ ___ ___ ___ Cooperative

Judging of the
Other Person ___ ___ ___ ___ ___ ___ ___ ___ ___ Empathetic

Controlling ___ ___ ___ ___ ___ ___ ___ ___ ___ Problem
Oriented

Superior ___ ___ ___ ___ ___ ___ ___ ___ ___ Equal

Positive ___ ___ ___ ___ ___ ___ ___ ___ ___ Provisional

Defensive ___ ___ ___ ___ ___ ___ ___ ___ ___ Supportive

3. How satisfied are you with the interaction?

Very
Dissatisfied ___ ___ ___ ___ ___ ___ ___ ___ ___ Very
Satisfied

4. How satisfied are you with the outcome or product of the discussion?

Very
Dissatisfied ___ ___ ___ ___ ___ ___ ___ ___ ___ Very
Satisfied

The Pfeiffer Book of Successful Communication Skill-Building Tools © 2004 John Wiley & Sons, Inc.

8

Mediated Message Exchange: Exploring the Implications of Distance Communication in the Workplace

Heidi A. Campbell

Goals

- To investigate the impact of computer-mediated distance communication on dialogue between two people.

- To allow individuals to reflect on ways that limitations and/or benefits of computer-mediated communication can shape their personal communication and their treatment of those with whom they communicate.

- To simulate the process of e-mail communication in a workshop setting to enable individuals to consider the implications this technology has for their own work.

- To consider the impact of industry trends toward distance working.

Group Size

Any size, but this activity is ideal for ten to twelve participants.

Time Required

Approximately forty-five to sixty minutes.

Materials

- One copy of the Mediated Message Exchange Background Sheet for each participant.
- One envelope containing the Mediated Message Exchange E-Mail Memo for each participant. (Two sets should be prepared in advance, numbered sequentially according to how many members are in the group. For twelve participants in two groups of six, you will have two sets of envelopes numbered from one to six.)
- At least four plain white envelopes per participant.
- Pens for all participants.
- At least four sheets of plain white paper for each participant.
- A stopwatch.

Physical Setting

Two small rooms or a large open space with a partition to divide the room so that when participants are separated into two groups neither group can see the other. If neither option is possible, a separation can be accomplished by participants sitting back-to-back in chairs, with a gap between the lines of chairs.

Process

1. Frame the activity as a simulation of a distance work situation involving e-mail. Give everyone a copy of the Mediated Message Exchange Background Sheet and give them time to read it. Then summarize the situation in the following way:

   "Thanks for coming to this meeting. You have been selected by your company, Star Enterprises, as a member of a virtual work group. The group has been assigned a special project: restructuring the company. You will be required to work closely with your assigned partners, but due to the organizational changes taking place and the timely nature of this project, you will be able to communicate with your partners only via e-mail.

You have already been assigned a partner, and when you return to your work station you will receive an e-mail message that will briefly explain the project and your role in it. In brief, you and your partner must present a short task report at a general meeting scheduled later today. This means you will have about twenty minutes to work together on this report, beginning when you receive your first message. You must begin by immediately reading your message, contacting your partner, and working on your assignment."

2. Inform the group that you will answer no questions once the activity starts. Ask if there are any questions at this time; if there are any, simply clarify the information you have already given.

3. Divide the group into two smaller groups and place each in a designated work space, either in separate rooms or behind partitions if possible. Number the people in each group separately and then assign partners according to the like number in the other group. Do not give people the name or any "real world" clues about their partners. If there is an odd number of participants, ask for a volunteer to help you in the role of a courier.

4. After everyone is settled, give each person an envelope corresponding with his or her number and containing a copy of the Mediated Message Exchange E-Mail Memo describing the project and the specific task.

5. Give everyone a few minutes to read their e-mail memos.

6. Choose one group to respond immediately to the e-mail message. Hand out writing paper, pens, and envelopes to everyone in that group. Tell them they have four minutes to write messages to their partners. Explain that, when they are finished, they should place their e-mail messages into plain envelopes, write their numbers on the envelopes, and send them to their partners via "courier." (Five minutes.)

7. Collect the envelopes and distribute them to the appropriate people in the second group. Give that group four minutes to read and respond to their messages, using either the sheets of paper they received or new sheets. Tell them to place their responses in envelopes, write their numbers on the outside, and send the envelopes back to their partners via the "courier." Again, collect all the envelopes and distribute them in the other group. (Five minutes.)

8. Repeat the process at least four times within the time constraints. It is important to keep track of time and adhere strictly to the exchange time. This helps to emphasize the constraints of electronic communication (quick

and brief) and ensures that individuals are able to exchange several messages within the total time limit.

9. Notify the groups when they are exchanging their last messages.

10. After the last e-mail exchange, ask everyone to take a few minutes to evaluate his or her own communication. Ask participants to write down their answers to the following questions:

   - How would you rate your ability to communicate with your partner during this exercise?

   - Were you able to work on the task effectively? Why or why not?

   - Did you form any opinions about your partner during the exchange of messages? If so, what were they?

   - What can be learned from your experiences?

   (Ten minutes.)

11. Bring the group together. Allow each pair to meet. Have the partners share their observations with one another for a few minutes. Then bring the entire group together and lead them in processing the activity. Allow each pair to share its observations with the total group; then pose the following questions:

   - How did you feel as you went through this activity?

   - What factors affected your communications with your partners?

   - Was it difficult to communicate? Why or why not?

   - Did you notice anything about your communication with your partner as the activity progressed?

   - If you were to do this activity again, what would you do differently?

   - How do distance and means impact one's ability to communicate?

   - If this had been an actual work situation, what would the benefits have been from communicating in this manner? The disadvantages? The consequences?

   - Are you currently involved in any work situations in which you have to use e-mail or other forms of technology to communicate with others at a distance?

   - What did you learn from this activity that you could apply to those situations?

   (Twenty minutes.)

Variations

- Each subgroup can be divided into pairs who together decide on the content of the messages and then exchange them with like pairs in the other subgroup. Then they can be introduced to one another and allowed to discuss the task for five minutes.

- The group can be divided into three subgroups. Individuals can then complete this same task in sets of threes, being required to communicate with two other trios. (This method requires another individual to help with the courier task.)

- Allow the individuals to come together after fifteen minutes and spend five to ten minutes to complete their task "in real time." Then ask them to compare their long-distance versus face-to-face interactions.

- The entire group can be given the same task, or each pair can be assigned a different one. The activity can be structured to be relevant to a specific group of workers or to a particular organization.

Originally published in The 2000 Annual, Volume 1, Training.

MEDIATED MESSAGE EXCHANGE BACKGROUND SHEET

We live in a world in which communication is becoming increasingly mediated through various forms of technology. It is common for individuals, alone or collaboratively, to conduct their work at a distance from the workplace using computer-mediated communication (CMC). Individuals frequently utilize various electronic mail and computer software to transmit and receive information based on text, images, and even sound over great distances with relative ease and efficiency. Within many organizations, face-to-face communication is often not possible, although the same levels of quality and clarity of communication are expected among its workers. Thus CMC is used to bridge the gap.

According to Barry Wellman (1997): "Many workers are involved in multiple work teams, rather than solidary groups, and they are as apt to work with colleagues across the country as with those in the next seat. The computerized flow of information drives their work, not the office clerk handing out the day's 'snail mail.'"

When direct contact is eliminated, there are unknown consequences. Because computer-meditated communication is void of face-to-face contact, many wonder at the implications for the workplace. Does mediated communication lead to a depersonalizing form of communication, second-best to face-to-face interaction? However, the human element is not altogether lacking in computer-mediated communication. After all, it is humans who produce and shape the communication. Yet the tools they use do influence this process. Workers can see themselves as interacting with text, rather than with other individuals. Workers and management must consider how the newer forms of communication may impact not only the process, but also the end products of their work.

Reference

Wellman, B. (1997). An electronic group is a social network. In S. Kielser (Ed.), *Cultures of the Internet*. Mahwah, NJ: Lawrence Erlbaum.

Mediated Message Exchange E-Mail Memo

Date sent: Mon, 1 Feb 00 10:54:00-0800
From: Star Enterprises <headquarters@star.com>
Organization: Star Enterprises
To: Partner groups <workgroup@star.com>
Subject: Work group assignments

Star Enterprises recently hired an independent consultant who proposed that
we switch to smaller satellite offices, connected electronically via e-mail and the
Internet, rather than expanding our current headquarters to meet our increasing
business demands. This move would mean a considerable cost savings.
The consultant also recommended that employees be allowed to telecommute,
that is, work from home connected to satellite offices via the company computer
network. Work done in the offices would then be broken into smaller, more
individually focused tasks. In order to remain competitive, Star Enterprises has
decided that it must follow these recommendations. The changes that must be
made will undoubtedly affect all employees.

You have been selected to serve on a special team that will plan this
restructuring and have been assigned a work partner from another department.
Your goals as a partnership are to evaluate how these changes would affect the
workplace.

Your first task is to produce a short report on how these potential changes
could impact your job in particular and the company as a whole. You and your
partner are to present a report—summarizing the ideas you both have—at this
afternoon's general company meeting, so you must work quickly. Remember
that your suggestions may influence the direction of the entire organization,
so your focused effort and clear input are extremely important.

The nature of your current assignment via e-mail is also intended as an
experiment to see how the proposed changes might affect communication
between and relationships among workers.

After reading this e-mail, contact your partner (unless your partner has been
chosen to contact you first). Then immediately proceed with your task.

Thank you for your efforts on behalf of Star Enterprises.
Hal Edwards, General Manager

9

Bugs: Improving Customer Service

James W. Kinneer

Goals

- To help the participants to identify universal problems in customer service.

- To enhance the participants' awareness of their own responses to customer service issues.

- To offer the participants the opportunity to share ideas about dealing with customer service problems.

Group Size

Twelve to twenty participants in subgroups of four or five members each.

Time Required

One hour and one-half hours to two hours.

Materials

- One pad of Post-it™ Notes for each participant.

- A pencil for each participant.

- Several sheets of newsprint and a felt-tipped marker for each subgroup.
- A newsprint flip chart and a felt-tipped marker for the facilitator's use.
- Masking tape for posting newsprint.

Physical Setting

Any room in which the group can work comfortably and which has ample space for posting newsprint. Movable chairs should be provided.

Process

1. The facilitator introduces the goals of the activity and distributes a pad of Post-it™ Notes and a pencil to each participant. He or she gives the following instructions:

   "Think about times in the past when you have been annoyed by poor customer service. These can be very specific instances, or general annoyances, such as unfriendly clerks. Write each customer service 'bug' or annoyance on a separate Post-it™ Note sheet. You will have five minutes to complete this portion of the activity."

   (Five minutes.)

2. After five minutes, the facilitator calls time and reconvenes the total group. He or she goes around the group, asking each person in turn to come to the flip chart, name annoyances that they have experienced, and attach their Post-it™ Notes to the flip chart page. If more than one participant has written the same annoyance, their Post-it™ Notes can be pasted on top of each other. The facilitator provides new flip-chart pages as needed, posting the filled sheets around the room. (Twenty to thirty minutes.)

3. When all of the Post-it™ Notes have been collected, the facilitator leads the participants in clustering and naming the clusters. He or she posts clean flip-chart pages for the clusters (e.g., the ones that deal with waiting, the ones about product knowledge, etc.) and moves the Post-it™ Notes to the appropriate page. (Ten to fifteen minutes.)

4. When all of the annoyances have been grouped, the participants are asked to form subgroups of four or five members each. Each subgroup chooses to work with one of the clusters of annoyances. (Five minutes.)

5. Each subgroup is given the appropriate cluster of Post-it™ Notes, several sheets of newsprint, and a felt-tipped marker. The facilitator instructs the subgroups to accomplish two goals:

- Draw a service "bug," an animal that represents that particular annoyance. This service "bug" should be given a name (e.g., Slowmotionitis or Idunno bug) and a description of its characteristics should be listed on the newsprint. If desired, the Post-it™ Notes may be used as part of the composition of the drawing.

- Brainstorm solutions to combat this type of service "bug" in your organizations and list these on another sheet of newsprint.

(Twenty minutes.)

6. The facilitator reconvenes the total group. Each subgroup posts its "bug" creation, describes its characteristics, and presents ideas for how to prevent it. (Fifteen to twenty minutes.)

7. The facilitator leads a concluding discussion based on the following questions:

- What similarities did you identify in these "bugs?" What differences did you notice? How do you account for the differences?

- Which of the approaches to satisfying customers appeal to you as a customer? Which do not? What are some reasons for the differences in your reactions?

- What is the most important thing you have learned about customer service?

- What new thoughts do you want to adopt? What new behaviors do you want to try in dealing with customers?

(Fifteen minutes.)

Variations

- Subgroups could name the bugs without drawing them.

- Participants could name and post their annoyances one at a time, with those already posted not being repeated.

- If extra time is allotted, subgroups could decide on the solution they think best from the brainstorming and develop a plan to implement the solution.

Originally published in The 1996 Annual, Volume 1, Training.

10

Enhancing Communication: Identifying Techniques to Use with Diverse Groups

Robert William Lucas

Goals

- To enhance awareness of the need to use certain techniques to enhance communication with diverse types of people.
- To identify techniques that can be used in order to clarify communication.

Group Size

Three to six groups of approximately four members each.

Time Required

One to one and one-half hours.

Materials

- A copy of the Enhancing Communication Sheet for each participant.
- A newsprint flip chart and felt-tipped markers for each group.
- A copy of the Enhancing Communication Lecturette for the facilitator.
- A newsprint flip chart and felt-tipped markers for the facilitator.
- Masking tape for posting newsprint.

Physical Setting

A room large enough for subgroups to work without disturbing other groups. Provide a chair for each participant. Tables for the subgroups are optional.

Process

1. The facilitator introduces the activity and delivers the Enhancing Communication Lecturette. (Five minutes.)

2. The facilitator asks the participants, "What are some of the diverse types of people that could cause problems in communicating with them?" If needed, the facilitator may give one of the following as an example:

   - Those people from other cultures who have difficulty speaking the language,

   - Those people who have different orientations because of their cultural backgrounds,

   - People who have hearing or speech disabilities,

   - People who have learning disabilities or people who are illiterate/uneducated,

   - Members of the opposite sex from the speaker, and

   - People who are angry or have an argumentative attitude.

   The facilitator lists the participants' responses on a flip chart but does not discuss them in detail at this time. (Five minutes.)

3. The participants are divided into groups of approximately four members each. Each group is provided with a newsprint flip chart and felt-tipped markers. Each group is instructed to select a "scribe," who will be responsible for listing all ideas presented by group members on the flip chart and reporting them later to all participants. (Five minutes.)

4. The facilitator either assigns to each group one of the types of people identified in Step 2 or instructs each group to select a type (with no duplication among groups).

5. Each group is asked to take five minutes to brainstorm a list of techniques for communicating effectively with people in its particular type, then to take five minutes more to select its top ten techniques. The group's scribe lists these on newsprint. The facilitator gives time warnings during this period. (Ten minutes.)

The Pfeiffer Book of Successful Communication Skill-Building Tools © 2004 John Wiley & Sons, Inc.

6. The facilitator tells the groups that they have an additional ten minutes to discuss why they would use each technique. The group scribes take notes and create lists on newsprint. (Ten minutes.)

7. At the end of the allotted time, the total group is reassembled, and the groups report on their discussions. The following procedure may be used:

   ■ Each group's scribe, in turn, announces the group's "type," one of his or her group's techniques, and the reason for it.

   ■ The facilitator lists all ideas under each "type" on newsprint. If an idea is duplicated, a check mark is placed next to it.

   ■ When all scribes have presented one idea, each presents a second. The facilitator records all ideas under each group's type.

   ■ The process is repeated until all group items have been presented and recorded.

   (Fifteen minutes to one-half hour.)

8. The facilitator notes that in most situations like the ones addressed by the groups, there are some common techniques that can aid in making communication more effective. The facilitator distributes the Enhancing Communication Sheet and discusses any items not addressed by the groups. (Five to ten minutes.)

9. The facilitator leads a discussion of the activity. The following questions may be asked:

   ■ How did it feel to focus your attention on diversity among people?

   ■ What do you now understand about potential communication difficulties with diverse types of people?

   ■ What techniques seem to you most useful to try with diverse types of people?

   ■ How can you use these techniques in your back-home and on-the-job situations?

   (Ten to fifteen minutes.)

Variations

■ If the participants deal with diverse customers in their work, the focus of the activity can be on identifying customer needs and responding to them.

- The activity can be focused on working with others in a diverse work force.
- If the participants are managers or trainers, the activity may be focused on what techniques they could teach employees that would aid in communicating effectively with a diverse customer base/work force.

Originally published in The 1996 Annual, Volume 1, Training.

ENHANCING COMMUNICATION SHEET

Communicating with a wide variety of people is a challenge. There are numerous types of people with whom conversing and extracting meaning may be difficult. The causes of communication problems may be physical (e.g., ineffective use of the voice, eyes, arms, or hands), or skill-based (i.e., lack of knowledge about verbal and nonverbal communication skills), or emotional (e.g., issues related to culture, age, sexual preference, gender, or disability).

To effectively present information and identify the other person's needs, the following general techniques can help.

Listen actively. Take the time to practice effective listening skills by focusing on what is said by the other person and rephrasing it in your own words to see if you have interpreted it accurately. Check for understanding before making assumptions or decisions.

Act responsively. Decide whether an action is required and select the appropriate response or action.

Reduce your rate of speech. When dealing with people who have a hearing, learning, or speech-related disability or who are not native speakers of your language, slow your rate of speech. This allows better comprehension and formulation of a response.

Speak audibly and clearly but not patronizingly. Communication with people who have difficulty understanding your verbal communication can be enhanced if you clearly enunciate your words. Do not shout or exaggerate your pronunciation. This may distort your words or confuse your meaning. If the person does not have a hearing disability, it may also offend him or her.

Look directly at the person. When communicating, face the other person so that he or she can see you speak the words and watch your nonverbal facial expressions and gestures. This aids comprehension and verification of your message. Even if the person is using an interpreter or companion to assist in communication, speak to the person, not to the assistant.

Be concise. Eliminate unnecessary words and expressions and say exactly what you mean. Ask simple, open-ended questions (those that allow more than a "yes" or "no" response). In some cultures, the word "no" is used sparingly or not at all, so allow the other person to communicate unwillingness or disagreement in another way.

Have patience. Take time when communicating; do not rush the other person or interrupt or finish his or her sentences. Encourage the other person to continue.

Repeat or rephrase. If necessary, repeat your message, ensuring that it is spoken clearly and slowly. If appropriate, select shorter words. It also may be helpful to give an example, illustration, or demonstration.

Watch for nonverbal cues. Watch the person's facial expressions and body language to help gauge his or her reactions and comprehension. For example, frowning may indicate lack of comprehension as well as disagreement. In some other cultures, the typical North American speaking distance is "too close" or "not close enough" for interpersonal communication.

Keep hands and objects away from your face. Avoid masking your speech or facial messages. Obstructing the other person's view of your face may send the message that you are embarrassed, lying, or uncertain about what you are saying (or that you are rude). Keeping your face in view also makes it easier for hearing-impaired people to read your lips.

Use standard language. Avoid using contractions (e.g., don't, shouldn't, can't), slang, technical terms and jargon, acronyms, or other verbal short cuts that may be unfamiliar or annoying to the other person.

Use pauses. Allow time for comprehension and for the other person to respond or react. Also allow opportunities for questions.

Use inclusive language. Ensure that your language does not omit anyone or any group (e.g., do not refer to a group of men and women as "you guys").

Avoid demeaning terminology. Do not use terms that have negative meanings when referring to individuals or groups (e.g., handicapped, girls, retard). Do not make slurs about other cultures or beliefs.

Put messages in writing. In addition to verbally transmitting messages, provide written copies. This aids people who have difficulty interpreting spoken language by allowing future reference or translation from the material.

ENHANCING COMMUNICATION LECTURETTE

Some specific changes that are creating a need for skills in communicating with diverse types of people are as follows.

Globalization of the Economy. The lowering of worldwide trade barriers has opened new markets and allowed worldwide access in product production, sales, and service. Organizations are servicing a more diverse customer base. To compete effectively, they must increase worker knowledge of cultural differences and similarities and look for new ways of meeting customer expectations.

Women in the Work Force. Because of their rapid entry into the workplace, women's traditional roles in society have shifted. Women as colleagues and consumers are changing the ways in which organizations conduct their business.

Demographic Shifts. Longer life expectancies and the decline of births in many countries have changed population profiles. There are more older people. In some areas, there is beginning to be an acute shortage of entry-level employees. Other demographic shifts include increases in the number of minorities and people with disabilities in the business environment. These people have diverse backgrounds, orientations, ways of relating and communicating, and needs.

Changing Legal Environment. In the U.S., a number of laws have been enacted in the past decades to guarantee equal treatment and opportunity to all, regardless of race, cultural background, age, gender, disability, or religion. Intentional or unintentional violations could lead to personal and organizational liability.

Part 3
Inventories, Questionnaires, and Surveys

The final section of this handbook contains instruments designed to provide insights into and hard data on three facets of the communication puzzle: the current communication habits of individual workshop participants, the health of the participant's relationships with other individuals or groups, and the nature of communication within the organization as a whole.

These self-scoring questionnaires and surveys, usually administered at the beginning of a training session or beforehand, can provide invaluable information to highlight problem areas or to ground a workshop in the actual communication patterns of an organization or a work group.

For instance, how do members of an intact work team perceive the communication style of the team leader? How effectively does an individual communicate with his supervisor or his peers? And how well do the organization's official communications with employees reflect its actual practices or even its stated goals?

Each survey includes the background information necessary to understand it, use it, and interpret it. Scoring sheets and scales are provided, as are data provided by the survey's authors about its reliability and validity. You are free to reproduce the questionnaires and to employ them for training purposes as you see fit.

We present these eight instruments as the best the Pfeiffer *Annuals* have to offer for gathering the sort of information that trainers, consultants, and participants are likely to find useful in their efforts to improve communication skills.

Choose an instrument to meet your particular needs. Following are brief descriptions of the kind of data each is designed to yield.

1. **The Communication Climate Inventory.** Measures behaviors of individual managers and supervisors that will determine the levels of honesty and openness in the work groups they oversee.

2. **Organizational Values and Voice Audit.** Looks for disconnects between the organization's preaching and its practices in various forms of communication, including employee training.

3. **Interpersonal Communication Inventory.** Trainees evaluate their own communication patterns with regard to speaking clearly, listening carefully, and expressing anger.

4. **Communication Audit: A Pairs Analysis.** How effectively does an individual communicate with his or her supervisor, with senior management, and with others at work and elsewhere?

5. **The Behavior Description.** A short personality-type instrument allowing trainees to rate themselves on scales of dominance, extroversion, stability, and control.

6. **Cross-Cultural Interactive Preference Profile.** Measures both individual preferences and ability to communicate effectively with people whose cultural conditioning differs from one's own.

7. **Organization Behavior Describer Survey (OBDS).** Can be used to assess communication behaviors of a boss, a subordinate, a peer, or oneself.

8. **The Negotiation-Stance Inventory.** Helps individuals clarify their attitudes toward negotiation as a process carried out in work teams or other organizational groups.

1

The Communication
Climate Inventory

James I. Costigan and Martha A. Schmeidler

The communication climate in any organization is a key determinant of its effectiveness. Organizations with supportive environments encourage worker participation, free and open exchange of information, and constructive conflict resolution. In organizations with defensive climates, employees keep things to themselves, make only guarded statements, and suffer from reduced morale.

Gibb (1961) identified six characteristics of a "supportive environment" and six characteristics of a "defensive one." Gibb affirmed that employees are influenced by the communication climate in the organization. He characterized a supportive climate as one having description, problem orientation, spontaneity, empathy, equality, and provisionalism and a defensive climate as having evaluation, control, strategy, neutrality, superiority, and certainty. These items are paired opposites. Capsule definitions of the terms follow:

EXPLORING

Characteristics of a Defensive Climate

Evaluation—The supervisor is critical and judgmental and will not accept explanations from subordinates.

Control—The supervisor consistently directs in an authoritarian manner and attempts to change other people.

Strategy—The supervisor manipulates subordinates and often misinterprets or twists and distorts what is said.

Neutrality—The supervisor offers minimal personal support for and remains aloof from employees' personal problems and conflicts.

Superiority—The supervisor reminds employees who is in charge, closely oversees the work, and makes employees feel inadequate.

Certainty—The supervisor is dogmatic and unwilling to admit mistakes.

Characteristics of a Supportive Climate

Descriptive—The supervisor's communications are clear, describe situations fairly, and present his or her perceptions without implying the need for change.

Problem Orientation—The supervisor defines problems rather than giving solutions, is open to discussion about mutual problems, and does not insist on employee agreement.

Spontaneity—The supervisor's communications are free of hidden motives and honest. Ideas can be expressed freely.

Empathy—The supervisor attempts to understand and listen to employee problems and respects employee feelings and values.

Equality—The supervisor does not try to make employees feel inferior, does not use status to control situations, and respects the positions of others.

Provisionalism—The supervisor allows flexibility, experimentation, and creativity.

DESCRIPTION OF THE INSTRUMENT

The Communication Climate Inventory uses the twelve factors described above as a means of assessing the communication climate within work groups in an organization. Thirty-six questions are presented in a Likert response format.

The odd-numbered questions describe a defensive atmosphere, and the even-numbered questions describe a supportive environment. The following chart shows which questions are linked to which characteristic.

Defensive Climate Supportive Climate

Questions 1, 3, 5 —Evaluation   Questions 2, 4, 6 —Provisionalism

Questions 7, 9, 11 —Control   Questions 8, 10, 12 —Empathy

Questions 13, 15, 17 —Strategy   Questions 14, 16, 18 —Equality

Questions 19, 21, 23 —Neutrality Questions 20, 22, 24 —Spontaneity

Questions 25, 27, 29 —Superiority Questions 26, 28, 30 —Problem
                                                   Orientation

Questions 31, 33, 35 —Certainty   Questions 32, 34, 36 —Description

GUIDELINES FOR INTERPRETATION

The Communication Climate Inventory is designed so that the lower the score, the greater the extent to which either climate exists in an organization. However, low defensive scores will probably be an indication that supportive scores are high and vice versa, simply because both climates would not exist together in an organization, although scores will vary according to the supervisor being evaluated.

If the communication climate of an organization appears to be supportive and nondefensive, then probably no changes need to be made. However, if the communication climate is defensive and nonsupportive, an intervention is called for to improve the climate. Structured experiences that develop interpersonal communication skills are useful for this purpose. Overall ratings can be gleaned by having each department plot its scores on the scale at the bottom of the scoring sheet and then looking at any trouble spots.

Scoring the Instrument

If a person agrees or strongly agrees (a score of 1 or 2) with the statements measuring a specific characteristic, that factor is important in the person's work environment. If the person scores the statement as a 4 or 5 (disagree or strongly disagree), it indicates that the characteristic being measured is not part of the person's work environment. A score of 3 indicates uncertainty or that the characteristic occurs infrequently in the environment.

The total of the scores from the odd-numbered questions indicates the degree to which the work environment is defensive, and the total of the scores from the even-numbered questions indicates the degree to which the work environment is supportive. For each individual characteristic, then, a total score of 3 to 6 indicates agreement or strong agreement on either the defensive or supportive scales, a total of 12 to 15 indicates disagreement or strong disagreement, and a total of 7 to 11 indicates a neutral or uncertain attitude.

The lowest possible overall climate score is 18 on either the defensive or supportive scales, which means that the respondent strongly agreed with all questions. The highest possible overall score is 90, which means that the respondent strongly disagreed with all questions. Both extremes are highly improbable.

If more than one person fills out the questionnaire, obtaining the mean score for each item is the most convenient method of scoring the inventory. Summing the means for the questions in each category provides the overall score for the type of climate (defensive or supportive), and comparing those two scores provides a rough estimate of the general organizational climate. The following scales can be used to provide a way of checking the communication climate.

Defensive Scale	**Supportive Scale**
Defensive, 18–40	Supportive, 18–40
Defensive to Neutral, 41–55	Supportive to Neutral, 41–55
Neutral to Supportive, 56–69	Neutral to Defensive, 56–69
Supportive, 70–90	Defensive, 70–90

In administering the inventory, it is important to be specific about which communication climate (which supervisor's communication) is being surveyed.

Uses of the Instrument

The Communication Climate Inventory can be used to measure the organization's total communication environment or the climate of individual work areas. The scores from this inventory can be used to plan needed changes in the communication environment or to indicate which practices should be encouraged.

Organizational consultants can use the inventory to determine whether the communication environment is causing problems. Educators can use it to help students understand the characteristics of supportive and defensive climates. Supervisors can use it to assess how their subordinates feel about their handling of communications in the work environments.

References

Combs, G.W. (1981). Defensive and supportive communication. In J.E. Jones & J.W. Pfeiffer (Eds.), *The 1981 annual handbook for group facilitators*. San Francisco, CA: Pfeiffer.

Gibb, J.R. (1961). Defensive and supportive communication. *Journal of Communications, 11,* 141–148.

Originally published in The 1984 Annual.

COMMUNICATION CLIMATE INVENTORY

James I. Costigan and Martha A. Schmeidler

Instructions: The statements below relate to how your supervisor and you communicate on the job. There are no right or wrong answers. Respond honestly to the statements, using the following scale:

1 Strongly Agree   2 Agree   3 Uncertain   4 Disagree   5 Strongly Disagree

_____ 1. My supervisor criticizes my work without allowing me to explain.

_____ 2. My supervisor allows me as much creativity as possible in my job.

_____ 3. My supervisor always judges the actions of his or her subordinates.

_____ 4. My supervisor allows flexibility on the job.

_____ 5. My supervisor criticizes my work in the presence of others.

_____ 6. My supervisor is willing to try new ideas and to accept other points of view.

_____ 7. My supervisor believes that he or she must control how I do my work.

_____ 8. My supervisor understands the problems that I encounter in my job.

_____ 9. My supervisor is always trying to change other people's attitudes and behaviors to suit his or her own.

_____ 10. My supervisor respects my feelings and values.

_____ 11. My supervisor always needs to be in charge of the situation.

_____ 12. My supervisor listens to my problems with interest.

_____ 13. My supervisor tries to manipulate subordinates to get what he or she wants or to make himself or herself look good.

_____ 14. My supervisor does not try to make me feel inferior.

_____ 15. I have to be careful when talking to my supervisor so that I will not be misinterpreted.

_____ 16. My supervisor participates in meetings with employees without projecting his or her higher status or power.

The Pfeiffer Book of Successful Communication Skill-Building Tools © 2004 John Wiley & Sons, Inc.

1 Strongly Agree   2 Agree   3 Uncertain   4 Disagree   5 Strongly Disagree

_____ 17. I seldom say what really is on my mind, because it might be twisted and distorted by my supervisor.

_____ 18. My supervisor treats me with respect.

_____ 19. My supervisor seldom becomes involved in employee conflicts.

_____ 20. My supervisor does not have hidden motives in dealing with me.

_____ 21. My supervisor is not interested in employee problems.

_____ 22. I feel that I can be honest and straightforward with my supervisor.

_____ 23. My supervisor rarely offers moral support during a personal crisis.

_____ 24. I feel that I can express my opinions and ideas honestly to my supervisor.

_____ 25. My supervisor tries to make me feel inadequate.

_____ 26. My supervisor defines problems so that they can be understood but does not insist that his or her subordinates agree.

_____ 27. My supervisor makes it clear that he or she is in charge.

_____ 28. I feel free to talk to my supervisor.

_____ 29. My supervisor believes that if a job is to be done right, he or she must oversee it or do it.

_____ 30. My supervisor defines problems and makes his or her subordinates aware of them.

_____ 31. My supervisor cannot admit that he or she makes mistakes.

_____ 32. My supervisor tries to describe situations fairly without labeling them as good or bad.

_____ 33. My supervisor is dogmatic; it is useless for me to voice an opposing point of view.

_____ 34. My supervisor presents his or her feelings and perceptions without implying that a similar response is expected from me.

_____ 35. My supervisor thinks that he or she is always right.

_____ 36. My supervisor attempts to explain situations clearly and without personal bias.

COMMUNICATION CLIMATE INVENTORY SCORING
AND INTERPRETATION SHEET

Instructions: Place the numbers that you assigned to each statement in the appropriate blanks. Now add them together to determine a subtotal for each climate description. Place the subtotals in the proper blanks and add your scores. Place an X on the graph to indicate what your perception is of your organization or department's communication climate. Some descriptions of the terms follow. You may wish to discuss with others their own perceptions and interpretations.

Part I: Defensive Scores

Evaluation	Neutrality
Question 1 _____	Question 19 _____
Question 3 _____	Question 21 _____
Question 5 _____	Question 23 _____
Subtotal _____	**Subtotal** _____

Control	Superiority
Question 7 _____	Question 25 _____
Question 9 _____	Question 27 _____
Question 11 _____	Question 29 _____
Subtotal _____	**Subtotal** _____

Strategy	Certainty
Question 13 _____	Question 31 _____
Question 15 _____	Question 33 _____
Question 17 _____	Question 35 _____
Subtotal _____	**Subtotal** _____

Subtotals for Defensive Scores

Evaluation _____

Control _____

Strategy _____

Neutrality _____

Superiority _____

Certainty _____

Total _____

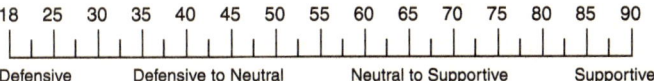

18 25 30 35 40 45 50 55 60 65 70 75 80 85 90

Defensive   Defensive to Neutral   Neutral to Supportive   Supportive

Part II: Supportive Scores

Provisionalism

Question 2 _____

Question 4 _____

Question 6 _____

Subtotal _____

Spontaneity

Question 20 _____

Question 22 _____

Question 24 _____

Subtotal _____

Empathy

Question 8 _____

Question 10 _____

Question 12 _____

Subtotal _____

Problem Orientation

Question 26 _____

Question 28 _____

Question 30 _____

Subtotal _____

Equality

Question 14 _____

Question 16 _____

Question 18 _____

Subtotal _____

Description

Question 32 _____

Question 34 _____

Question 36 _____

Subtotal _____

Subtotals for Supportive Scores

Provisionalism _____

Empathy _____

Equality _____

Spontaneity _____

Problem Orientation _____

Description _____

Total _____

```
18   25   30   35   40   45   50   55   60   65   70   75   80   85   90
|__|__|__|__|__|__|__|__|__|__|__|__|__|__|__|__|__|__|__|__|__|__|__|
Supportive      Neutral to Supportive      Defensive to Neutral      Defensive
```

The Pfeiffer Book of Successful Communication Skill-Building Tools © 2004 John Wiley & Sons, Inc.

2

Organizational Values and Voice Audit

Diane M. Gayeski

Abstract: Many organizations suffer from poor employee performance and attitudes because policies do not support the firm's stated goals and initiatives. Nowhere is this more significant than in employee communication and training practices, as these are the primary "voices" of the company to its constituencies. The Organizational Values and Voice Audit is an instrument through which organizational members can pinpoint areas that, in their perception, may be out of alignment with their organization's values and goals. A table of common disconnects is used to guide a discussion in which participants share their own responses to the questionnaire and can then recommend changes in communication and training practices.

INTRODUCTION

The phrase "walking the talk" is a common reference to managers' ability and willingness to behave in ways that encourage their subordinates to act in accordance with the organization's espoused values and culture. Unfortunately, employees in all types of organizations often perceive that management does not, in fact, walk the talk. This leads to a lack of executive credibility, employee cynicism, mixed messages, and lack of focus, all of which contribute to impaired individual and organizational performance.

Although the actions of individual members in an organization carry strong messages, so do its internal and external communications and training policies and practices. Training courses, manuals, newsletters, and employee meetings all represent the "voice" of the company. When the messages contained in these channels are mixed or when policies and practices around communication and training do not reinforce the organization's stated values and goals, the organization's culture and success are impaired. Often, employees are unaware of the source of their discontent and confusion; the Organizational Values and Voice Audit helps to uncover misaligned policies and practices so that discrepancies can be resolved.

The audit is an aid to discussion and helps to suggest possible changes in organizational communication and training management; those who administer it should therefore have a thorough grounding in these areas. It is used most fruitfully with small groups of employees (six to thirty people at one time) who have some exposure to management values and goals, as well as to the organization's communication and training practices. Therefore, the participants should be training or communication practitioners or managers who frequently request and use training and communication interventions.

DESCRIPTION OF THE INSTRUMENT

The instrument consists of two sets of lists. The first asks participants to identify the initiatives that their organization is pursuing or espousing. The second asks participants to identify common communication and training practices in their organization. Participants fill out the instrument individually, but then discuss their responses in a facilitated session. An Interpretation Sheet is provided that helps participants to see which initiatives actually are misaligned with typical training and communication policies and approaches.

ADMINISTRATION OF THE INSTRUMENT

The process takes twenty to forty minutes, depending on the size of the group, and should take place in a room where there is a convenient writing surface for each person and where group discussion can take place. The ideal size of the

The Pfeiffer Book of Successful Communication Skill-Building Tools © 2004 John Wiley & Sons, Inc.

group is about fifteen people, although the audit can be done with fewer or with more. The facilitator will need an overhead projector and screen, along with at least one felt-tipped marker; it is often useful to have flip charts or blank acetate to jot down remarks as they are made during the discussion. Make a copy of the Organizational Values and Voice Audit for each respondent and make a separate copy of the Interpretation Sheet for each person.

It is important that the people selected to participate have a clear idea of the organization's espoused values and goals, as well as of the typical ways that training and communication programs (including employee communication and customer communication) are generated and accessed. Before the meeting, make an overhead transparency of each question set and of the Interpretation Sheet.

Begin the assessment by introducing its purpose: to identify common disconnects between organizational values and goals and the way that organizational communication and learning actually take place. It is important to point out that every organization has at least a few misalignments in this regard, even the best-performing ones. Instruct the respondents to think over their own experiences in the organization and to use their own perceptions and opinions, rather than to try to represent the views of others.

Hand out the instrument and give the respondents about five minutes to fill it out. Ask them not to discuss their responses with one another during the process.

THE SCORING PROCESS

If the group is small, read each item and ask people to raise their hands if they checked it off. If the group is larger, collect the instruments and let the participants take a break or begin discussion while you (and/or an assistant) tally up the total number of check marks for each item. In either case, write the number of total check marks next to each item on the overhead transparency copy of the question sets.

Once you have the totals, ask the participants what this activity made them think about their organization's values and policies. Prompt them to recognize that many of the practices in the second list are actually at odds with the statements in the first list. Explain that many training and communication activities the organization engages in are sending the wrong messages to their employees about what's really important in the organization. Either the value statements (such as empowerment, diversity, and participatory management) are not really supported or are unattainable, or the communication about these issues is at odds with the activities.

Hand out a copy of the Interpretation Sheet to each person, and display the sections one at a time on the overhead projector. Highlight and discuss the ones that were most frequently mentioned by participants. Ask them what effect they believe the "disconnects" are having or will have on their organization's productivity, image, and morale. Then ask them what other values or initiatives the organization is pursuing and to think about which communication and training practices strengthen those values or initiatives and which appear to be at odds with them. Take notes on the overhead transparency or on a flip chart.

OTHER SUGGESTED USES FOR THE AUDIT

This instrument can be used as part of a formal employee communications or training audit, along with other typical measures of employee satisfaction with those functions. Additionally, it can be used as a part of a professional development program for public relations, employee communication, and training/development staffs to help them think about how their policies and projects impact organizational goals.

Originally published in The 2002 Annual, Volume 1, Training.

ORGANIZATIONAL VALUES AND VOICE AUDIT

Diane M. Gayeski

Instructions: Check each of the initiatives or approaches from the list below that your organization currently is pursuing.

☐ Continuous improvement/total quality management

☐ Cost-containment/downsizing

☐ Diversity awareness/diversity appreciation

☐ Employee empowerment

☐ Globalization

☐ High-performance workplace/performance-based compensation

☐ Just-in-time manufacturing

☐ Learning organization/continual learning

☐ Participatory decision making

☐ Relationship marketing/customer orientation

☐ Self-managed teams/teamwork

☐ Work-life balance/family-friendly workplace

On the list that follows, check the items that characterize your organization's *typical* communication and training practices.

☐ Communication interventions such as training and newsletters are evaluated (if at all) by "smile sheets" measuring how much the audience liked them.

☐ Communication/training/marketing staff are rewarded for the amount of materials or programs they produce, rather than on their return on investment.

☐ Company materials do not include or acknowledge input of employees or customers.

☐ Employees are typically sent to training courses or conferences either because of an organization-wide or department-wide mandate or as a "reward" for good performance.

- ☐ Employees are typically sent to training courses or conferences by managers, rather than making the decision to attend themselves.

- ☐ Most learning activities consist of courses led by a professional instructor.

- ☐ Most meetings with management consist of announcements and/or formal presentations.

- ☐ People are often expected to attend training courses and meetings before or after work or on weekends.

- ☐ People are not rewarded for doing what they've been taught in training.

- ☐ People often throw out memos and newsletters or delete email and voice mail messages before even reading/listening to them.

- ☐ Policies and procedures documentation is often not kept up-to-date.

- ☐ There is no established way to solicit and organize good ideas from customers and employees.

- ☐ Training and documentation generally present one "best" way to approach a task, based on the input of one or two subject-matter experts.

- ☐ Training and employee communication programs are based on requests from managers who think that the person has a training or communication problem.

- ☐ We don't really know how much the company spends on communication and training each year (including the time employees are away from their "real" work).

ORGANIZATIONAL VALUES AND VOICE AUDIT INTERPRETATION SHEET

Instructions: Look at each of the initiatives you checked off on the audit form and determine whether you also checked any of the negative characteristics that provide a "disconnect" between that espoused value and its practice in your organization. Consider how each affects your own work life and be ready to discuss your thoughts with others.

Initiative(s)	Possible Disconnects
Continuous improvement/ total quality management	Communication interventions such as training and newsletters are evaluated (if at all) by "smile sheets" measuring how much the audience liked them. (Is this any way to measure improvement or focus on quality?)
	Communication/training/marketing staff are rewarded for the amount of materials or programs they produce, rather than on their return on investment. (Is this a good metric of quality?)
	Policies and procedures documentation is often not kept up-to-date. (If we improve processes, why is this information often not accessible?)
	There is no established way to solicit and organize good ideas from customers and employees. (Do process improvement ideas only happen in meetings or quality circles?)
	We don't really know how much the company spends on communication and training each year (including the time employees are away from their "real" work). (Is this any way to manage resources?)
Cost containment/downsizing	Communication/training/marketing staff are rewarded for the amount of

Initiative(s)	Possible Disconnects

Initiative(s)

Possible Disconnects

materials or programs they produce, rather than their return on investment. (Do we reward waste?)

We don't really know how much the company spends on communication and training each year, including the time employees are away from their "real" work. (We cut costs by laying off hourly workers, yet spend untold resources disseminating information to those who are left.)

Diversity awareness/diversity appreciation/globalization

Employees are typically sent to training courses or conferences either because of an organization-wide or department-wide mandate or as a "reward" for good performance. (Forget about what you need or want as an individual; you are just a part of a group.)

Training and documentation generally present one "best" way to approach a task, based on the input of one or two subject-matter experts. (Forget about acknowledging or encouraging diversity.)

Employee empowerment/ participatory decision making/ self-managed teams/teamwork

Company materials do not include or acknowledge input of employees or customers. (So much for partnerships; it's just top-down communication as usual.)

Employees are typically sent to training courses or conferences by managers rather than making the decision to attend themselves. (So this is empowerment?)

There is no established way to solicit and organize good ideas from customers and employees. (Do process improvement ideas only happen in meetings or quality circles?)

Initiative(s)	Possible Disconnects
	Training and documentation generally present one "best" way to approach a task, based on the input of one or two subject-matter experts. (Is there any way to encourage and capture new approaches?)
	Training and employee communication programs are based on requests from managers who think that the employee has a training or communication problem. (Does the employee or team get to decide? Could there be other problems that are not training or communication related, such as the way people or projects are managed?)
High-performance workplace/ performance-based compensation	Employees are sent to courses or conferences by managers either because of an organization-wide or department-wide mandate or as a "reward" for good performance. (Ignore individual performance gaps; just put everybody through a course or train people when they don't really need it.)
	People are not rewarded for doing what they've been taught in training. (Let's just ignore that investment and teach people to be cynical.)
Relationship marketing/ customer orientation	Company materials do not include or acknowledge input of employees or customers. (Where can people see evidence of their own input in the partnership?)
	There's no established way to solicit and organize good ideas from customers and employees. (How can we forge relationships with people we don't really pay attention to?)

Initiative(s)	Possible Disconnects
Just-in-time manufacturing	Policies and procedures documentation is often not kept up-to-date. (We can eliminate millions of dollars of inventory, but we can't replace our old pages in manuals.)
Learning organization/ continual learning	Company materials do not include or acknowledge input of employees or customers. (Who's in the best position to decide what is examined and discussed?)
	Most learning activities consist of courses led by a professional instructor. (Forget about sharing knowledge informally; learning consists of taking courses.)
	Most meetings with management consist of announcements and/or formal presentations. (Is this any way to gather new information or challenge assumptions?)
	There is no established way to solicit and organize good ideas from customers and employees. (Where do good ideas come from anyway?)
Work-life balance/ family friendly workplace	People are often expected to attend training courses and meetings before or after work or on weekends. (Does this provide a hardship for people with family or community obligations?)

The Pfeiffer Book of Successful Communication Skill-Building Tools © 2004 John Wiley & Sons, Inc.

3

Interpersonal Communication Inventory

Millard J. Bienvenu, Sr.

The ability to be an effective communicator seems to be based on five interpersonal components:

1. An adequate self-concept, the single most important factor affecting people's communication with others;

2. The ability to be a good listener, a skill that has received little attention until recently;

3. The skill of expressing one's thoughts and ideas clearly, which many people find difficult to do;

4. Being able to cope with one's emotions—particularly angry feelings—and expressing them in a constructive way; and

5. The willingness to disclose oneself to others truthfully and freely. Such self-disclosure is necessary for satisfactory interpersonal relationships.

In the early 1970s, several research techniques and devices were developed to study interpersonal communication in several areas: marriage counseling, parent-child counseling, group therapy, and small-group communication.

The Interpersonal Communication Inventory (ICI) is applicable generally to social interaction in a wide variety of situations. It is an attempt to measure general tendencies in interpersonal communication and it may be used as a counseling tool, as a teaching device, as a supplement to an interview, by management, or for further research.

A fifty-four-item scale measures the process of communication as an element of social interaction; it is not intended to measure content but to identify patterns, characteristics, and styles of communication.

The items included were drawn from a review of the literature in the field and from the author's counseling experience and his work on related communication scales.

The instrument is probably best suited for individuals of high school age or older. It can be adapted to either sex and any marital status.

Items in the ICI are designed to sample the dimensions of self-concept, listening, clarity of expression, difficulties in coping with angry feelings, and self-disclosure.

This instrument is closely linked to Dr. Myron R. Chartier's article, "Five Components Contributing to Effective Interpersonal Communications," which appears in the Lecturettes section of *The 1974 Annual.* The lecturette discusses and develops aspects of the "Interpersonal Communication Inventory."

Engaged in ongoing research, the author would like to collaborate with others using the ICI. He has also developed a guide to the ICI which may be obtained from him on request.

References

Bienvenu, M.J., Sr. (1969). Measurement of parent-adolescent communication. *The Family Coordinator, 18,* 117–121.

Bienvenu, M.J., Sr. (1970a). Measurement of marital communication. *The Family Coordinator, 19,* 26–31.

Bienvenu, M.J., Sr. (1970b). Parent-adolescent communication and self-esteem. *Journal of Home Economics, 62,* 344–345.

Bienvenu, M.J., Sr. (1971). An interpersonal communication inventory. *The Journal of Communication, 21*(4), 381–388.

Originally published in The 1974 Annual.

INTERPERSONAL COMMUNICATION INVENTORY

Millard J. Bienvenu, Sr.

This inventory[1] offers you an opportunity to make an objective study of the degree and patterns of communication in your interpersonal relationships. It will enable you to better understand how you present and use yourself in communicating with persons in your daily contacts and activities. You will find it both interesting and helpful to make this study.

Instructions:

- The questions refer to persons other than your family members or relatives.

- Please answer each question as quickly as you can according to the way you feel *at the moment* (not the way you usually feel or felt last week).

- Please do not consult anyone while completing this inventory. You may discuss it with someone after you have completed it. Remember that the value of this form will be lost if you change *any* answer during or after this discussion.

- Honest answers are very necessary. Please be as frank as possible, since your answers are confidential.

- Use the following examples for practice. Put a check (✔) in *one* of the three blanks on the right to show how the question applies to your situation.

	Yes (usually)	No (seldom)	Some- times
Is it easy for you to express your views to others?	_____	_____	_____
Do others listen to your point of view?	_____	_____	_____

- The **Yes** column is to be used when the question can be answered as happening *most of the time or usually*. The **No** column is to be used when the question can be answered as *seldom or never*.

- The **Sometimes** column should be marked when you definitely cannot answer **Yes** or **No**. *Use this column as little as possible.*

---

[1]Copyright © 1969 by Millard J. Bienvenu, Sr. Reprinted with permission of the author. This inventory was previously published in the *Journal of Communication* in December 1971.

- Read each question carefully. If you cannot give the exact answer to a question, answer the best you can but be sure to answer each one. There are no right or wrong answers. Answer according to the way *you* feel *at the present time*. Remember, do not refer to family members in answering the questions.

	Yes (usually)	**No** (seldom)	**Some-** **times**
1. Do your words come out the way you would like them to in conversation?	_____	_____	_____
2. When you are asked a question that is not clear, do you ask the person to explain what he or she means?	_____	_____	_____
3. When you are trying to explain something, do other persons have a tendency to put words into your mouth?	_____	_____	_____
4. Do you merely assume that the other person knows what you are trying to say without your explaining what you really mean?	_____	_____	_____
5. Do you ever ask the other person to tell you how he or she feels about the point you may be trying to make?	_____	_____	_____
6. Is it difficult for you to talk with other people?	_____	_____	_____
7. In conversation, do you talk about things that are of interest to both you and the other person?	_____	_____	_____
8. Do you find it difficult to express your ideas when they differ from the ideas of those around you?	_____	_____	_____
9. In conversation, do you try to put yourself in the other person's shoes?	_____	_____	_____
10. In conversation, do you have a tendency to do more talking than the other person?	_____	_____	_____
11. Are you aware of how your tone of voice may affect others?	_____	_____	_____
12. Do you refrain from saying something that you know will only hurt others or make matters worse?	_____	_____	_____

	Yes (usually)	No (seldom)	Some- times
13. Is it difficult for you to accept constructive criticism from others?	_____	_____	_____
14. When someone has hurt your feelings, do you discuss this with him or her?	_____	_____	_____
15. Do you later apologize to someone whose feelings you may have hurt?	_____	_____	_____
16. Does it upset you a great deal when someone disagrees with you?	_____	_____	_____
17. Do you find it difficult to think clearly when you are angry with someone?	_____	_____	_____
18. Do you fail to disagree with others because you are afraid they will get angry?	_____	_____	_____
19. When a problem arises between you and another person, can you discuss it without getting angry?	_____	_____	_____
20. Are you satisfied with the way you settle your differences with others?	_____	_____	_____
21. Do you pout and sulk for a long time when someone upsets you?	_____	_____	_____
22. Do you become very uneasy when someone pays you a compliment?	_____	_____	_____
23. Generally, are you able to trust other individuals?	_____	_____	_____
24. Do you find it difficult to compliment and praise others?	_____	_____	_____
25. Do you deliberately try to conceal your faults from others?	_____	_____	_____
26. Do you help others to understand you by saying how you think, feel, and believe?	_____	_____	_____
27. Is it difficult for you to confide in people?	_____	_____	_____
28. Do you have a tendency to change the subject when your feelings enter into a discussion?	_____	_____	_____

	Yes (usually)	No (seldom)	Some-times
29. In conversation, do you let the other person finish talking before reacting to what he or she says?	_____	_____	_____
30. Do you find yourself not paying attention while in conversation with others?	_____	_____	_____
31. Do you ever try to listen for meaning when someone is talking?	_____	_____	_____
32. Do others seem to be listening when you are talking?	_____	_____	_____
33. In a discussion, is it difficult for you to see things from the other person's point of view?	_____	_____	_____
34. Do you pretend that you are listening to others when actually you are not?	_____	_____	_____
35. In conversation, can you tell the difference between what a person is saying and what he or she may be feeling?	_____	_____	_____
36. While speaking, are you aware of how others are reacting to what you are saying?	_____	_____	_____
37. Do you feel that other people wish you were a different kind of person?	_____	_____	_____
38. Do other people understand your feelings?	_____	_____	_____
39. Do others remark that you always seem to think you are right?	_____	_____	_____
40. Do you admit that you are wrong when you know that you are wrong about something?	_____	_____	_____

Total Score [   ]

INTERPERSONAL COMMUNICATION INVENTORY
SCORING KEY AND NORMS

Instructions: Look at how you responded to each item in the ICI. In front of the item write the appropriate weight from the table on this page. For example, if you answered "Yes" to item 1, you would find below that you get three points; write the number 3 in front of item 1 in the inventory and proceed to score item 2. When you have finished scoring each of the forty items, add up your total score. You may wish to compare your score with the norms listed below.

	Yes	No	Sometimes		Yes	No	Sometimes
1.	3	0	2	21.	0	3	1
2.	3	0	2	22.	0	3	1
3.	0	3	1	23.	3	0	2
4.	0	3	1	24.	0	3	1
5.	3	0	2	25.	0	3	1
6.	0	3	1	26.	3	0	2
7.	3	0	2	27.	0	3	1
8.	0	3	1	28.	0	3	1
9.	3	0	2	29.	3	0	2
10.	0	3	1	30.	0	3	1
11.	3	0	2	31.	3	0	2
12.	3	0	2	32.	3	0	2
13.	0	3	1	33.	0	3	1
14.	3	0	2	34.	0	3	1
15.	3	0	2	35.	3	0	2
16.	0	3	1	36.	3	0	2
17.	0	3	1	37.	0	3	1
18.	0	3	1	38.	3	0	2
19.	3	0	2	39.	0	3	1
20.	3	0	2	40.	3	0	2

The Pfeiffer Book of Successful Communication Skill-Building Tools © 2004 John Wiley & Sons, Inc.

Means and Standard Deviations for the ICI

Age Groups	Males		Females	
17–21	*Mean*	81.79	*Mean*	81.48
	S.D.	21.56	*S.D.*	20.06
	N.	53	*N.*	80
22–25	*Mean*	86.03	*Mean*	94.46
	S.D.	14.74	*S.D.*	11.58
	N.	38	*N.*	26
26 and up	*Mean*	90.73	*Mean*	86.93
	S.D.	19.50	*S.D.*	15.94
	N.	56	*N.*	45
All Age Groups by Sex	*Mean*	86.39	*Mean*	85.34
	S.D.	19.46	*S.D.*	18.22
	N.	147	*N.*	151

All Age Groups	*Mean*	**85.93**
Males and Females	*S.D.*	**19.05**
Combined	*N.*	**298**

4

Communication Audit: A Pairs Analysis

Scott B. Parry

Abstract: If we consider all the skills needed to succeed in our work and to enjoy life to the fullest, the ability to communicate effectively probably leads the list. Our desire to understand others and to be understood is one of humankind's most basic needs. *Effective* communication requires much more than grammar and vocabulary. Words such as trust, openness, respect, and empathy come to mind as qualities that must accompany the written or spoken message if it is to achieve its intended results. This audit enables respondents to assess their ability to communicate both within the workplace and within more intimate groups.

INTRODUCTION

Communication is the cement that holds an organization together; lack of communication can cause it to fall apart. This is true whether the organization referred to is a society, an organization, a department, a work group, a marriage, a family, a club, or a social group.

This Communication Audit enables respondents to identify the strengths and weaknesses that are characteristic of the communications in which they engage. Part One is an assessment of one's workplace and the "state of health" of the communication that comes from three sources within it: senior management, the respondent's immediate supervisor, and him- or herself. Part Two is an assessment of the quality of the interpersonal communications that regularly take place between the respondent and those closest to him or her—family, friends, or immediate work group members.

Three major benefits can be expected from taking the Communication Audit. The first is that respondents will take stock of their strengths and weaknesses of communication on two levels: organizational and interpersonal. The Audit can be thought of as a needs analysis in which respondents can pinpoint those attributes of their communication that are healthy and those that require work.

The second benefit is that the Audit will equip respondents with a set of criteria and a common vocabulary for describing interpersonal communications. This allows them to gain a better understanding of and ability to discuss the process with one another.

A third benefit comes from respondents' discussion of their perceptions with others who also fill out the Audit (for Part One, their supervisors; for Part Two, others with whom they communicate on a regular basis). Within the workshop setting, you can help manager and employee or two co-workers to develop action plans to improve the quality of their communications.

Administration of the Audit

Instructions for completing the Communication Audit are given at the beginning of each part. Hand copies out to participants and ask them to read the instructions and begin. If the workshop is focused only on communication between manager and employee, ask that they fill in only Part One. If they will also have a chance to discuss their communication style with co-workers, ask them to also complete Part Two, but assign pairs before beginning. You may also wish to make extra copies of the Audit for those who would like to use it at home or in a nonwork setting at a later date.

Part One

Tell everyone that the Audit they will complete focuses on communication between them and their managers and upper management at work. Explain that they will not be able to fill in the totals until after you've provided scoring instructions, which you will do later.

The Pfeiffer Book of Successful Communication Skill-Building Tools © 2004 John Wiley & Sons, Inc.

After everyone has completed the Audit, give respondents the appropriate Instructions for Scoring and Interpreting the results. Guidelines for analyzing scores are provided, along with some interpretation implications and suggestions for taking appropriate actions.

Part Two

In this next section of the Audit, respondents will examine their interpersonal communications with those with whom they work. Explain that there are fourteen sets of adjectives and they are to decide where along a continuum they would rate the other person's and their own communication behavior. Tell them that you will give them copies of the instrument (two per communication partner) if they want to use it at home or in another setting to focus on their interpersonal communications.

Hand out the second part of the Audit and ask everyone to complete it according to the instructions. Remind them to be honest in assessing their own behavior.

SCORING AND INTERPRETING THE RESULTS

Tell participants that they are now ready to score their responses, interpret the results, share their insights, and decide what actions are appropriate for improving the quality of their interactions. Say that you first want to discuss briefly the importance of interpersonal communication. The following text can be used to provide a basis for the discussion.

> "If we consider all the skills needed to succeed in our work and to enjoy life to the fullest, we will probably conclude that the ability to communicate effectively is the most important set of skills we will ever develop. Indeed, many of the other skills in our jobs depend heavily on the quality of our communication—time management and prioritizing, negotiating, persuading others, evaluating alternatives, and so on.
> "In short, the quality of our relations with others at work, at home, and at play depend on our ability to communicate effectively. Our ability to solve problems, make decisions, set realistic goals and a timetable for accomplishing them, assess people and situations, and perform the hundreds of activities that fill our daily work depends on the ability to communicate. It's what makes marriage or a relationship

with a lifetime partner a success. It's what keeps us together—as a family, a team, a club, a class, a social group. It's what occupies us during most of the work day. And our time spent communicating at work typically divides as follows:"

List the following categories on a flip chart:

	Giving Information	**Receiving Information**
Spoken	Speaking 30%	Listening 45%
Written	Writing 9%	Reading 16%

"Given the critical importance of speaking and listening, which together make up three-quarters of our communications, anything we can do to improve the quality of our interactions will be time well-invested. And there should be add-on benefits through our improvement in many of the other skills that depend so heavily on interpersonal communications."

Now distribute copies of the Scoring and Interpreting sheets and direct the participants to score Part One of the Audit. Then ask participants to get together with their pre-assigned partners and to compare their ratings of themselves with the ratings of them by the other person. Rarely do managers see themselves as their subordinates see them, and nowhere is this more true than in their communication effectiveness. Partners should then be given time to complete the interpretation for Part Two of the Audit.

After the participants have completed the Scoring and Interpreting sheets, say to them:

"Organizations differ greatly with regard to their style of communication. I want you to explore this topic by discussing the following questions in your pre-assigned pairs:

- If you were to describe this style of your organization to an outsider, what adjectives would you use?
- What analogies would you make?
- What characteristics of the organization are illustrated by the style of communication that's prevalent here?
- On which items do you and your supervisor differ most?"

Post these questions and allow the pairs ten or fifteen minutes to discuss them.

Making Action Plans

After paired discussions between supervisor and employee and between co-workers, hand out copies of the Communication Audit Action Planning Samples and discuss how to write an action plan. Have partners write similar plans for enhancing their own communications with one another.

Originally published in The 2001 Annual, Volume 2, Consulting.

COMMUNICATION AUDIT

Scott B. Parry

PART ONE: COMMUNICATION WITH SUPERVISORS

Instructions: Listed below are a number of phrases describing how *senior management* in your organization, your *supervisor,* and *you* behave while communicating with one another. Evaluate each of the others and yourself by circling the letter for each relationship that indicates whether this is a behavior the person does "always," "usually," "sometimes," "rarely," or "never."

If you wish, you may go through the twenty items three separate times, or answer the question for all three communication relationships as you go.

A = Always   U = Usually   S = Sometimes   R = Rarely   N = Never

	Senior Management	Your Supervisor	Yourself
1. Listens closely to find out others' facts and feelings before reacting.	A U S R N	A U S R N	A U S R N
2. Plays games with others and manipulates their responses.	A U S R N	A U S R N	A U S R N
3. Asks good questions and is effective in drawing others out.	A U S R N	A U S R N	A U S R N
4. Is defensive and displays an element of distrust.	A U S R N	A U S R N	A U S R N
5. Summarizes and restates to increase mutual understanding.	A U S R N	A U S R N	A U S R N
6. Fills the "parent" role and puts others in the "child" role.	A U S R N	A U S R N	A U S R N
7. Sticks to the subject and the aim of the communication.	A U S R N	A U S R N	A U S R N
8. Is unable to establish an open climate of trust and candor.	A U S R N	A U S R N	A U S R N

A = Always   U = Usually   S = Sometimes   R = Rarely   N = Never

	Senior Management	Your Supervisor	Yourself
9. Gives good feedback to show understanding of what the other person has said.	A U S R N	A U S R N	A U S R N
10. Uses time asked for by others to meet personal agendas.	A U S R N	A U S R N	A U S R N
11. Remains neutral (low bias) to elicit the feelings of others.	A U S R N	A U S R N	A U S R N
12. Has difficulty expressing ideas clearly and concisely.	A U S R N	A U S R N	A U S R N
13. Uses analogies, examples, etc., to bring a message to life.	A U S R N	A U S R N	A U S R N
14. Interrupts, making it hard for others to express themselves.	A U S R N	A U S R N	A U S R N
15. Is persuasive; others go along because they are convinced.	A U S R N	A U S R N	A U S R N
16. High bias leads others to say what is expedient and expected.	A U S R N	A U S R N	A U S R N
17. Maintains favorable climate, reflecting mutual respect and benefit.	A U S R N	A U S R N	A U S R N
18. Pulls rank and tends to dominate when with subordinates.	A U S R N	A U S R N	A U S R N
19. Uses probes well to draw out the feelings of others.	A U S R N	A U S R N	A U S R N
20. Fails to follow up to see whether message was acted on.	A U S R N	A U S R N	A U S R N
Totals:			

Part Two: Interpersonal Communication

Instructions: Listed below are fourteen pairs of adjectives. They describe the major attributes of most interpersonal communications. A seven-point rating scale separates each pair, with the range extending from + + + (extremely high on the adjective at the left) to – – – (extremely high on the adjective at the right). Circle the rating for each pair of adjectives that best describes your interactions with *the person with whom you are completing this Audit.*

Remember that your rating does not necessarily indicate praise or censure of the other person. Rather, it describes the nature of the interpersonal communication that regularly takes place between you. *Both of you* are responsible for the quality of this communication. When you are finished, you will discuss what each of you has said.

goal-directed	+ + +	+ +	+	0	–	– –	– – –	unclear, unfocused
constructive	+ + +	+ +	+	0	–	– –	– – –	destructive
unhurried	+ + +	+ +	+	0	–	– –	– – –	rushed
useful	+ + +	+ +	+	0	–	– –	– – –	waste of time
complete	+ + +	+ +	+	0	–	– –	– – –	fragmented
supportive	+ + +	+ +	+	0	–	– –	– – –	defensive
candid	+ + +	+ +	+	0	–	– –	– – –	hidden agenda
accepting	+ + +	+ +	+	0	–	– –	– – –	fault-finding
open	+ + +	+ +	+	0	–	– –	– – –	guarded
adult-adult	+ + +	+ +	+	0	–	– –	– – –	parent-child
informal, relaxed	+ + +	+ +	+	0	–	– –	– – –	formal, rigid
unbiased	+ + +	+ +	+	0	–	– –	– – –	biased
trusting	+ + +	+ +	+	0	–	– –	– – –	distrusting
"win-win"	+ + +	+ +	+	0	–	– –	– – –	"win-lose," manipulative

The Pfeiffer Book of Successful Communication Skill-Building Tools © 2004 John Wiley & Sons, Inc.

Now multiply the numbers on the rules below by the number of times you circled the response in the column above it. Write the totals in the blanks provided.

Point value of each column x number of items in column

+ + +	+ +	+	0	–	– –	– – –
7 ×	6 ×	5 ×	4 ×	3 ×	2 ×	1 ×
_____	_____	_____	_____	_____	_____	_____

Now add all your points together and write your total score below.

Total Score: _____

GUIDELINES FOR SCORING AND INTERPRETING PART ONE

Instructions: The paragraphs that follow contain guidelines for scoring your responses and questions to help you interpret the results and take appropriate actions.

As you may have noticed, every odd-numbered statement on the Audit describes a *desirable* trait. On these items an "always" response is worth 5 points, a "usually" is worth 4 points, a "sometimes" rates 3 points, a "seldom" gets 2 points, and a "never" is worth 1 point. In other words, on the odd-numbered items, the scores descend from left to right—from 5 to 1.

Look back at your answers on the odd-numbered items only (1, 3, 5, 7, 9, 11, 13, 15, 17, 19). Place a number beside each letter that you circled to indicate its point value—from 5 to 1.

Now look at the even-numbered statements, which describe undesirable traits. On these items an "always" is worth 1 point, a "usually" is worth 2 points, a "sometimes" rates 3 points, a "seldom" gets 4 points, and a "never" is worth the full 5 points. Use this reverse scale to mark your score on the even-numbered items (2, 4, 6, 8, 10, 12, 14, 16, 18, 20).

You are now ready to determine the total score you have given senior management at your organization, your direct supervisor, and yourself. Add all numbers in the five senior management columns and enter the numbers at the bottom of the senior management columns. Then add these number together to obtain the score you have given to senior management. Then follow the same procedure to determine the score you have given your supervisor and yourself.

There are twenty items, each worth up to five points, so a perfect score is 100 points. A score of 85 or better indicates that communications are quite healthy. Scores that are significantly below this level indicate a need to work on weak areas—those behaviors that received ratings of only 1 or 2 points each.

GUIDELINES FOR INTERPRETING PART TWO

Instructions: After you have completed this Audit and discussed your results with your partner, it's time to draw some conclusions about your own communication style. This will be especially instructive for you if you have completed the Audit and discussed the results with several different partners.

Fill out the answers to the questions below:

1. Of the fourteen adjective pairs (qualities) listed, which ones seemed to be the strongest aspects of your interpersonal communications? What qualities were consistently rated very high, regardless of who your partner was?

2. As you evaluate your results, were there any adjective pairs (qualities) that were rated low, regardless of the person with whom you were communicating? Are these qualities that you may be lacking?

3. There are fourteen qualities and a maximum of seven points for each. Thus, a "perfect" score is ninety-eight points. How big was the gap between your total score and your partner's total score? (Do this for each partner.) What does the size of the gap tell you? Discuss this with your partner(s).

4. Was there a tendency for you to rank your interactions more favorably or less favorably than your partner(s) did? Or did the ratings tend to balance out? How do you interpret this?

5. Which of the fourteen qualities are ones that you and your partner(s) see a need to improve? What made you pick these?

6. Can the qualities that you listed above be improved through individual work? Are they closely tied to personality and so deeply rooted that they are not likely to change much over time?

7. What actions do you each plan to take to improve the quality of your interpersonal communications on those attributes you've selected?

Communication Audit Action Planning Samples

The following samples are provided so that you can write your own plan for change.

- "I've identified four areas in the interactions with my supervisor that need improvement. I plan to sit down with her to discuss them and, hopefully, to agree on things we can each do to improve these areas (Numbers 5, 9, 10, 14)."

- "The members of my special project team don't always understand me. I often find out too late that they're doing things differently from what I said (or thought I said). So I'm going to focus on improving in three of the areas listed: Numbers 3, 5, and 13. I'll remember three key words—*ask* (Number 3), *summarize* (Number 5), and *illustrate* (Number 13)—as my constant reminder whenever I'm talking to someone, to make sure I do these things until they become natural for me."

- "Two other people with whom I work closely took Part Two. Although I met with each separately to discuss our scores, the ratings of each were very similar. And we were all in agreement on the qualities that were weak in all of us. So the three of us got together and agreed to concentrate on changing from 'unfocused, rushed, and fragmented' interactions to taking more time to clue the others in, so that we all have the same picture in our heads. Often it's a case of our assuming that the others know the background and understand what we're talking about."

- "My wife and I went through Part Two. We both agreed that our interactions were becoming 'destructive, fault-finding, parent-child, win-lose, and manipulative.' We couldn't agree on why this was happening and lapsed into fault-finding when we tried to! However, we did agree that when either of us felt that the other was doing it, we would call 'time out' before continuing. This should increase our awareness and sensitivity, and thus reduce our destructive comments."

- "Six people work with me in our section. I'm the group leader. I plan to make extra copies of the Communication Audit so that we can each go through it as individuals. Then we'll get together and compare answers. In the middle column of Part One they will be evaluating me, so we can make this part confidential or discuss it openly, whichever they prefer. Either way, I'm sure we can identify the things that they and I need to work on to improve our communications."

5

The Behavior Description

John E. Oliver

The concept of individual differences can be one of
the most interesting and stimulating topics in the
study of human resource management. Sometimes,
however, people who are studying this concept do not
receive an in-depth understanding of personality traits
or they are not impressed with the importance of personality differences in personnel-placement decisions,
communication, motivation, and other efforts to create effective organizations. Using a personality inventory is one way to raise their interest and involvement,
which in turn lead to greater understanding.

Because many personality inventories are expensive and take a great deal of
time to administer, score, and interpret, a short, quickly scored, and easily
explained instrument (the Behavior Description) was designed as a focus for
discussing individual personality traits and related subjects.

DEVELOPMENT OF THE INSTRUMENT

The theory of Marston (1928), which is similar to that of Emery and Ackoff
(1972) in dealing with the response of a person to environmental stimuli, was

used to create this instrument. The resulting four behavioral traits may be viewed in combination to illustrate various kinds of behaviors that may affect job performance and communication. Marston labeled the traits *dominance, inducement, submissiveness,* and *compliance.* Some other authors have relabeled the traits to make them more acceptable in modern times in teaching managers, personnel professionals, sales people, and others to analyze behavior when trying to improve job performance and interpersonal relations. For example, Merrill and Reid (1981) call them *driver, expressive, amiable,* and *analytical.* The traits are also included among the 17,953 identified by Allport and Odbert (1936) and are similar to some of the sixteen source traits pinned down by Cattell (1973).

The Behavior Description refers to these traits as *dominance, extroversion, stability,* and *control.* Implicitly, these labels suggest four continuums as did Cattell's: dominant-submissive, extrovert-introvert, stable-unstable, and controlled-independent. This article presents the Behavior Description and its underlying theory; analyzes the reliability, validity, and meaning of scores on the Behavior Description; and discusses the use of the instrument in teaching or training settings.

THE INSTRUMENT

Format

The Behavior Description contains sixteen items. Each item is a group of three adjectives that describe behaviors associated with the four source traits. For example, the words "polished," "diplomatic," "enthusiastic," and "popular" are found in items one, nine, two, and ten and represent behaviors associated with extroversion. The respondent is asked to rank the words by assigning a weight of three to the word that best describes himself or herself, a weight of one to the least descriptive word, and a weight of two to the remaining word.

Scoring

A score is computed on each of the four traits. The scores are computed by transferring the numerical rankings of the words from the instrument to the scoring sheet and totaling the numbers in each column on the scoring sheet. Thus, the *dominance* score will be the total of all the numbers assigned to the twelve words that describe dominant behavior. The three remaining scores are computed similarly. The scores are then plotted on the graph so that combinations and patterns of traits can be seen and discussed.

Composition of Normative Sample

Data gathered for analyzing the instrument were taken from 220 respondents in classrooms and work places. Included in this normative sample were undergraduate and graduate students; members of a chapter of the American Society for Personnel Administration; accountants; teachers; social workers; engineers; salespeople; clerical workers; postal employees; nurses; technicians; therapists; investigators; analysts; chemists; architects; planners; negotiators; pilots; navigators; and managers from manufacturing, banking, military, government, hospital, police, laboratory, and sales organizations. Male and female respondents were about equal in number.

Reliability and Validity

Descriptive statistics from the samples are shown in Table 1. The internal consistency of scores as indicated by coefficient alpha averaged .59, and test-retest reliability averaged .66.

The scale intercorrelations in Table 2 indicate some relationships between scales. For instance, dominance is positively related to extroversion and negatively related to control. In other words, individuals who score high on dominance would also tend to score high on extroversion and lower on control, whereas those scoring low on dominance might be expected to score low on extroversion and higher on control.

Construct validity of the theory and the items was established by correlating each of the adjectives with the four total scores. Adjectives that were chosen to represent each behavior correlated positively (in the range of .2 to .5) with the total score that represented its related construct and correlated negatively with (or were unrelated to) the other construct scores. For example, the correlation between the word "adventurous" and the dominance score was .28, whereas its correlations with the extroversion, stability, and control scores were −.01, −.21, and −.08, respectively. External validity of the Behavior Description would require correlation between test scores and actual behaviors. Such data are not available at this time.

Table 1. Descriptive Statistics (N = 220)

	Dominance	Extroversion	Stability	Control
Possible Range	12-36	12-36	12-36	12-36
Actual Range	14-34	13-33	13-35	16-34
Mean	23.7	22.8	24.8	24.6
Standard Deviation	4.1	4.0	3.7	3.6
Standard Error	.3	.3	.2	.2
Coefficient Alpha*	.63	.65	.54	.54
Test-Retest*	.73	.64	.72	.56

*Significant at $p < .001$; $n = 41$.

Table 2. Scale Intercorrelations

	Extroversion	Stability	Control
Dominance	.43	.26	−.41
Extroversion		.25	−.38
Stability			.01

Interpretation

The four interpretation sheets, which follow the scoring sheet, show the relative strengths of each adjective according to the percentage of people in the sample who assigned a maximum value to the adjective. Because appropriateness of behavior is relative to the situation in which the behavior occurs, the same behaviors that appear to be positive and successful in one situation may appear negative or inappropriate in another situation. The right-hand column on the interpretation sheets gives negative interpretations of the adjectives that are in the left-hand column.

The theory for the Behavior Description is built on the assumption that most people tend to describe themselves and to behave in relatively fixed styles. In other words, the ability to adapt one's own behavior to changing circumstances is a personality trait that is more or less normally distributed in the general population. Individuals who score very high or very low on a given scale will probably show less flexibility in changing that behavior. Those who score

The Pfeiffer Book of Successful Communication Skill-Building Tools © 2004 *John Wiley & Sons, Inc.*

about average on all four scales could be expected to show more behavioral flexibility.

ADMINISTERING THE BEHAVIOR DESCRIPTION

After the respondents have completed the instrument, they should be given the theory associated with the Behavior Description, including an explanation of the four basic traits. Then they should be asked to predict their own scores. After the scoring process, the interpretation sheets should be distributed to the respondents, and the facilitator should be available to help with interpreting the scores. Scores can be posted, and the respondents should be asked to discuss both the process and the results.

The person administering the instrument could also lead a discussion on the measurement levels, normal distribution, reliability, and validity. Such a discussion would help the respondents to assess the value of the self-description provided by the instrument. Other appropriate topics for discussion are the pitfalls of using information provided by instruments that measure traits poorly and Stagner's (1958) classic article, "The Gullibility of Personnel Managers." These topics can generate a high degree of interest.

Other Discussion Topics

Combinations of the traits can be observed in the graph of the scores and may lead to stimulating discussions and insights into the behaviors of the respondents and their acquaintances or co-workers. The pattern-association sheet, which follows the interpretation sheets, lists behaviors that are associated with various patterns of scores. The greater the spread between two scores, the greater is the probability that the behavior will be exhibited and the lower is the likelihood that opposite traits will be exhibited. Respondents could be asked to judge the validity of the Behavior Description by relating "what I am" and "what I am not" (opposite traits) to behavioral incidents they can recall.

The Johari Window concept developed by Luft and Ingham (Luft, 1970) is useful in discussing how the Behavior Description can help in differentiating between self-images and perceptions by others. The Behavior Description opens one pane of the Johari Window by allowing the respondents to describe themselves as they believe they are. These self-descriptions may or may not match perceptions by others and may or may not be accurate descriptions of actual behavior.

An interesting question for discussion is whether individuals might be expected to behave at all times in a manner indicated by their behavior descriptions. This type of discussion might include topics such as situational variables, changing values and goals, and role theory.

If role theory is discussed, respondents might focus on the limiting effect that self-image has on the variety of roles a person can play. It is easier to play a role that requires only a slight adjustment in behavior than a role opposite from one's self-image.

Respondents may be asked how their described behavior might affect their success as managers (or some other position). They may say, for example, that as a decision maker a dominant individual would act before gathering enough information, the extrovert would choose popular alternatives, the stable person might debate too long, and the control person would avoid taking risks. Or looking at the strengths of each type, they might suggest that the dominant person would be able to overcome obstacles in reaching a decision, the extrovert would excel in interpersonal relations, a stable individual would give due consideration to a problem, and the control person would minimize the risks.

BEHAVIORAL STYLES AND ROLE STRESS

If organizations would place employees in roles that suit their natural behavioral styles, not only would the employees be more satisfied and possibly more successful, but the organization could be more effective. The stress that is created by playing roles that do not match one's self-image may exact both a physical and emotional toll. Congruence between personality and role would reduce some types of role stress and thereby reduce physical and emotional illness in the workplace. However, the Behavior Description measures only the self-perception and not a person's actual behavioral style. Valid descriptions of actual behaviors would be needed to match individuals to jobs that require them to act in their most natural ways.

Knowledge of the differences in individuals' personality traits can be used to create more effective organizations by improving communication, motivation, personnel placement, assignment of problems, and the structure of the organization and groups within the organization. Nevertheless, before personality differences can be used in making assignments, they must be reliably measured and their importance must be properly weighed in the decision process. In placement decisions, for instance, differences in specific skills, knowledge,

The Pfeiffer Book of Successful Communication Skill-Building Tools © 2004 John Wiley & Sons, Inc.

abilities, intelligence, commitment, and motivation may outweigh personality differences and may far outweigh the self-perceived traits in the Behavior Description.

CONCLUSION

Awareness of individual behavioral traits, such as those included in the Behavior Description, is helpful to managers or potential managers because it can be used to help understand people in organizations, to improve communications and motivation, and to aid in understanding placement decisions. Therefore, the Behavior Description is useful as a learning device. It was not, however, designed for use in counseling, career development, or job placement. Therefore, care should be taken not to misuse it.

References

Allport, G.W., & Odbert, H.S. (1936). Trait names, a psycholexical study. *Psychological Monograph, 47,* 211.

Cattell, R.B. (1973, July). Personality pinned down. *Psychology Today,* pp. 40–46.

Emery, F.E., & Ackoff, R.L. (1972). *On purposeful systems.* Chicago: Aldine-Atherton.

Luft, J. (1970). *Group processes: An introduction to group dynamics.* Palo Alto, CA: Mayfield.

Marston, W.M. (1928). *Emotions of normal people.* New York: Harcourt Brace.

Merrill, D.W., & Reid, R.H. (1981). *Personal styles and effective performance.* Radnor, PA: Chilton.

Stagner, R. (1958). The gullibility of personnel managers. *Personnel Psychology, 11,* 346–352.

_____

Originally published in The 1988 Annual.

Behavior Description

John E. Oliver

Instructions: For each of the following groups of three terms, place a "3" by the term that describes you best, "1" by the term that least describes you, and a "2" by the remaining term.

1. a. Adventurous _____
   b. Polished _____
   c. Stable _____

2. a. Receptive _____
   b. Determined _____
   c. Enthusiastic _____

3. a. Steady _____
   b. Exacting _____
   c. Original _____

4. a. Poised _____
   b. Patient _____
   c. Orderly _____

5. a. Forceful _____
   b. Persuasive _____
   c. Settled _____

6. a. Cautious _____
   b. Bold _____
   c. Outgoing _____

7. a. Persistent _____
   b. Cooperative _____
   c. Brave _____

8. a. Attractive _____
   b. Controlled _____
   c. Correct _____

9. a. Competitive _____
   b. Diplomatic _____
   c. Accommodating _____

10. a. Careful _____
    b. Decisive _____
    c. Popular _____

11. a. Dependable _____
    b. Accurate _____
    c. Inventive _____

12. a. Convincing _____
    b. Consistent _____
    c. Open minded _____

13. a. Positive _____
    b. Cordial _____
    c. Even tempered _____

14. a. Conservative _____
    b. Eager _____
    c. Entertaining _____

15. a. Amiable _____
    b. Systematic _____
    c. Self-reliant _____

16. a. Sociable _____
    b. Unhurried _____
    c. Precise _____

The Pfeiffer Book of Successful Communication Skill-Building Tools © *2004 John Wiley & Sons, Inc.*

BEHAVIOR DESCRIPTION SCORING SHEET

Instructions: Enter your scores from the Behavior Description form in the spaces below. Then add the scores in each column and enter the total for the column in the space provided.

Behavior

Dominance	Extroversion	Stability	Control
1a _____	1b _____	1c _____	2a _____
2b _____	2c _____	3a _____	3b _____
3c _____	4a _____	4b _____	4c _____
5a _____	5b _____	5c _____	6a _____
6b _____	6c _____	7a _____	7b _____
7c _____	8a _____	8b _____	8c _____
9a _____	9b _____	9c _____	10a _____
10b _____	10c _____	11a _____	11b _____
11c _____	12a _____	12b _____	12c _____
13a _____	13b _____	13c _____	14a _____
14b _____	14c _____	15a _____	15b _____
15c _____	16a _____	16b _____	16c _____
Total _____	*Total* _____	*Total* _____	*Total* _____

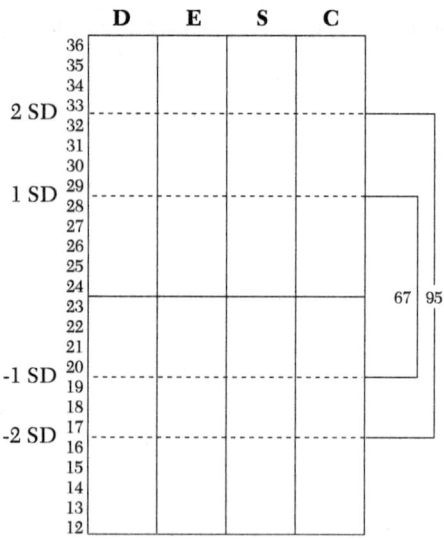

Notes:

1. The horizontal line in the middle of the graph represents the means or average scores in the normative sample.

2. Sixty-seven percent of the population is expected to score between ± 1 standard deviation (SD) from the mean.

3. Ninety-five percent of the population is expected to score between ± 2 SD from the mean.

4. Scores outside ± 2 SD are rare, indicating extreme preferences.

 The Pfeiffer Book of Successful Communication Skill-Building Tools © 2004 John Wiley & Sons, Inc.

BEHAVIOR DESCRIPTION INTERPRETATION SHEET NO. 1

Dominants

Positive Description	% Selecting	Negative Description[1]
Brave	19	Reckless
Inventive	19	Inflexible
Bold	21	Brash
Forceful	23	Pushy
Determined	29	Stubborn
Decisive	30	Overbearing
Eager	35	Overly eager
Adventurous	37	Too risky
Original	44	Dissatisfied
Competitive	46	Overly competitive
Positive	51	Reckless
Self-reliant	52	Too independent

Dominants do *not* describe themselves as sociable, stable, patient, accurate, systematic, receptive, steady, accommodating, or cooperative. An individual scoring extremely high in dominance may be seen by others either as a forceful, dynamic leader or as a belligerent troublemaker, depending on the circumstances.

Positive adjectives that might be applied to a person scoring relatively *low* on the dominance scale include mild-mannered, conservative, peaceful, modest, nice, and cautious. Negative adjectives would include timid, hesitant, unsure, and fearful. An individual who scores extremely low on the dominance scale might be seen by others as a cooperative team player or as weak and self-deprecating, depending on the situation.

---

[1]Possible negative interpretation of the behavior when it is inappropriate for the situation.

BEHAVIOR DESCRIPTION INTERPRETATION SHEET No. 2

Extroverts

Positive Description	% Selecting	Negative Description[2]
Poised	15	Inattentive
Attractive	16	Flashy
Persuasive	20	Too talkative
Popular	21	Time wasting
Polished	22	Too slick
Convincing	23	Inclined to oversell
Sociable	31	Flighty
Diplomatic	31	Wordy
Outgoing	32	Superficial
Entertaining	37	Self-centered
Cordial	37	Unoriginal
Enthusiastic	41	Shallow

Extroverts do *not* describe themselves as being stable, persistent, accurate, systematic, receptive, consistent, controlled, careful, or cautious. An individual scoring extremely high in extroversion may be seen by others either as enthusiastic, popular, and influential or as superficial and nonproductive, depending on the situation.

Positive adjectives that might be applied to a person scoring relatively *low* on the extroversion scale include logical, factual, probing, thoughtful, and incisive. Negative adjectives would include cold, aloof, blunt, shy, and skeptical. An individual who scores extremely low on the extroversion scale might be seen by others as either a thoughtful, quiet, logical problem solver or a noncommunicative, blunt recluse, depending on the situation.

---

[2]Possible negative interpretation of the behavior when it is inappropriate for the situation.

The Pfeiffer Book of Successful Communication Skill-Building Tools © 2004 John Wiley & Sons, Inc.

BEHAVIOR DESCRIPTION INTERPRETATION SHEET NO. 3

Stables

Positive Description	% Selecting	Negative Description[3]
Unhurried	19	Slow
Accommodating	29	Noncompetitive
Consistent	32	Inflexible
Patient	34	Unmotivated
Amiable	34	Too easy going
Settled	34	Unambitious
Even tempered	38	Resentful
Steady	42	Too slow
Controlled	42	Unemotional
Stable	43	Slow starting
Persistent	47	Dogged
Dependable	51	Too predictable

Stables do *not* describe themselves as being adventurous, original, bold, inventive, exacting, decisive, eager, determined, popular, entertaining, or correct. An individual scoring extremely high in stability may be seen by others either as a patient, persistent team player or as a stubborn roadblock to progress and change, depending on the situation.

Positive adjectives that might be applied to a person scoring relatively *low* on the stability scale include alert, self-starting, flexible, and responsive. Negative adjectives include impatient, impulsive, erratic, and explosive. An individual who scores extremely low on the stability scale might be seen by others as either an alert self-starter or an impulsive decision maker, depending on the situation.

---

[3]Possible negative interpretation of the behavior when it is inappropriate for the situation.

Behavior Description Interpretation Sheet No. 4

Controls

Positive Description	% Selecting	Negative Description[4]
Correct	20	Too perfect
Cooperative	21	Easily swayed
Exacting	29	Inflexible
Orderly	29	Too neat
Cautious	29	Scared
Precise	31	Picky
Conservative	35	Old fashioned
Open minded	37	Wishy-washy
Systematic	40	Bound by procedure
Careful	41	Fearful
Receptive	50	Easy to convince
Accurate	61	Too detailed

Controls do *not* describe themselves as original, bold, persuasive, forceful, competitive, convincing, enthusiastic, outgoing, decisive, eager, self-reliant, popular, entertaining, or cordial. An individual scoring extremely high in control may be seen by others as a precise, systematic, cooperative worker or as an overly dependent, fearful person, depending on the situation.

Positive adjectives that might be applied to a person scoring relatively *low* on the control scale include independent, individualistic, strong, and firm. Negative adjectives include stubborn, unbending, arbitrary, and uncommunicative. An individual who scores extremely low on the control scale might be seen by others as either an independent individualist with high ideals or an obstinate, arbitrary rebel, depending on the situation.

---

[4]Possible negative interpretation of the behavior when it is inappropriate for the situation.

The Pfeiffer Book of Successful Communication Skill-Building Tools © 2004 John Wiley & Sons, Inc.

BEHAVIOR DESCRIPTION PATTERN-ASSOCIATION SHEET

If this score is high	And if this score is low	This trait is likely to be present	Opposite Trait
Dominance	Extroversion	Logical	Companionable
	Stability	Driving	Patient
	Control	Fighting	Giving
Extroversion	Dominance	Companionable	Logical
	Stability	Outgoing	Concentrative
	Control	Argumentative	Perfectionistic
Stability	Dominance	Patient	Driving
	Extroversion	Concentrative	Outgoing
	Control	Rigid	Empathic
Control	Dominance	Giving	Fighting
	Extroversion	Perfectionistic	Argumentative
	Stability	Empathic	Rigid

The greater the spread between the two scores, the greater the likelihood that the high-scoring trait will be exhibited and the lower the likelihood that the opposite trait will be exhibited. Greater spreads may also lead respondents to perceive that the Behavior Description is more valid than it actually is.

6

Cross-Cultural Interactive Preference Profile

Morris Graham and Dwight Miller

Many people encounter problems interacting in environments that are culturally different from their own. Everyone has preferences regarding interpersonal interactions, and these may vary from culture to culture as well as from individual to individual.

One important dimension of culture is *context*, which ranges from *high context* (collectivism) to *low context* (individualism). The Cross-Cultural Interactive Preference (CCIP) Profile measures an individual's preferences for level of context as well as his or her ability to interact effectively across contexts. This profile comprises the following factors: socialization of information, socialization of people, spatial orientation, and time orientation. As a result of understanding his or her own preferences, a person can become more aware of the role that context plays in individual and group interactions.

Most people do not do really well when interacting in an environment that is foreign to their own or with people of cultural preferences different from their own. This is particularly true within cross-cultural or cross-functional groups. Preferences regarding interpersonal interactions, group interactions, and information may vary from one culture to another, just as they also vary from one individual to another, regardless of cultural origin. People's interactive preferences need to be understood in order to facilitate productive group work. Such understanding can help to reduce potential interpersonal conflicts and can increase group effectiveness.

In cross-cultural or cross-functional group settings, what we can learn about ourselves through others is as important as what we can learn about others and their cultures. The ways in which we feel, think, and behave can be checked in terms of how others perceive and interact with us. Things take on new meanings in the context of other cultural orientations. Moreover, things that we may consider to be uniquely individual about our "selves" are actually shaped by our culture, which determines, to a large extent, how we respond in different situations.

The Cross-Cultural Interactive Preference Profile (CCIP Profile) identifies how the respondents would prefer to interact in group activities or in situations in which more than one cultural orientation is involved.

DEFINITIONS OF TERMS

Understanding any subject area requires a basic working vocabulary. In the cross-cultural field, this vocabulary has grown with the advance of research. However, only the essential terms are defined here, for the purpose of interpreting the CCIP Profile.

Assimilate: To become absorbed into the cultural traditions of another ethnic population or group.

Context: The information that surrounds an event and is inextricably bound up with the meaning of the event. The elements that combine to produce a given meaning—events and context—vary in proportion from culture to culture. The cultures of the world can be compared on a scale from low context to high context (Hall & Hall, 1990).

Cross-Cultural Activities: Activities that involve more than one cultural set, viewpoint, or environment. Such activities deal with an individual's personal and cultural self-awareness, other-awareness, intercultural communication barriers, and interaction skills (Brislin, 1990).

Culture: A collection of many beliefs, values, perspectives, behaviors, activities, institutions, and learned patterns of communication largely shared in common by a group of people.

High-Context Message: Communication in which the vast majority of the information is either internalized in the individual or the physical context of the situation. Very little is in the explicit transmission or coding of the message (Hall, 1977; Hall & Hall, 1990).

Judgment: The process of forming conclusions about what has been perceived by an individual.

Low-Context Message: Communication in which the mass of information is in the explicit coding of the message and not resident within the individuals involved or within the situation or context (Hall, 1977).

Microculture: A subculture or new culture formed by the interaction of two or more major cultures such as business organizations, nations, or persons. A formulation of beliefs, behaviors, values, characteristics, patterns of communication, etc., shared by a specific group of people, that originates from diverse, major cultural groupings (Fontaine, 1989).

Multicultural Individual: An individual who has assimilated understanding, precepts, knowledge, and characteristics of more than his or her own native culture by experiencing microcultural activities of cross-cultural groups. Adler (1986) notes that members of multicultural groups should recognize and integrate all the cultures represented.

Multiculturalism: Situations in which people from more than one culture (and frequently more than one country) interact regularly, thus forming a number of perspectives, approaches, and—in the case of businesses—business methods (Adler, 1986).

Personality: The result of conditioning by culture; the total of the individual's characteristic reactions to his or her environment.

Predisposition: The condition of being inclined beforehand or having a susceptibility to act or react in a particular way.

CONCEPTUAL BACKGROUND: LOW-CONTEXT AND HIGH-CONTEXT ORIENTATIONS

Theorists have identified a major dimension of cultural variability, called "context" (Chinese Culture Connection, 1987; Hall, 1977; Hall & Hall, 1990; Hofstede, 1984; Kluckhohn & Strodtbeck, 1961; Marsella, DeVos, & Hsu, 1985; Triandis, 1988). The two basic dimensions of are low context (individualism) and high context (collectivism).

Low-Context Cultures (Individualism)

Low-context, or "individualistic," people and cultures place emphasis on individualism and individual goals, facts, the management of time, nonverbal communication, privacy, and compartmentalization.

The cultural norms associated with low context, which dominate most North American and Northern European societies, are essentially task-oriented, focusing on data to provide the answers to living well. Progress is measured in tangibles. Goals are action-oriented and geared to produce short-term material profits. The driving force of a low-context culture is work, which is the usual context in which a person is honored. Societies are structured to honor individuals who succeed financially. Emotions are suspect and considered inappropriate in most social and work settings.

Low-context people are highly individualistic, assertive, directive, dominating, results-oriented, independent, strong-willed, competitive, quick to make decisions, impatient, time-conscious, solution-oriented, control-seeking, well-organized, and self-contained. The individual has a high need to be recognized for his or her performance.

Individualistic social skills include meeting people quickly, putting them at ease, finding topics of conversation that others can discuss readily, being interesting so that the others will have memories of the interaction six months later, and so forth. These skills are useful, as they allow people to obtain information from others, central to the pursuit of individual goals (Brislin, 1993).

In a group setting, low-context individuals need less time to develop new, progressive programs that can be changed easily and quickly. However, these individuals can create less cohesion and stability in the group. Also, they are less committed to group agreements or planned actions.

In low-context cultures, when there is a conflict between an individual's goals and those of a valued group (i.e., co-workers), consideration of the individual's goals is of major importance. Individualists report (Brislin, 1993) that they would feel stifled if they were surrounded by others. There would be too many people whose opinions would have to be considered before an individualist could act in the pursuit of his or her goals. Individualists find that clearing their plans with others interferes too much with their desire "to do their own thing."

High-Context Cultures (Collectivism)

High-context, or "collectivistic," individuals and cultures place emphasis on relationships, group goals, the process and surrounding circumstances, time as natural progression, verbal communication, communal space, and interrelationships.

High-context cultural norms are primarily group-oriented, i.e., honoring the relationships of their cultural group before that of an "out-group," such as a university, company, or country. Family and community ties are strong; feelings and emotions are valued and encouraged to be expressed; religious and spiritual beliefs are deep.

The Pfeiffer Book of Successful Communication Skill-Building Tools © 2004 John Wiley & Sons, Inc.

In a high-context culture, behavior is viewed in a complex way. People look beyond the obvious to note nuances in meaning, nonverbal communication cues, and the status of others in context. In general, Asian cultural orientations are high context.

Personal characteristics include being indirect, highly affiliative, team-oriented, systematic, steady, quiet, patient, loyal, dependable, informal, servicing, sharing, slow in making decisions, respectful, and good listeners. A longer amount of time is needed for individuals to become acquainted with and trusting of one another; after that, communication is fast. The culture is rooted in the past; it is a slow-to-change, highly stable, unified group.

Collectivists feel comfortable with the constant psychological presence of a group. Important collective social attributes are loyalty to the group, cooperation, contributing to the group without the expectation of immediate reciprocity, and public modesty about one's abilities (Triandis, 1988). People are more likely to downplay their own goals in favor of the goals of the valued group. Individuals are more committed to group agreements and planned actions.

Contextual Factors

The factors or dimensions of context are time and space (Hall, 1977; Hall & Hall, 1990). These factors can be considered across all cultures; they are not specific to one culture or another or have meaning in and of themselves. Hall notes the importance of these factors as information is disseminated and acted on.

Hall uses the terms "monochronic" and "polychronic" to describe the individual orientations to time. In monochronic time, one pays attention to and does only one thing at a time. Events, functions, people, communication, and information flow are compartmentalized. In monochronic cultures, people are governed by time and work and they communicate in a linear fashion. In polychronic time, many things may happen or receive attention at the same time. In polychronic cultures, there is great involvement with people and events. People take precedence over time and schedules, and there is an emphasis on completing human transactions.

Monochronic cultures are basically low-context cultures that control and restrict information flow and communication. Polychronic cultures are basically high-context cultures in which information flows freely among all participants. Because the information is available to all, one is expected to use intuition and to understand automatically.

The purpose of meetings and communication in low-context cultures is to pass and/or determine information in order to evaluate and make decisions.

In high-context cultures, the purpose of meetings is to reach consensus about what is already known. The two processes are mutually exclusive in that in the low context, meaning is derived primarily from the coding of the messages. In the high context, the individuals already have the information or message within them. Hall and Hall (1990, p. 19) strongly emphasize the fact that "one must always be contexted to the local time systems" when working across cultures.

Spatial changes influence and often give definition to communications and human interaction even to the extent of overriding the spoken word. Spatial cues are perceived by all of the senses. Some cultures may attune more to the auditory, some to kinesthetic, others to visual, and so on. Each individual is surrounded by invisible boundaries of personal space or territories. These often communicate ownership or power when linked to physical location. With low-context monochronic societies and individuals, personal space is private, controlled, and often large. In contrast, in high-context polychronic societies or individuals, space is often shared with subordinates and centralized or shared in an information network. Time and space are often closely linked in that access to individuals is often dictated by both location and timing. An individual's availability is often determined by how well he or she is screened or separated from others.

Context and Communication

In his book, *Beyond Culture,* Hall (1977) identifies the critical need for individuals to transcend cultural barriers. He challenges us to " . . . recognize and accept the multiple hidden dimensions of unconscious culture . . . " (p. 2), because each culture has its own hidden or unconscious dimensions. In analyzing communication factors, Hall notes that it is impossible to know the meaning of a communication without knowing the context. Barker (1968) established that as the ecology or environment changed, so did people's responses.

With regard to context in relation to meaning, Hall (1977) states that context will largely determine the message that a person receives. Hall defines the collectivistic, high-context (HC) message or communication as one in which the vast majority of the information is either internalized in the individual or in the physical context of the situation. Very little is in the explicit transmission or coding of the message. With the individualistic, low-context (LC) message, the mass of information is in the explicit coding of the message, not within the individual or the situation (context).

Individuals perform the critically important function of correcting for distortions or omissions in the messages they receive. The key to being effective in communicating across cultures is in knowing the degree of information—context—that must be supplied and in the correct reading of another individual's verbal and nonverbal behavior. The context—the information surrounding an event that gives it meaning—varies from culture to culture and is often the determining factor in whether or not individuals from different cultures will communicate effectively, reach understanding, and make decisions. The integration of both verbal message and context is the basis of effective communication (Hall, 1977; Hall & Hall, 1990).

THE PROFILE

High versus low context, individualism versus collectivism, and the factors of time and space are not the only dimensions by which culture can be analyzed. However, they are ways in which a determination can be made as to how to communicate and work with individuals, regardless of their cultural orientations. Although many comparisons of major ethnic and national groups have been made based on contextual needs and decision-making processes, few, if any, have been developed to measure individual responses. The Cross-Cultural Interactive Preference Profile (CCIP Profile) was developed to reveal an individual's preferences in terms of contextual needs and socialization in interactive, group-decision-making processes so that effective communication, facilitation, and training designs could be established.

Development

The profile items were developed from a review of the literature and were given to seven experts who had extensive knowledge and experience in cross-cultural environmental learning and group interaction. A conceptual review was completed first. To establish content validity on revisions, a Delphi panel was asked to review each of the profile items for appropriateness and inclusion. This panel was selected on the basis of working experience in highly cross-cultural learning environments and experience in designing either assessment tools or training materials that had been applied in that environment. Panel members also had worked as consultants or employees in business and industry. They reviewed items based on appropriateness to the culturally defined categories, readability, comprehension, and the exclusion of culturally charged contextual items. Individual reviews and further revisions continued until at least 75 percent of panel members agreed on each of the forty-eight retained items.

The profile was pilot tested with a culturally mixed group of university students, and feedback was solicited about the profile through focus groups and an interview process. Particular attention was paid to comprehensibility of the language. Minor adjustments were made before administering the CCIP Profile to 512 freshmen and sophomore students (247 males and 265 females) at Brigham Young University-Hawaii, where fifty cultural orientations were represented. Approximately 20 percent of the students were from the mainland United States and other (predominantly European) Western cultural mixes, 25 percent were from Hawaii, 25 percent were from the South Pacific, 25 percent were from the Asian-rim countries, and the remainder were from other parts of the world. It was observed that most foreign students, after their arrival on campus, would develop and retain socialization patterns that maintained close ties to their own cultural groups through culture-based clubs and organizations. Thus, the majority of the students surveyed were close to their native orientations.

The CCIP Profile is intended for use with individuals who are involved in cross-cultural activities that result in the development of knowledge and skills. The profile is designed to foster awareness of, and sensitivity to, contextual orientation that affect interactive behavior in culturally diverse groups.

Validity

The content validity of the profile was assured through the implementation of the literature review, the iterative Delphi panel, and interviews during the pilot-testing stages.

Construct validity was determined by assessing the relationship of test items with cultural groups through the use of factor analysis and multidiscriminant analysis. The profile employs a Likert scale, which resulted in a single factor or construct when factor analysis was applied. Factor loadings were above a level of .45. To assure validity, more than ten respondents per item were utilized. Item analysis utilizing two-tail probability showed a p-value .001 on all items.

Overall validity was based on the strength of the factor-1 loadings and the significance levels of the individual items. However, it is noted that there are some weaknesses to be dealt with through a continued analysis with additional populations.

Reliability

There are no current tests or standards with which to compare the results of the profile administration. A coefficient of internal consistency was determined utilizing a single-test administration. Cronbach's Coefficient Alpha was used to test reliability, as the profile relies on a nondichotomous, six-level Likert scale to circumvent a neutral or nonresponse, and a method of rational equivalence could not be used. Reliability coefficients (alphas) were: .49 in seven of the eight factor groupings, with the eighth at .34.

Suggested Use

The CCIP Profile can be used in various aspects of group decision making, cross-cultural conflict resolution, training and development, and team development in diverse work and educational settings. It is particularly useful as a clarification tool with newly organized groups or teams. Facilitators can be assured that finding out about one's own and others' preferences is a releasing experience, not a restricting one, as may be feared. Finding out about cultural preferences frees group members to recognize their own natural predispositions and to respect and learn how to effectively interact with the differences in the group with a minimum of conflict. Groups can become less polar or fragmented and more multiculturally sensitive and unified in their interactions.

References

Adler, N.J. (1986). In D.A. Ricks (Ed.), *International dimensions of organizational behavior* (The Kent International Business Series). Boston, MA: Kent Publishing.

Barker, R.G. (1968). *Ecological psychology*. Stanford, CA: Stanford University Press.

Brislin, R. (1993). *Understanding culture's influence on behavior*. Fort Worth, TX: Harcourt Brace College.

Brislin, R.W. (Ed.). (1990). *Applied cross-cultural psychology* (Cross-Cultural Research and Methodology Series No. 14). Newbury Park, CA: Sage.

Chinese Culture Connection. (1987). Chinese values and the search for culture-free dimensions of culture. *Journal of Cross-Cultural Psychology, 18,* 143–164.

Fontaine, G. (1989). *Managing international assignments*. Englewood Cliffs, NJ: Prentice Hall.

Hall, E.T. (1977). *Beyond culture*. Garden City, NY: Anchor Press/Doubleday.

Hall, E.T., & Hall, M.R. (1990). *Understanding cultural differences*. Yarmouth, ME: Intercultural Press.

Hofstede, G. (1984). Culture's consequences: International differences in work-related values. Newbury Park, CA: Sage.

Kluckhohn, F., & Strodtbeck, F. (1961). *Variations in value orientations.* New York: Row, Peterson.

Marsella, A.J., DeVos, G., & Hsu, F.L.K (Eds.). (1985). *Culture and self: Asian and Western perspectives.* New York: Tavistock.

Triandis, H.C. (1988). Collectivism vs. individualism: A reconceptualization of a basic concept in cross-cultural psychology. In G. Verma & C. Bagley (Eds.), *Cross-cultural studies of personality, attitudes and cognition* (pp. 60–95). London: Macmillan.

Triandis, H.C. (1990). Cross-cultural studies of individualism-collectivism. In J. Berman (Ed.), *Nebraska Symposium on Motivation 1989* (Vol. 35, pp. 41–53). Lincoln, NE: University of Nebraska Press.

Originally published in The 1995 Annual, Volume 1, Training.

CROSS-CULTURAL INTERACTIVE PREFERENCES PROFILE

Morris Graham and Dwight Miller

There are no right or wrong answers on this questionnaire. The answers will be useful only if you respond honestly and candidly. By doing this, you will help us to better understand the ways in which you prefer to interact within a group where there is more than one culture represented.

    Instructions: The following items describe how you might interact within a work or problem-solving group. Respond to each item by filling in the circle that best describes your preference, that is, how strongly you agree or disagree with the statement. This should take about fifteen minutes.

SD = Strongly Disagree   MA = Mildly Agree
D = Disagree   A = Agree
MD = Mildly Disagree   SA = Strongly Agree

Example:

You would mark your questionaire	**If you strongly agreed with this statement:**
	It's O.K. for new situations or ideas to be presented to the group for a decision even if some details are not included.

You would mark your questionaire	**If you disagreed with this statement:**
	I would let members do their own work the way they think best.

SD = Strongly Disagree   MA = Mildly Agree
D = Disagree   A = Agree
MD = Mildly Disagree   SA = Strongly Agree

(SD) (D) (MD) (MA) (A) (SA) 1. I need the leader of the group to explain the details before I can make a decision.

(SD) (D) (MD) (MA) (A) (SA) 2. I work best when we share information and then reach consensus as a group.

(SD) (D) (MD) (MA) (A) (SA) 3. Information should be held in common and not controlled by specific individuals or parts of the group.

(SD) (D) (MD) (MA) (A) (SA) 4. It is better to quietly acknowledge that a person may be incorrect or needs to change rather than to openly confront him/her in the group.

(SD) (D) (MD) (MA) (A) (SA) 5. It is best for all decisions to be approved by the whole group.

(SD) (D) (MD) (MA) (A) (SA) 6. Experts within a group should be allowed to make decisions for the group.

(SD) (D) (MD) (MA) (A) (SA) 7. Getting the details of needed information is more important than knowing who provided them.

(SD) (D) (MD) (MA) (A) (SA) 8. I am impatient when someone tries to explain something I already know.

(SD) (D) (MD) (MA) (A) (SA) 9. Individuals within a group do not need to share the information they have with the rest of the group until it is absolutely necessary.

(SD) (D) (MD) (MA) (A) (SA) 10. It is not important that all members of a group contribute ideas.

(SD) (D) (MD) (MA) (A) (SA) 11. I would compromise with others in order to maintain harmony in the group.

(SD) (D) (MD) (MA) (A) (SA) 12. I would expect the team leader to direct members away from problems or issues that would upset the balance of the group.

(SD) (D) (MD) (MA) (A) (SA) 13. I would trust the group members and support their shared interests even if I do not agree with them.

SD = Strongly Disagree MA = Mildly Agree
D = Disagree A = Agree
MD = Mildly Disagree SA = Strongly Agree

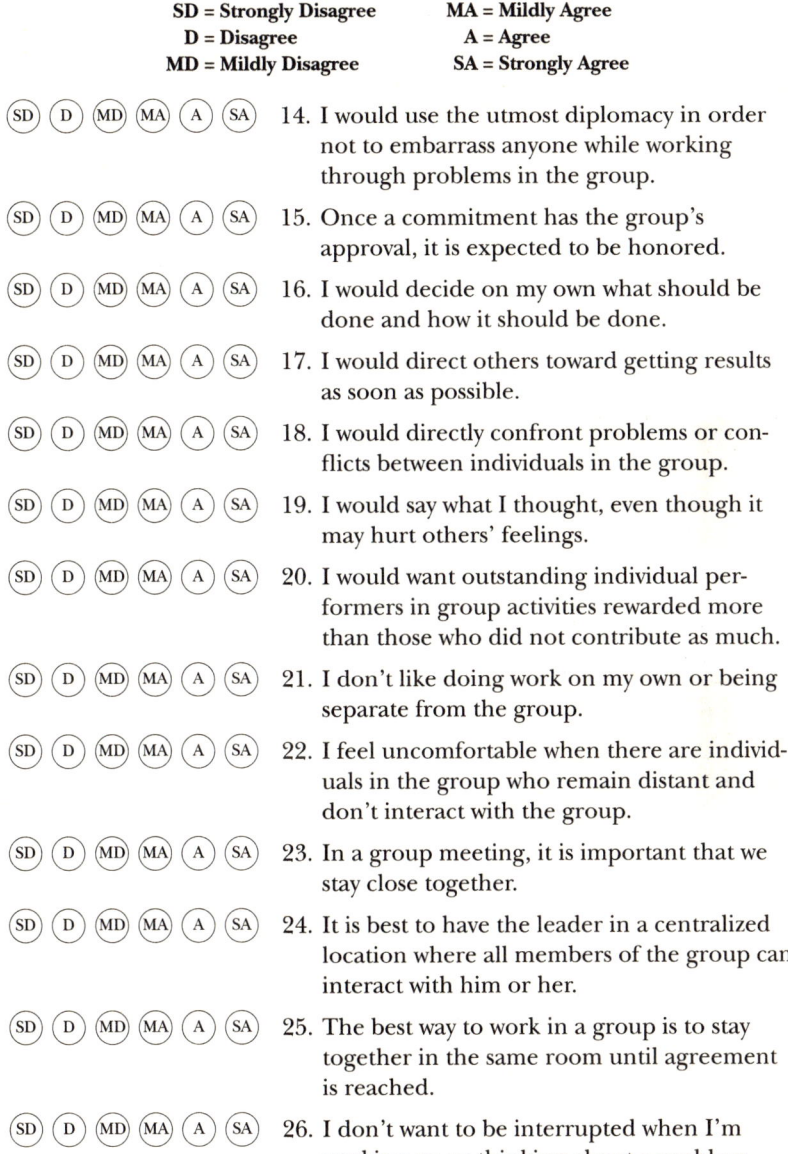

(SD) (D) (MD) (MA) (A) (SA)   14. I would use the utmost diplomacy in order not to embarrass anyone while working through problems in the group.

(SD) (D) (MD) (MA) (A) (SA)   15. Once a commitment has the group's approval, it is expected to be honored.

(SD) (D) (MD) (MA) (A) (SA)   16. I would decide on my own what should be done and how it should be done.

(SD) (D) (MD) (MA) (A) (SA)   17. I would direct others toward getting results as soon as possible.

(SD) (D) (MD) (MA) (A) (SA)   18. I would directly confront problems or conflicts between individuals in the group.

(SD) (D) (MD) (MA) (A) (SA)   19. I would say what I thought, even though it may hurt others' feelings.

(SD) (D) (MD) (MA) (A) (SA)   20. I would want outstanding individual performers in group activities rewarded more than those who did not contribute as much.

(SD) (D) (MD) (MA) (A) (SA)   21. I don't like doing work on my own or being separate from the group.

(SD) (D) (MD) (MA) (A) (SA)   22. I feel uncomfortable when there are individuals in the group who remain distant and don't interact with the group.

(SD) (D) (MD) (MA) (A) (SA)   23. In a group meeting, it is important that we stay close together.

(SD) (D) (MD) (MA) (A) (SA)   24. It is best to have the leader in a centralized location where all members of the group can interact with him or her.

(SD) (D) (MD) (MA) (A) (SA)   25. The best way to work in a group is to stay together in the same room until agreement is reached.

(SD) (D) (MD) (MA) (A) (SA)   26. I don't want to be interrupted when I'm working on or thinking about a problem.

SD = Strongly Disagree   MA = Mildly Agree
D = Disagree   A = Agree
MD = Mildly Disagree   SA = Strongly Agree

(SD) (D) (MD) (MA) (A) (SA)   27. I need to be away from the group in order to think and make a decision.

(SD) (D) (MD) (MA) (A) (SA)   28. I prefer to work alone until I am ready to get with the group.

(SD) (D) (MD) (MA) (A) (SA)   29. The leader of a group or organization needs to be separate but where I can go to him or her when I need to.

(SD) (D) (MD) (MA) (A) (SA)   30. When working in a group, I prefer to work with individuals who think as I do.

(SD) (D) (MD) (MA) (A) (SA)   31. I would desire lots of time and flexibility to accommodate the different personalities in the group.

(SD) (D) (MD) (MA) (A) (SA)   32. If there were disagreement in the group, I would be patient while others worked through and resolved conflicts before proceeding.

(SD) (D) (MD) (MA) (A) (SA)   33. It is more important to take the time needed to develop or share ideas before making a decision than it is to meet deadlines.

(SD) (D) (MD) (MA) (A) (SA)   34. It is O.K. to stop a group discussion and take a break whenever needed.

(SD) (D) (MD) (MA) (A) (SA)   35. Plans should always be open to change.

(SD) (D) (MD) (MA) (A) (SA)   36. A group should not stop working or discussing until a solution is found or a decision is made.

(SD) (D) (MD) (MA) (A) (SA)   37. I would not tolerate postponements.

(SD) (D) (MD) (MA) (A) (SA)   38. It is very important that a schedule be maintained.

(SD) (D) (MD) (MA) (A) (SA)   39. The group should deal with only one thing at a time until a decision is made.

(SD) (D) (MD) (MA) (A) (SA)   40. When the group has finished its work, it is best to move on and form new relationships.

CCIP PROFILE SCORING SHEET

Instructions: Convert each rating that you gave to a profile item to a number, as shown, and place that number in the appropriate spaces on this sheet.

SD = 0   D = 1   MD = 2   MA = 3   A = 4   SA = 5

Factor	Subscores
Socialization of Information	
Item—Highly Shared Flow	**Item—Controlled Flow**
1.	6.
2.	7.
3.	8.
4.	9.
5.	10.
Total	Total
Socialization of People	
Item—Collectivist	**Item—Individualist**
11.	16.
12.	17.
13.	18.
14.	19.
15.	20.
Total	Total

SD = 0   D = 1   MD = 2   MA = 3   A = 4   SA = 5

Factor	Subscores
Spatial Orientation	
Item—Shared/Central	**Item—Personalized**
1.	6.
2.	7.
3.	8.
4.	9.
5.	10.
Total	Total
Time Orientation	
Item—Polychronic	**Item—Monochronic**
11.	16.
12.	17.
13.	18.
14.	19.
15.	20.
Total	Total

Place the *total* scores in the appropriate boxes on the following sheet.

CCIP PROFILE INTERPRETATION GRAPH

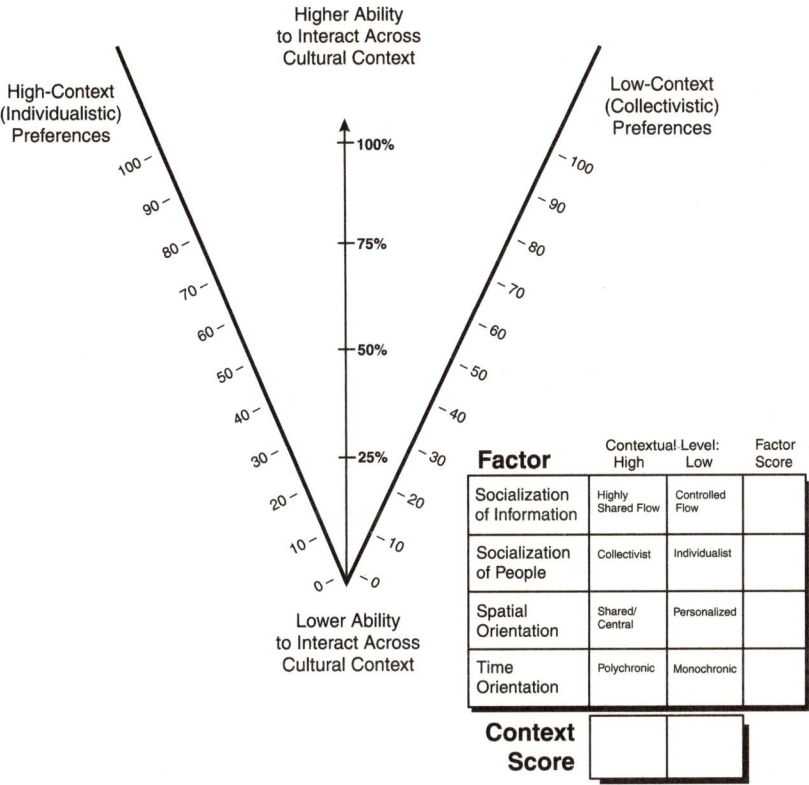

Factor	Contextual Level: High	Low	Factor Score
Socialization of Information	Highly Shared Flow	Controlled Flow	
Socialization of People	Collectivist	Individualist	
Spatial Orientation	Shared/ Central	Personalized	
Time Orientation	Polychronic	Monochronic	
Context Score			

Instructions:

1. Place the total scores from the CCIP Profile Scoring Sheet in the Factor boxes above.

2. Sum each row across to determine the Factor Score. Sum each column down to determine the Context Score.

3. Plot the "contextual level scores" on the graph, with the high-context score on the left axis and the low-context score on the right axis. Draw a line between the two plotted points.

CCIP Profile Interpretation Sheet

Background

As individuals develop within their cultures and in interactions with others, they form preferences about various aspects of interpersonal interactions. Many of these preferences have been identified in terms of what is called "context." Two basic contexts are "individualistic" and "collectivistic." The context in which one is interacting affects how one relates to others, communicates, interprets information, and so on.

Individualistic

Individualistic people and cultures focus on individual goals, tasks, facts, solutions, time management, and privacy. Individualists are assertive, directive, controlling, results-oriented, independent, strong-willed, competitive, quick to make decisions, impatient, organized, self-contained, and have a high need to be recognized for their performance. Goals are action-oriented to produce short-term material profits, and financial success is esteemed. Emotions are considered inappropriate in most social and work settings.

Individualists tend to have a monochronic time focus. One pays attention to and does only one thing at a time. Events, functions, people, communication, and information flow are compartmentalized.

Individualistic communication is "low context," which means that interactions are linear and specific and do not carry a lot of cultural "context" within them. Meaning is derived primarily from the coding of the message. Social skills include meeting people quickly, finding topics of conversation that others can discuss readily, being interesting so that the others will have memories of the interaction six months later, and obtaining information from others in pursuit of individual goals (Brislin, 1993).

Individualists' plans are progressive and can be changed quickly. However, such individuals can create less cohesion and stability in a group. They are less committed to group agreements, and when there is a conflict between an individual's goals and those of the group, the individual's goals are of major importance. Individualists do not like to have to consider the opinions of others before they act. Clearing their plans with others interferes too much with their desire "to do their own thing" (Brislin, 1993).

The Pfeiffer Book of Successful Communication Skill-Building Tools © 2004 John Wiley & Sons, Inc.

Collectivistic

Collectivistic individuals and cultures place emphasis on relationships, group goals, the process and surrounding circumstances, time as natural progression, verbal communication, communal space, and interrelationships. Cultural norms are primarily group oriented. Family and community ties are strong; expression of feelings is valued and encouraged; religious and spiritual beliefs are deep. These mutual understandings and beliefs supply the "high context" of this orientation.

In such a culture, behavior is viewed in a complex way. People look beyond the obvious to note nuances in meaning, nonverbal communication cues, and the status of others in the context of a shared history and understanding. Thus, language need not be as specific; relationships are part of the message. Because the information is available to all, one is expected to use intuition and to understand automatically.

Personal characteristics include being indirect, affiliative, informal, team-oriented, loyal, systematic, quiet, patient, dependable, cooperative, sharing, slow in making decisions, respectful, a good listener, contributing to the group without the expectation of immediate reciprocity, and public modesty about one's abilities (Triandis, 1990). A longer amount of time is needed for individuals to become acquainted with and trusting of one another; after that, communication is fast. The culture is rooted in the past; it is slow-to-change, highly stable, unified.

People are more likely to downplay their own goals in favor of the goals of the group, and individuals are more committed to group agreements.

Collectivists tend to have a polychronic time focus. Many things may happen or receive attention at the same time. There is great involvement with people and events. People take precedence over time and schedules, and there is an emphasis on completing human transactions.

Hall (1977) notes that it is impossible to know the meaning of a communication without knowing the context. Context largely determines what one pays attention to or does not pay attention to. The information surrounding an event that gives it meaning varies from culture to culture. The key to being effective in communicating across cultures is in knowing the degree of information—context—that must be supplied and in the correct reading of another individual's verbal *and* nonverbal behavior.

Individual Application

People who score high on one side of the CCIP Profile Interpretation Graph and low on the opposite side (a steeply sloped profile) may interact well with those who have profiles similar to theirs, but not with others.

People whose scores are relatively high on both sides of the graph (a flat profile) probably have little difficulty in interacting within groups in which there are varying levels of contextual requirements. These people are better able to move between situations and/or groups with ease, to be more flexible and adaptable in interpretation and decision-making situations, and to be more responsive in learning and decision making. The higher the flat profile, the greater the flexibility.

The factor scores represent relative levels in each of the factor preference areas. Where flexibility and adaptability problems exist, low scores may indicate which orientation or requirement may be responsible. Sub scores will indicate the dominance of the characteristic. The differences between sub scores indicate level of flexibility for a characteristic (higher differences represent higher flexibility). In general, low scores represent a potential difficulty in interacting across contextual boundaries.

Note: Language, religion, philosophical, and other communication or social barriers are not included in this profile.

References

Brislin, R. (1993). *Understanding culture's influence on behavior.* Fort Worth, TX: Harcourt Brace College.

Hall, E.T. (1977). *Beyond culture.* Garden City, NY: Anchor Press/Doubleday.

Triandis, H.C. (1990). Cross-cultural studies of individualism-collectivism. In J. Berman (Ed.), *Nebraska Symposium on Motivation 1989* (Vol. 35, pp. 41–53). Lincoln, NE: University of Nebraska Press.

7

Organization Behavior Describer Survey (OBDS)

Roger Harrison and Barry Oshry

The Organization Behavior Describer Survey (OBDS) was developed to assess the behavior of line and staff managers and administrators in group and interpersonal situations arising during the course of work. It can be used as a self-evaluation form or to obtain descriptions of behavior from others.

The OBDS originally was developed deductively from Argyris's (1962) theory of interpersonal behavior in organizations. Argyris postulates two kinds of administrative competence: rational-technical competence and interpersonal competence. Rational-technical competence is the ability to meet intellectual-knowledge and technical-skill requirements of the job; interpersonal competence is the individual's willingness and ability to deal directly and openly with the emotional aspects of interpersonal relationships in the organization.

Argyris's theory is similar to other two-factor theories of organizational behavior, notably Fleishman's Initiating Structure and Consideration, Blake's Managerial Grid, and McGregor's Theory X and Theory Y. Another Fleishman instrument, the *Supervisory Behavior Questionnaire,* was already available for assessing supervisory behavior on the dimensions of Initiating Structure and Consideration. It focused on supervisor-subordinate relationships and was primarily designed for the first-line level of supervision. In contrast, the OBDS was designed to produce a more general measure of interpersonal behavior, not only downward in the organization but laterally and upward as well.

In the first attempt to construct the instrument, twenty items were deductively composed—ten representing rational—technical aspects of interpersonal behavior and ten describing interpersonal competence as defined by Argyris. These items were factor analyzed, using 321 descriptions of managers in a technical manufacturing firm at middle levels of responsibility. Instead of the two expected factors, three important dimensions emerged from the analysis: rational-technical competence (24 percent of the variance), interpersonal competence (22 percent of the variance), and emotional expressiveness (11 percent of the variance).

These results indicated that the expressive and receptive aspects of interpersonal competence were not seen by respondents as closely related to each other. Being open to the ideas and feelings of others was seen as quite different from being open in expression of one's feelings. This seemed an important finding, because it identified another factor beyond the two usually considered important in organizational behavior and because it implied that aspects of interpersonal behavior that trainers and organizational consultants have carelessly tended to think of together may be quite separate processes.

Correlations were calculated between the three scales of the OBDS and the rating on Fleishman's *Supervisory Behavior Questionnaire.* As expected, the interpersonal competence scale showed moderately high correlations (median = .62) with Fleishman's Consideration Scale. Both the rational-technical and emotional expressiveness scales of the OBDS were moderately correlated with Fleishman's Initiating Structure Scale (median – .47). The emotional expressiveness scale showed negligible correlations with Fleishman's Consideration Scale and lower correlations with the OBDS interpersonal competence scale than with the rational-technical scale. This provided further evidence that the receptive and expressive aspects of interpersonal behavior may be seen quite differently.

Based on these preliminary results, development of the OBDS was carried out. A thirty-six-item questionnaire was constructed, and the descriptions by 189 subordinates of middle managers attending human relations training workshops were factor analyzed. An essentially similar factorial structure was obtained. This was tested by further factor analysis of descriptions of middle managers by fellow participants in a human relations training laboratory (T-group). In this artificial and specialized interaction situation, similar factors were found to those obtained from on-the-job descriptions. The resulting scales are presented here for use in studies of organizational behavior, evaluation of training, and the analysis of interpersonal behavior in groups.

In the current version of the OBDS, four scales are used. These are not altogether independent factorially. The basic factor structure is still three dimensional. However, the items in each of the four scales cluster rather neatly together and have a unity of connotation that argues for separate scoring. The median interscale correlations and reliability estimates of these scales are given in Table 1.

Interscale correlations are based on twelve samples (median N = 51), including:

1. descriptions by fellow members of managers participating in a T-group laboratory;

2. descriptions of industrial managers by self, supervisor, subordinate, and peer;

3. descriptions of managers in an applied-research organization by the categories of describers in (2); and

4. descriptions of YMCA executives by the categories of describers in (2).

Table 1. Median Interscale Correlations and Reliability Estimates of OBDS Scales

Scale	Rational-Technical Competence	Verbal Dominance	Consideration	Emotional Expressiveness
Rational-Technical Competence	.73 (pre-post)[1] .83 (split half)[2]	.69	.36	−.03
Verbal Dominance		.71 (pre-post) .84 (split half)	.23	.13
Consideration			.70 (pre-post) .92 (split half)	−.29
Emotional Expressiveness				.70 (pre-post) .89 (split half)

[1] Pre-post correlations are with intervening training experience and are based on eleven samples (median N=49).
[2] Speaman-Brown split-half reliabilities are based on four samples (median N=80).

Inspection of Table 1 shows reasonable independence of the scales, with the exception of verbal dominance and rational-technical competence, which are closely related. It is interesting to note the low negative correlation between consideration and emotional expressiveness in view of the attempts by practitioners of laboratory training to encourage increases in behavior on both dimensions. There is, in fact, a consistent tendency in our research for managers who rank high on emotional expressiveness to be seen in generally negative ways by their associates.

The reliabilities reported in Table 1 are adequate, especially considering the shortness of the scales. The pre-test correlations are also evidence of considerable stability, considering that they are based on pre-test time differences averaging two months and that they encompass an intervening human relations training experience designed to produce change along the dimensions measured by the OBDS.

With an instrument measuring behavior through descriptions, it is important to consider not only intradescriber reliability but also to assess interdescriber reliability: the degree of agreement among observers of the same individual's behavior. Accordingly, correlations were calculated between descriptions of the same person by self, supervisor, and subordinate. The findings, presented in Table 2, are based on the same populations as the figures in Table 1.

Table 2. Median Interdescriber Correlations, OBDS Scales

Scale	Correlations Based on Different Roles (13 Samples)		Correlations Based on Same Role (Subordinate) (2 Samples)	
	Median r	Range	r	N
Rational-Technical Competence	.14	−.03 to .27 .	.39 24	70 28
Verbal Dominance	.20	−.05 to .47	.28 .40	61 22
Consideration	.14	−.07 to .40	.15 .45	69 26
Emotional Expressiveness	.30	.09 to .56	.50 .56	66 29

Note: Median N = 53; range of N's: 15 to 66.

The Pfeiffer Book of Successful Communication Skill-Building Tools © 2004 John Wiley & Sons, Inc.

These findings are not very encouraging if one hopes to obtain a composite measure from several describers of an individual's interpersonal style in his or her organizational setting. When compared with the respectable intradescriber reliabilities, these figures are small indeed.

The inclusion of self-subordinate and self-supervisor correlations in this determination may be questioned on the grounds that self-descriptions are more subject to distortion than are descriptions by associates. There is, however, no indication from the distribution of correlations that this is the case. Roughly the same range of relationships was found in those correlations involving self-descriptions as in those based on observations by subordinate and supervisor. The data suggest, rather, that there is in fact considerable inconsistency in personal style, depending on some combination of the perceptual idiosyncracies of the observer and the behavior-determining role relationships between the observer and the individual described. From the data in Table 2, it can be seen that correlations between descriptions by two subordinates of the same supervisor are, on all scales, higher than the median of correlations based on different roles. This suggests that some of the unreliability between raters is indeed due to role relationships that influence interpersonal style. However, even within the same role, the interrater correlations leave a great deal to be desired.

It also is of interest that the correlations tend to be higher for verbal dominance and emotional expressiveness than they do for rational-technical competence and consideration. The items in the latter two scales require a higher degree of inference and refer less directly to observable behavior than do the items in the verbal-dominance and emotional-expressiveness scales. The more inference we require from the describer, of course, the more we can expect his or her judgment to be affected by his or her own psychological processes. For this reason the "best" scale should be one that is based most heavily on concrete descriptions of observable behavior.

In this connection it is interesting to compare Fleishman's *Supervisory Behavior Questionnaire* with the OBDS. In the study in which the OBDS was first developed, we also obtained descriptions on Fleishman's instrument from self, supervisor, peer, and subordinate (N = 50). The median interrater correlations were .39 for initiating structure and .16 for consideration. Thus, the OBDS and the *Supervisory Behavior Questionnaire* compare favorably in interrater reliability on the consideration dimension, but Fleishman's instrument has a better showing on initiating structure than the OBDS has on verbal dominance, the closest OBDS scale in content.

The rather high mean scores on the OBDS suggest that the responses could be designed to produce a greater spread of scores. For example:

4 Always

3 Most of the time

2 Often

1 Occasionally

0 Seldom

References

Argyris, C. (1962). *Interpersonal competence and organizational effectiveness.* New York: John Wiley.

Blake, R.R., & Mouton, J.S. (1964). *The managerial grid.* Houston, TX: Gulf.

Fleishman, E.A. (date unknown). *Initiating structure and consideration.*

Fleishman, E.A. (date unknown). *Supervisory behavior questionnaire.*

McGregor, D.M. (1960). *The human side of enterprise.* New York: McGraw-Hill.

———————

Originally published in The 1976 Annual.

Organization Behavior Describer Survey (OBDS)

Roger Harrison and Barry Oshry

Instructions: Listed below are twenty-five descriptions of ways that people behave in staff and problem-solving meetings. Choose an actual person in your organization and select the alternative in each item that comes closest to describing that person's behavior at work. Select a number using the five-point scale given below and write in the number in the first blank. Write only one alternative for each item. Keep in mind that you are limiting yourself to a description of how this person behaves only in *meetings* and *work-oriented situations or conversations*.

The person I am describing is: (check one)

_____ Myself

_____ My superior

_____ My subordinate

_____ Someone who works at the same level as I

_____ Other (specify)

I have known this person for approximately _____ years.

I spend about _____ hours per month with this person in *meetings* and/or *work-oriented situations or conversations*.

4 = Always   3 = Most of the time   2 = Often   1 = Occasionally   0 = Seldom

_____ _____ 1. He/She tries to understand the feelings (anger, impatience, rejection) expressed by others in the group.

_____ _____ 2. He/She shows intelligence.

_____ _____ 3. He/She sympathizes with others when they have difficulties.

_____ _____ 4. He/She expresses ideas clearly and concisely.

_____ _____ 5. He/She expresses his/her own feelings, e. g., when he/she is ignored, angry, impatient.

_____ _____ 6. He/She is tolerant and accepting of other people's feelings.

_____ _____   7. He/She thinks quickly.

_____ _____   8. He/She is angry or upset when things do not go his/her way.

_____ _____   9. He/She is persuasive, a "seller of ideas."

_____ _____   10. You can tell quickly when he/she likes or dislikes what others do or say.

_____ _____   11. He/She listens and tries to use the ideas raised by others in the group.

_____ _____   12. He/She demonstrates high technical or professional competence. He/She "knows his/her stuff."

_____ _____   13. He/She is warm and friendly with those who work with him/her.

_____ _____   14. He/She is able to attract the attention of others.

_____ _____   15. His/Her feelings are transparent; he/she does not have a "poker face."

_____ _____   16. He/She comes up with good ideas.

_____ _____   17. He/She encourages others to express their ideas before he/she acts.

_____ _____   18. He/She tries to help when others become angry or upset.

_____ _____   19. He/She tries out new ideas.

_____ _____   20. He/She is competitive; he/she likes to win and hates to lose.

_____ _____   21. He/She presents his/her ideas convincingly.

_____ _____   22. If others in the group become angry or upset, he/she listens with understanding.

_____ _____   23. He/She offers effective solutions to problems.

_____ _____   24. He/She tends to be emotional.

_____ _____   25. When he/she talks, others listen.

TOTALS   [   ] **R-TC**   [   ] **VD**   [   ] **EE**   [   ] **C**

OBDS Scoring and Interpretation Sheet

Scoring Instructions:

1. Go back over your responses to the twenty-five items on the Organization Behavior Describer Survey and assign a number value to each of your responses, using the scale below:

   4 = Always

   3 = Most of the time

   2 = Often

   1 = Occasionally

   0 = Seldom

2. In the second blank in front of each item, write one of the following codes:

Items	Code
2, 7, 12, 16, 19, 23	R-TC
4, 9, 14, 20, 21, 25	VD
5, 8, 10, 15, 24	EE
1, 3, 6, 11, 13, 17, 18, 22	C

3. Sum the scores of the items for each code and enter them in the four boxes at the end of the instrument.

Interpretation: Your profile of scores describes a person's behavior according to the following four major dimensions.

   R-TC: Rational-Technical Competence. This is the degree to which the person behaves intelligently and quickly, demonstrates competence, has good ideas, tries out new ideas, and offers effective solutions to problems.

   VD: Verbal Dominance. This score reflects your assessment of the degree to which the person tends to behave competitively, persuasively, and in an attention-getting manner; presents ideas convincingly; commands attention; and expresses ideas clearly and concisely.

   EE: Emotional Expressiveness. This is the degree to which the person becomes emotional (e.g., acts angry or upset when things do not go his or her way), expresses his or her own feelings and emotions, and expresses how he or she feels about what other people say.

   C: Consideration. This score reflects the degree to which the person listens and responds to the ideas raised by others, encourages others to express their ideas, tries to understand the feelings expressed by others, tries to help when others become angry or upset, listens empathically, and is warm and friendly with those who work with him or her.

Because the four scales do not have an equal number of items, you can make them comparable by utilizing the following procedure:

1. Copy your four total scores below.

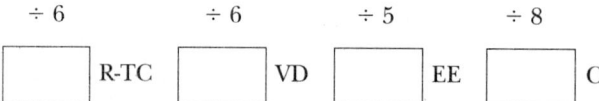

2. Divide each score by the appropriate number below and enter the result in the boxes.

$\div 6$ $\div 6$ $\div 5$ $\div 8$

□ R-TC   □ VD   □ EE   □ C

These scores can be plotted on the following diagram and compared with the norms on the following page.

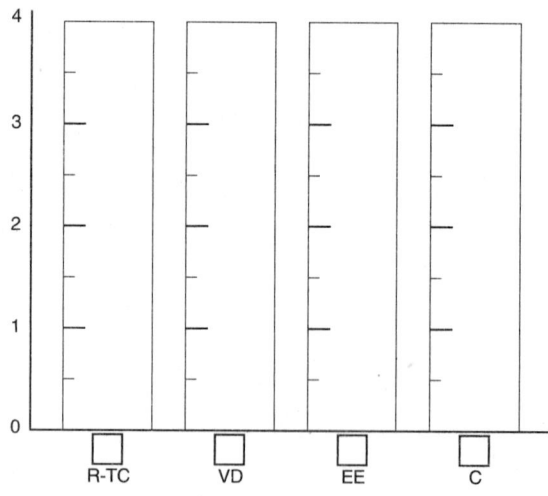

Your Average Scores

The Pfeiffer Book of Successful Communication Skill-Building Tools © 2004 John Wiley & Sons, Inc.

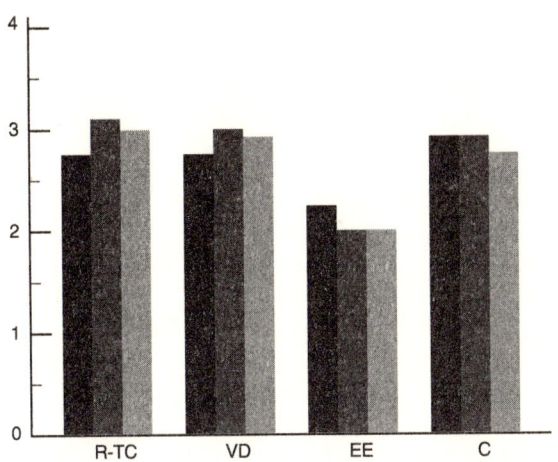

Norms

Combined norms of human relations laboratory participants,
research and development managers, and YMCA managers
(groups virtually identical on the OBDS)

Self N = 214
Subordinate N = 365
Superior N = 201

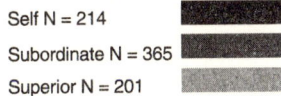

The Negotiation-Stance Inventory

H.B. Karp

With the emphasis on both teamwork and individual empowerment in today's organizations, the development of negotiation skills is particularly important. However, there is an important step that precedes that skill development: learning how one views the process of negotiation. Some people see negotiation as an odious experience to be avoided at all costs; some see it as an opportunity to obtain essential resources, thereby benefiting themselves, their opponents in the negotiation, and the organization. There are also stances between these two extremes.

The author's contention is that some people may possess the necessary skills to negotiate, but they are unwilling to participate in the process. For these people, training in negotiation skills would be inappropriate. Therefore, the author has designed an instrument that helps the respondent to clarify his or her own attitude toward negotiation. This instrument would provide an excellent beginning to a workshop on negotiation: It can be completed in about ten minutes, respondents score their own inventories, and the instrument is accompanied by both an interpretation sheet and a rationale sheet.

Introduction

Organizations are becoming increasingly more team oriented and, at the same time, more focused on the empowerment of the individual worker. With this orientation, the need to negotiate from a position of strength and confidence has become extremely important to those who are accountable for decisions at all levels of the organization. Both teams and individuals are expected to be more effective in obtaining what they need in the work setting and less dependent on those in higher authority to simply grant or deny their requests.

A clear and easily understood definition of *negotiation* is "a process in which two or more parties, with common and conflicting interests, come together to discuss ways to reach agreement." The need to negotiate effectively has always been apparent in traditional situations such as management-labor relations or the purchase of supplies and equipment. Now, however, negotiation is becoming just as important in nontraditional situations. For example, it is used in dealing with customers' service issues, in setting prices, in bartering with fellow team members concerning the allocation of assets and opportunities (such as vacation times or work load), and in other situations in which resources or opportunities are limited.

People may have difficulty with the negotiation process because either (1) they do not possess the skills needed to engage others effectively or (2) they do not possess the fortitude or perspective to engage fully in the negotiation process. Those in the first category need to learn the tactics and strategies of effective negotiating and bargaining. Many excellent training programs address the needed skills; and many experts can show people how to engage in negotiations, maintain the upper hand, and determine where the pitfalls lie.

If skills were the only consideration, organizations could have all employees trained and ready to negotiate at a moment's notice. However, the greater problem is a lack of fortitude or perspective. Regardless of latent ability, many people avoid negotiating because they see themselves as weaker or less aggressive than the other party and/or because they are painfully uncomfortable with the negotiation process. For example, many people are willing to pay almost list price for an automobile because they want to escape from a conflict-ridden, pressure-laden encounter.

The option is to see the negotiation process from a more positive perspective. To do that, a person has to recognize how he or she presently views negotiation.

     The Pfeiffer Book of Successful Communication Skill-Building Tools © 2004 John Wiley & Sons, Inc.

The Negotiation-Stance Inventory helps participants to discover how they experience the negotiation process and to what extent they resist it. A high score on the Negotiation-Stance Inventory indicates that regardless of the effectiveness of a negotiation-skills program, the participant is unlikely to internalize or value the learning. Consequently, the first step after completing the inventory is to establish a view of negotiating as a positive and essential process.

The Instrument

The Negotiation-Stance Inventory helps a participant understand the extent to which he or she is comfortable in engaging in negotiations with another person. It consists of fifteen items, each of which the participant answers with a number on a seven-point scale, ranging from "Strongly Disagree" to "Strongly Agree."

The Negotiation-Stance Inventory Scoring Sheet allows participants to score the inventory themselves. They can then read the Negotiation-Stance Inventory Interpretation Sheet, draw their own conclusions about the implications of their scores, and use those conclusions as a basis for group discussion and for developing a positive attitude toward negotiation.

The Negotiation-Stance Inventory Rationale Sheet, which is based on Gestalt theory,[1] emphasizes the need for individual strength and self-support in the negotiating process. The preferred answer for each item is explained in terms of the participant's:

- Not taking responsibility for the other person's feelings or actions;

- Being willing to recognize his or her own right to be successful and obtain what is wanted; and

- Recognizing and respecting the other person as an opponent, instead of viewing the opponent as an adversary with evil intentions.

Validity and Reliability

No validity or reliability data are available on the Negotiation-Stance Inventory. However, the instrument has face validity, as its purpose is to make participants more aware of their views on negotiating.

---

[1]The facilitator does not have to be familiar with Gestalt theory to use the inventory.

Uses of the Instrument

The Negotiation-Stance Inventory was designed as part of a training module on negotiation and is valuable when administered as the opening activity. However, other uses are possible (for example, as a warm-up activity prior to actual negotiations).

Administering and Scoring the Instrument

A copy of the Negotiation-Stance Inventory is distributed to each participant, who is given approximately ten minutes to complete the fifteen-item form.

After all participants have completed the instrument, the facilitator distributes copies of the Negotiation-Stance Inventory Scoring Sheet and explains the scoring process, *reminding participants that the scoring is reversed on items 2, 10, and 15.* Scoring takes about seven minutes.

Interpretation

When the scoring process has been completed, the facilitator distributes copies of the Negotiation-Stance Inventory Interpretation Sheet. Either the participants read this handout silently, or they follow along as the facilitator reads it aloud. If the participants read silently, the facilitator reviews the highlights of the sheet afterward.

Next the facilitator distributes copies of the Negotiation-Stance Inventory Rationale Sheet and asks the participants to read this sheet. Subgroups of three to five members each are then formed, and the members of each subgroup are asked to devise a list of ideas, issues, and questions that they would like to discuss in the total group. The facilitator clarifies that items on the list should be focused on how to improve attitudes toward negotiation.

One important point that the facilitator should make is that the participants' scores have to do with the way they feel about negotiating, not with their negotiation skills. Those who made the "poorest" scores (that is, those who had the highest numbers) may be the most effective negotiators—when they allow themselves to negotiate. The most important question for this discussion is "How are we stopping ourselves from negotiating when we already know how to do it?"

Once this point has been made, the balance of the training can take one of several directions, such as the following:

The Pfeiffer Book of Successful Communication Skill-Building Tools © 2004 John Wiley & Sons, Inc.

tator's guide, which offers advice on administering the instrument and interpreting the collected data, and an initial set of instruments. Additional instruments are available separately. Pfeiffer, though, is investing heavily in e-instruments. Electronic instrumentation provides effortless distribution and, for larger groups particularly, offers advantages over paper-and-pencil tests in the time it takes to analyze data and provide feedback.

LECTURETTE A short talk that provides an explanation of a principle, model, or process that is pertinent to the participants' current learning needs. A lecturette is intended to establish a common language bond between the trainer and the participants by providing a mutual frame of reference. Use a lecturette as an introduction to a group activity or event, as an interjection during an event, or as a handout.

MODEL A graphic depiction of a system or process and the relationship among its elements. Models provide a frame of reference and something more tangible, and more easily remembered, than a verbal explanation. They also give participants something to "go on," enabling them to track their own progress as they experience the dynamics, processes, and relationships being depicted in the model.

ROLE PLAY A technique in which people assume a role in a situation/scenario: a customer service rep in an angry-customer exchange, for example. The way in which the role is approached is then discussed and feedback is offered. The role play is often repeated using a different approach and/or incorporating changes made based on feedback received. In other words, role playing is a spontaneous interaction involving realistic behavior under artificial (and safe) conditions.

SIMULATION A methodology for understanding the interrelationships among components of a system or process. Simulations differ from games in that they test or use a model that depicts or mirrors some aspect of reality in form, if not necessarily in content. Learning occurs by studying the effects of change on one or more factors of the model. Simulations are commonly used to test hypotheses about what happens in a system—often referred to as "what if?" analysis—or to examine best-case/worst-case scenarios.

THEORY A presentation of an idea from a conjectural perspective. Theories are useful because they encourage us to examine behavior and phenomena through a different lens.

TOPICS

The twin goals of providing effective and practical solutions for workforce training and organization development and meeting the educational needs of training and human resource professionals shape Pfeiffer's publishing program. Core topics include the following:

Leadership & Management
Communication & Presentation
Coaching & Mentoring
Training & Development
E-Learning
Teams & Collaboration
OD & Strategic Planning
Human Resources
Consulting

Pfeiffer Publications Guide

This guide is designed to familiarize you with the various types of Pfeiffer publications. The formats section describes the various types of products that we publish; the methodologies section describes the many different ways that content might be provided within a product. We also provide a list of the topic areas in which we publish.

FORMATS

In addition to its extensive book-publishing program, Pfeiffer offers content in an array of formats, from fieldbooks for the practitioner to complete, ready-to-use training packages that support group learning.

FIELDBOOK Designed to provide information and guidance to practitioners in the midst of action. Most fieldbooks are companions to another, sometimes earlier, work, from which its ideas are derived; the fieldbook makes practical what was theoretical in the original text. Fieldbooks can certainly be read from cover to cover. More likely, though, you'll find yourself bouncing around following a particular theme, or dipping in as the mood, and the situation, dictate.

HANDBOOK A contributed volume of work on a single topic, comprising an eclectic mix of ideas, case studies, and best practices sourced by practitioners and experts in the field.

An editor or team of editors usually is appointed to seek out contributors and to evaluate content for relevance to the topic. Think of a handbook not as a ready-to-eat meal, but as a cookbook of ingredients that enables you to create the most fitting experience for the occasion.

RESOURCE Materials designed to support group learning. They come in many forms: a complete, ready-to-use exercise (such as a game); a comprehensive resource on one topic (such as conflict management) containing a variety of methods and approaches; or a collection of like-minded activities (such as icebreakers) on multiple subjects and situations.

TRAINING PACKAGE An entire, ready-to-use learning program that focuses on a particular topic or skill. All packages comprise a guide for the facilitator/trainer and a workbook for the participants. Some packages are supported with additional media—such as video—or learning aids, instruments, or other devices to help participants understand concepts or practice and develop skills.

- *Facilitator/trainer's guide* Contains an introduction to the program, advice on how to organize and facilitate the learning event, and step-by-step instructor notes. The guide also contains copies of presentation materials—handouts, presentations, and overhead designs, for example—used in the program.

- *Participant's workbook* Contains exercises and reading materials that support the learning goal and serves as a valuable reference and support guide for participants in the weeks and months that follow the learning event. Typically, each participant will require his or her own workbook.

ELECTRONIC CD-ROMs and web-based products transform static Pfeiffer content into dynamic, interactive experiences. Designed to take advantage of the searchability, automation, and ease-of-use that technology provides, our e-products bring convenience and immediate accessibility to your workspace.

METHODOLOGIES

CASE STUDY A presentation, in narrative form, of an actual event that has occurred inside an organization. Case studies are not prescriptive, nor are they used to prove a point; they are designed to develop critical analysis and decision-making skills. A case study has a specific time frame, specifies a sequence of events, is narrative in structure, and contains a plot structure—an issue (what should be/have been done?). Use case studies when the goal is to enable participants to apply previously learned theories to the circumstances in the case, decide what is pertinent, identify the real issues, decide what should have been done, and develop a plan of action.

ENERGIZER A short activity that develops readiness for the next session or learning event. Energizers are most commonly used after a break or lunch to stimulate or refocus the group. Many involve some form of physical activity, so they are a useful way to counter post-lunch lethargy. Other uses include transitioning from one topic to another, where "mental" distancing is important.

EXPERIENTIAL LEARNING ACTIVITY (ELA) A facilitator-led intervention that moves participants through the learning cycle from experience to application (also known as a Structured Experience). ELAs are carefully thought-out designs in which there is a definite learning purpose and intended outcome. Each step—everything that participants do during the activity—facilitates the accomplishment of the stated goal. Each ELA includes complete instructions for facilitating the intervention and a clear statement of goals, suggested group size and timing, materials required, an explanation of the process, and, where appropriate, possible variations to the activity. (For more detail on Experiential Learning Activities, see the Introduction to the *Reference Guide to Handbooks and Annuals*, 1999 edition, Pfeiffer, San Francisco.)

GAME A group activity that has the purpose of fostering team sprit and togetherness in addition to the achievement of a pre-stated goal. Usually contrived—undertaking a desert expedition, for example—this type of learning method offers an engaging means for participants to demonstrate and practice business and interpersonal skills. Games are effective for team-building and personal development mainly because the goal is subordinate to the process—the means through which participants reach decisions, collaborate, communicate, and generate trust and understanding. Games often engage teams in "friendly" competition.

ICEBREAKER A (usually) short activity designed to help participants overcome initial anxiety in a training session and/or to acquaint the participants with one another. An icebreaker can be a fun activity or can be tied to specific topics or training goals. While a useful tool in itself, the icebreaker comes into its own in situations where tension or resistance exists within a group.

INSTRUMENT A device used to assess, appraise, evaluate, describe, classify, and summarize various aspects of human behavior. The term used to describe an instrument depends primarily on its format and purpose. These terms include survey, questionnaire, inventory, diagnostic survey, and poll. Some uses of instruments include providing instrumental feedback to group members, studying here-and-now processes or functioning within a group, manipulating group composition, and evaluating outcomes of training and other interventions.

Instruments are popular in the training and HR field because, in general, more growth can occur if an individual is provided with a method for focusing specifically on his or her own behavior. Instruments also are used to obtain information that will serve as a basis for change and to assist in workforce planning efforts.

Paper-and-pencil tests still dominate the instrument landscape with a typical package comprising a facili-

1. If the group is Gestalt oriented, the facilitator can link negotiation to the Gestalt-theory base of the inventory and demonstrate how developing clear personal boundaries can enhance one's effectiveness as a negotiator.

2. The awareness gained from the inventory can support a discussion of various strategies and tactics of negotiating.

3. The participants may engage in role plays designed to provide practice in negotiating in a nonthreatening environment. After the role plays, experiential outcomes would be discussed.

Originally published in The 1997 Annual, Volume 1, Training.

NEGOTIATION-STANCE INVENTORY

H.B. Karp

Instructions: This inventory consists of fifteen statements. You are asked how strongly you agree or disagree with each. Evaluate each statement as honestly as you can. Although you may realize that exceptions occur, use your best judgment and choose the response that describes your point of view most of the time. Use the following scale to indicate your choices:

SD = Strongly Disagree   AS = Agree Slightly
D = Disagree   A = Agree
DS = Disagree Slightly   SA = Strongly Agree
N = Neutral

_____ 1. Negotiating is basically an undignified and messy process.

_____ 2. I am fundamentally comfortable with conflict and confrontation.

_____ 3. If I cannot have it all, I would just as soon have nothing.

_____ 4. I refuse to negotiate with people I do not like.

_____ 5. I do not like taking a strong stance with others, because it could hurt their feelings.

_____ 6. If people just knew why I wanted what I want, they would be more willing to give it to me.

_____ 7. If I am a good team player or organizational member, I should not have to negotiate for what I want.

_____ 8. When I am in a negotiating position with another person, part of my responsibility is to see that we both obtain as much of what we want as we can.

_____ 9. People who resist the rules and demands of the organization are just being selfish and do not have the organization's best interests at heart.

_____ 10. Resistance is a natural part of the negotiating process. It should be honored and dealt with openly.

_____ 11. In any negotiation, it is important for both sides to maintain a friendly, cooperative stance from the outset.

The Pfeiffer Book of Successful Communication Skill-Building Tools © 2004 John Wiley & Sons, Inc.

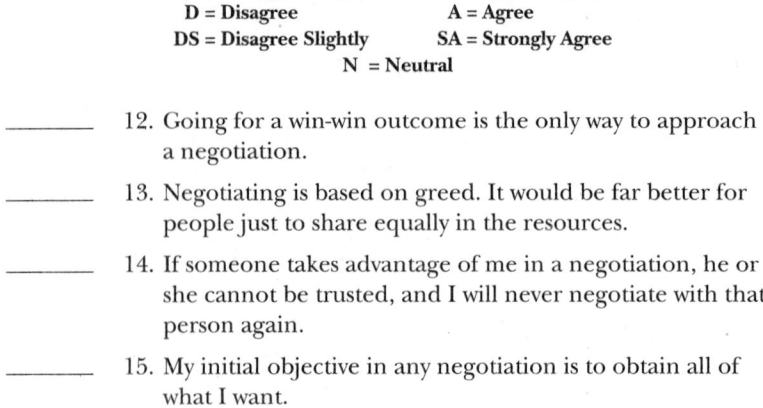

SD = Strongly Disagree AS = Agree Slightly
D = Disagree A = Agree
DS = Disagree Slightly SA = Strongly Agree
N = Neutral

_____ 12. Going for a win-win outcome is the only way to approach a negotiation.

_____ 13. Negotiating is based on greed. It would be far better for people just to share equally in the resources.

_____ 14. If someone takes advantage of me in a negotiation, he or she cannot be trusted, and I will never negotiate with that person again.

_____ 15. My initial objective in any negotiation is to obtain all of what I want.

Negotiation-Stance Inventory Scoring Sheet

Instructions: For all items *except numbers 2, 10, and 15,* the scoring is as follows:

SD = 1 point
D = 2 points
DS = 3 points
N = 4 points
AS = 5 points
A = 6 points
SA = 7 points

For items **2, 10,** and **15** only, the scoring reverses and the points are assigned as follows:

SD = 7 points
D = 6 points
DS = 5 points
N = 4 points
AS = 3 points
A = 2 points
SA = 1 point

Add the numbers you assigned to your responses for the fifteen items, and write the sum in the blank below.

Total Score

The Pfeiffer Book of Successful Communication Skill-Building Tools © 2004 John Wiley & Sons, Inc.

Negotiation-Stance Inventory Interpretation Sheet

Range of Scores	Interpretation
15–33	You have an excellent negotiation stance. You are strong and flexible and maintain a realistic perspective of the negotiating process. Your time-and-place orientation is "right now, right here." Although you respect others and acknowledge that they have just as much right to want what they want as you do, you realize that they will take care of themselves. You recognize that in a universe of limited resources, negotiating is the most effective and civilized way of obtaining what you want.
34–50	You are usually a willing negotiator, but a few areas (those items on which you scored 6 or 7 points) tend to be blind spots for you. You can and will negotiate, but you sometimes wish there were an easier way to obtain what you want. You are reasonably comfortable with conflict if it does not last too long or become too heated. You maintain good working relationships, for the most part, but prefer others to be a little more cooperative in helping you obtain what you want.
51–69	Negotiating is difficult for you. Although others may have needs, you believe those needs are, frankly, just not as important as yours. Although you can and will negotiate on some things, you believe you should not have to. You believe that you have earned the right to the resource; and, if others want to be considered, they should work as hard or be as entitled as you. You are uncomfortable with conflict and confrontation; you view negotiating as conflict producing and, therefore, harmful to those involved.
70–88	You consider negotiating to be compromising, and you want little to do with it. You view people who are competing with you for some resource or outcome as the "enemy" and untrustworthy. You abhor conflict and confrontation and will go to almost any length to avoid them. You believe that the most important thing is for you to be treated fairly; no one else should receive more of the resource or outcome than you. If resources have to be shared, then you believe they should be shared equally, as a point of policy.

Range of Scores	Interpretation
89+	You refuse to negotiate. If you have to negotiate to obtain what you want, you will do without it. You do not want anyone but yourself to receive anything, but you are unwilling to "fight" about it. Your philosophy is "If, for some reason, I can't have it all, then I don't want any of it. That'll show them!"

The Pfeiffer Book of Successful Communication Skill-Building Tools © 2004 John Wiley & Sons, Inc.

NEGOTIATION-STANCE INVENTORY RATIONALE SHEET

For each item of the Negotiation-Stance Inventory, the original statement is listed below, along with the preferred response and the rationale for preferring that response.

1. *Negotiating is basically an undignified and messy process.*

   Preferred Response: SD

   As long as people approach negotiation from this position, they will view the process as being beneath them. It is a way for them to avoid the difficulty of negotiating while maintaining an acceptable self-image.

2. *I am fundamentally comfortable with conflict and confrontation.*

   Preferred Response: SA

   Viewing conflict as a natural and positive condition among people who have different needs or perspectives is essential for developing creative solutions. Being hurt is not inevitable in a conflict situation.

3. *If I cannot have it all, I would just as soon have nothing.*

   Preferred Response: SD

   This position not only blocks any chance of coming out of the negotiation with anything of value; it also identifies the person who holds this position as a self-styled martyr. This position will also reduce the probability of positive outcomes in any future negotiations.

4. *I refuse to negotiate with people I do not like.*

   Preferred Response: SD

   Negotiation is not a social event. Liking or disliking should play no part in how one conducts a negotiation. In fact, liking an adversary too much can often lead a person to softening his or her position inappropriately, because a "friend" is being dealt with. At the minimum, negotiators need to achieve some social distance from each other.

5. *I do not like taking a strong stance with others, because it could hurt their feelings.*

   Preferred Position: SD

   In any conflict situation, there is a chance that someone's feelings will be hurt. Behavior that will hurt someone should be avoided whenever feasible,

but fear of hurting should never be used as an excuse not to engage in negotiations. Once it is discovered that someone takes this position, all the other person has to do to "win" is appear to be emotionally injured.

6. *If people just knew why I wanted what I want, they would be more willing to give it to me.*

Preferred Position: SD

Unless there is a hidden benefit for the other person to receive what you want, this negotiating position is a myth. Once you attempt to convince the other person that your motivation is superior to his or hers, you immediately lower your position and take a defensive stance. In other words, once you begin explaining why you want what you want, the other person can easily say, "Sorry, not good enough." Rather than revealing your reasons, you can put the other person in a defensive position by demanding, "What is your objection to my having this?"

7. *If I am a good team player or organizational member, I should not have to negotiate for what I want.*

Preferred Position: SD

This position suggests that one is rewarded for good work by having the system anticipate and meet one's needs. That is not the way the system works. One is rewarded by pay, bonus, or opportunity for growth and development. The available resources, on the other hand, go to the people who can make the best case for receiving them. In fact, the "good team player and organizational member" is frequently identified by his or her ability and willingness to negotiate effectively.

8. *When I am in a negotiating position with another person, part of my responsibility is to see that we both obtain as much of what we want as we can.*

Preferred Position: SD

The objective of any negotiation is to come to an agreement that all parties can actively support. This goal is best accomplished by taking full responsibility for getting what you want and allowing the other person to do the same. Beware the salesperson who wants to make a deal on an automobile that is "fair" to both of you. If you are looking out for the salesperson's welfare and he or she is also looking out for his or her own welfare, then who is looking out for your welfare? Offer to pay the list price and see if the salesperson counters with "Oh, no, no, no! That's way too much! We can do much better than that!"

The Pfeiffer Book of Successful Communication Skill-Building Tools © 2004 *John Wiley & Sons, Inc.*

9. *People who resist the rules and demands of the organization are just being selfish and do not have the organization's best interests at heart.*

Preferred Response: SD

The most positive aspect of negotiating is that it provides a process for people who have different views to surface as much information as possible. Discussing or arguing these differences increases the number of options. If a win-win strategy is adopted, the broader the view the better.

10. *Resistance is a natural part of the negotiating process. It should be honored and dealt with openly.*

Preferred Response: SA

If receiving what is best for yourself and the organization is the preferred situation, then resisting what is worst is every bit as beneficial. People will naturally resist things that they view as harmful to themselves and their objectives, regardless of who says that they should or should not. Openly expressing that resistance gives you and the other person an opportunity to discover where the blocks occur and an opportunity to address them.

11. *In any negotiation, it is important for both sides to maintain a friendly, cooperative stance from the outset.*

Preferred Response: SD

The time to develop and maintain a friendly, cooperative relationship is after the negotiations have been concluded. Placing a value on warm relationships may ease the negotiating process, but it also softens the edges and diminishes the probability that all parties will emerge with the best possible outcome. Although hostile and aggressive positions should also be avoided, a reasonable amount of distance is desirable.

12. *Going for a win-win outcome is the only way to approach a negotiation.*

Preferred Position: SD

A win-win outcome is the preferred position in most negotiations but not in every case. A win-win solution is particularly important when there is an ongoing relationship between the negotiators, when there is a condition of mutual accountability for the outcome, or when this negotiation will have an impact on future negotiations. However, a win-lose outcome may be preferred if a fixed amount of resource is available with no options, if there is a tradition of competition between the parties, or if only a win-lose option is available (for example, when buying an automobile).

13. *Negotiating is based on greed. It would be far better for people just to share equally in the resources.*

    Preferred Position: SD

    This position, although appearing somewhat reasonable, is the ultimate strategy of the conflict avoider. Not only does it disempower people and keep them dependent; it also does not take into account the outcome. This position does not consider what is needed, why it is needed, and by whom it is needed. The inevitable result would be a mediocre to poor solution.

14. *If someone takes advantage of me in a negotiation, he or she cannot be trusted, and I will never negotiate with that person again.*

    Preferred Response: SD

    Although this position is an understandable response to being taken advantage of, it is an ineffective approach to negotiation. The painful reality is that if you were taken advantage of, you let it happen and you should assume responsibility for your behavior. A much better response is to learn from the experience and take a different approach next time. Rather than refusing to deal with the person again, let him or her know that you are aware of the past behavior, and point out that he or she is going to find it much tougher now to get anything from you as a result of it. Then demand some kind of collateral or escrow up-front to guard against that person's unethical tactics.

15. *My initial objective in any negotiation is to obtain all of what I want.*

    Preferred Response: SA

    The operative term here is "initial." The clearer you are about what you want in the beginning, the easier it will be to make reasonable concessions later. If you walk into the negotiations ready to compromise from the first word, you will have little left to bargain with when you arrive at the tougher points.

About the Editor

Jack Gordon is the former chief editor of *Training* Magazine. His articles and columns on workplace training have appeared in *The Wall Street Journal, San Diego Chronicle, Minneapolis Star Tribune,* and *Learning & Training Innovations.* He has written on other subjects for numerous publications, including *The Economist, The Journal of Law & Politics,* and *Independent Banker.* He has served as editor of numerous books, including *The Pfeiffer Book of Successful Conflict Management Tools* and *The Pfeiffer Book of Successful Leadership Development Tools.*